W9-ABV-775

Shaw the Dramatist

Shaw the Dramatist

BY

LOUIS CROMPTON

UNIVERSITY OF NEBRASKA PRESS · LINCOLN

Chapters Seven, Nine, and Ten originally appeared in slightly different form in the *Prairie Schooner*, Chapter Seven as "Shaw's Challenge to Liberalism," XXXVII (Fall 1963), 229–244; Chapter Nine as "Improving *Pygmalion*," XLI (Spring 1967), 73–83; and Chapter Ten as "Shaw's Heartbreak House," XXXIX (Spring 1965), 17–32.

First printing: March, 1969
Second printing: January, 1970

Manufactured in the United States of America

Preface

This book is an attempt to elucidate Shaw's major plays through a consideration of their social, philosophical, and historical backgrounds. If one were to make a survey of performances of serious drama in English-speaking countries today, he would find Shaw second only to Shakespeare and the runners-up nowhere at all. The ten plays which are currently competing with Shakespeare's masterpieces on the classical stage are *Man and Superman, Major Barbara, Saint Joan, Heartbreak House, Caesar and Cleopatra, Candida, Pygmalion, Arms and the Man, The Doctor's Dilemma,* and *The Devil's Disciple.* In this book I have devoted an essay to each of these. I have added a chapter on the *Unpleasant Plays* by way of introduction, and one on *Back to Methuselah*, which, whatever its deficiencies as theater, nevertheless remains Shaw's most ambitious philosophical essay in dramatic form.

My intention has been to write a general introduction to Shavian drama which would incorporate the results of a study of the manuscripts of the plays and of Shaw's unpublished lectures and essays in the libraries of the British Museum and the University of Texas and in the Berg Collection of the New York Public Library. I have tried to let such new material inform my understanding of Shaw's plays while confining the scholarly apparatus largely to the notes. In interpreting them I have not tried to be original, but to give a true and comprehensive view. And I have hoped to write a book that would be of interest both to the literate layman and to the specialist.

Modern formalist criticism is strongly anti-ideological in bias. Our New Critics are historically the sons of Walter Pater, and the New Criticism (not so new any more) is Pater's aesthetic without its hedonism. By contrast, this book is in the classical tradition of

v

87181

English literary criticism, which, from Sir Philip Sidney down to Johnson, Shelley, and Ruskin, has been that of moral realism. It represents an effort to break with the formalism that has dominated the academies for the last generation and to connect literature once more with life and society.

"Learn everything," Shaw once advised novelists in a lecture on fiction, "and when you know it, stick to naturalism, and write every word as if you were on your oath in a witness box." It is not generally realized how seriously Shaw took his own advice as far as naturalism was concerned. Most training in literary tradition is in fact a positive impediment in understanding Shaw. When Shaw introduces literary conventions into his plays, it is most often to demonstrate how absurdly they misrepresent human behavior, or how silly the moral assumptions behind them are. The effect of boldly introducing what he had observed in life onto the stage fell so far short of theatrical expectations that audiences frequently mistook Shaw's realism for perverse farce. Sometimes the character types Shaw copied were common everywhere but in the playhouse. Sometimes his characters were the highly individualistic men and women who formed part of the same radical circles Shaw moved in at the turn of the century. To free Shaw from the charge of arbitrarily fantasticating, I have regularly related the characters in the plays to their real-life prototypes where they were identified by Shaw himself or where I felt I could make a reasonably safe guess at Shaw's models. If this leaves me open to the charge of counting Lady Macbeth's children, I can only reply that, in the long run, such efforts are less debilitating to literature than making it an autonomous activity sealed off from the rest of our existence.

Is Shaw dated? The answer is yes, as every classic is dated. The specific personalities and political crises that moved him to write are now part of history, as Plato's and Aristophanes' debaters and statesmen are. The images of his plays belong to an eternal world, as his ideas on government, economics, sex, psychology, logic, and art, now seen apart from the novel and amusing expression he gave them, form part of a perennial philosophy which we can call "Shavian." But there is still a third aspect of the question. One might perhaps hope that the particular social outrages Shaw wrote about in his "problem" plays might by now be things of the past. Nothing could be more gratifying than to pronounce Shaw hopelessly out of date in such matters. Unfortunately, I cannot see that this is so. To take two clear-cut examples: the demoralization of men by poverty is still the world's first problem, and our national system of criminology is still outrageously perverse in its intentions and pernicious in its results.

In my attempt to see Shaw's plays whole I have often taken issue with Shaw's critics. If the reader is struck by the frequency with which I disagree with others, he should remember, first, that debate makes for livelier reading than concurrence, and, second, that I have tacitly accepted much of what previous writers have discovered. If I have not acknowledged all my debts, it is because in some cases I do not know what is stolen and what is my own. I have more than once congratulated myself on a new insight, only to find it later in the pages of some book whence it had lodged itself subconsciously in my memory. I am especially aware of what I owe to Eric Bentley, Desmond MacCarthy, William Irvine, Archibald Henderson, and Martin Meisel. Nevertheless, I must candidly declare that Shaw's critics have on the whole taken me only a short way toward what seemed an adequate understanding of the plays. Where I have challenged them, the reader will sometimes find me relying on my background reading or my own intuition. More frequently, however, I have fallen back on Shaw himself as his own most helpful explicator. In doing this I have been surprised at the number of clues Shaw has provided that critics have overlooked or ignored.

LOUIS CROMPTON

Contents

Shaw the Dramatist

CHAPTER ONE

Unpleasant Prelude

Shaw was not a playwright who struck his own unique vein immediately. His first experiments in drama, the *Unpleasant Plays*, have few of the qualities we think of as typically Shavian. They do not have the complex characterization, the imaginative intensity, or the breadth of vision of the *Pleasant Plays*, the *Plays for Puritans*, or the great philosophical comedies. Nevertheless they are neither unformed nor tentative pieces. Shaw had served his literary and intellectual apprenticeship in grinding out his five unprofitable novels. When he sat down to write the first act of *Widowers' Houses* in 1885, he was a man whose opinions and judgment were fully mature. Essentially, he said nothing in the *Unpleasant Plays* he would have wished unsaid in later years. Even the fact that they are skeletal diagrams rather than fully fleshed Shavian masterpieces makes them all the more revealing as guides to the underlying assumptions of his sociology. This directness is further sharpened by their lack of the geniality characteristic of Shaw's better-known plays. Indeed, anyone who, unwarned by the title, comes to them expecting Shaw's usual high spirits and comedic brilliance will inevitably be shocked by their grimness.

In one play, Rembrandt's famous "Lesson in Anatomy" figures prominently in the setting. This picture, which shows a lecturer displaying the bared tendons and veins in a corpse's arm, might serve as an emblem of the *Unpleasant Plays* as a whole. To use one of Shaw's own favorite metaphors, they are Shavian surgical operations performed without the benefit of the usual laughing gas. In this they embody the spirit of the literary movement that inspired them: nineteenth-century naturalism. Like the novels of Zola and the plays of Becque and the youthful Strindberg, they are ruthless exposés of

1

social plague spots. We may say of them what Shaw said of the works of his naturalistic forebears, that they show "the bourgeoisie, after a century and a half of complacent vaunting of its own probity . . . turning bitterly on itself with accusations of hideous sexual and commercial corruption."[1] Where Shaw differs from Zola and Gorki, however, is that he does not, like the Frenchman or the Russian, directly depict Nana plying her trade or slum-dwellers in the full degradation of their misery, but instead shows how the middle class, while purporting to hold such things in horror, in fact condones and even profits from them.

To the Victorian bourgeois, private property and the domestic hearth seemed the very foundations of social morality. In these plays Shaw maintains that the first of the two institutions is inevitably antisocial, and the second potentially so, since devotion to the welfare of one's family may well be at the expense of society as a whole, and the model father or son may be anything but a model employer or landlord. Private property, on the other hand, because of the capricious distribution of nature's bounty, necessarily leads to social inequality. In his Fabian essay, "The Economic Basis of Socialism," Shaw demonstrates how the first settlers in a country or city pre-empt the best land for farming or business and later retire as *rentiers* to live idly off the advantages their favored position provides. For Shaw, this system is tolerated only because of the corruption of our social morality by what he calls the gambling spirit: "As against Socialism, the gambling spirit urges man to allow no rival to come between his private individual powers and Stepmother Earth, but rather to secure some acres of her and take his chance of getting diamonds instead of cabbages."[2] The result of the pre-emption of land and natural resources by the favored few is the squalor of our city and rural proletariat.

Shaw's sense of social justice was originally fired by his reading of the American Henry George (who based his criticism of private property on land speculation in San Francisco) and the German Marx, but the cool temper of his English Fabianism kept him from the besetting sin of the naturalists—the exploitation of sensational material for melodramatic or sentimental effects. There are no idealized workmen, no large-hearted philanthropists or capitalist villains in Shaw's plays.[3] Instead, he chooses irony as his weapon and keeps close to the bald facts, basing his first play, *Widowers' Houses*, on the dry-as-dust pages of a government bluebook. The *Report of the Royal Commission on the Housing of the Working Classes of 1885*[4] provided, with relentless reiteration of cases, a comprehensive survey of living conditions in the poorer sections of Europe's largest city. Historically, London showed a typical development. Huge tracts of land were in the hands of aristocrats who had acquired them by grant or purchase in earlier centuries. Most of these distinguished "head landlords" had let out their holdings on ninety-nine-year leases to middlemen who in turn sublet them, so they had no direct control of their property. At the end of the chain were the "house knackers," men who turned single-family homes designed for six or seven people into tenements holding sixty or seventy, with a family or more in every room. The appalling result had prompted the passage of housing laws in 1851 and 1861, but these were circumvented by the landlords, who simply got themselves or their henchmen elected to the city vestries and prevented enforcement of the reform codes.

As a socialist, Shaw wanted the municipalization of housing, the public ownership of land, and the end of rent payments to private landlords. But *Widowers' Houses*[5] is not directed to socialists. It is aimed at sympathetic conservatives, that is, at that section of the British Tory aristocracy which professed belief in *noblesse oblige* and waxed indignant at what they regarded as middle-class exploitation of the poor in slums and factories. Harry Trench, the nominal hero of *Widowers' Houses*, is a young man of just such aristocratic bias, who is genuinely shocked when he learns that the wealth of his prospective father-in-law, Sartorius, comes from neglected and decaying slum properties. But unfortunately, Trench has never thought for two minutes about economic questions. When he makes his embarrassed refusal of Sartorius' money, the older man easily overwhelms him with the standard middle-class defenses—the poor are naturally improvident, and improvements will be wasted on slum-dwellers, since "when people are very poor, you cannot help them, no matter how much you may sympathize with them."[6] To these arguments Trench's friend Cokane adds the two clichés of laissez

faire economics, declaring that "rent must be paid," and ascribing
the suffering of the poor to the "increase of the population," the
latter having been a standard excuse for tolerating social misery from
the days of Malthus onward. Trench is further overwhelmed when
he finds that his own small income, which he has always thought
untainted because it came from a "respectable" aristocratic source,
that is, land rents, is actually paid by Sartorius out of the money he
screws from his starving tenants. Shaw's point here is that under the
free enterprise system there is literally no way for a man to escape
tainted money.

Shaw wants us to realize the futility of mere sympathy and good
feelings apart from economic knowledge and effective action. For
the eighteenth-century philosopher of ethical sentimentalism, Lord
Shaftesbury, to have the feelings "right and entire" was in itself
virtue and integrity. Shaw demonstrates the absurdity of such an
idea in a world controlled by the principles of capitalism. Lickcheese,
the impoverished rent collector, begins by begging Trench to "have
some feeling for the poor." But later he, too, grows rich at the
expense of poor men. And at the conclusion of the play, Trench, the
balked sentimentalist, has become in reaction the completest cynic;
if guilt is inescapable he will reject even the anodynes to conscience
the tactful Cokane offers and act on strictly commercial considerations. Nor will Shaw allow the conventional playgoer any of the
traditional gratifications of sentimental domestic comedy. The
lovers' quarrel between Trench and Sartorius' daughter is patched
up primarily because the financial relations between the two men
make it desirable. Lickcheese approves the match on the ground that
"a bit of romance" will cost nothing and be highly gratifying,
since "we all have our feelins: we aint mere calculatin machines."[7]
Thus the play ends with a wedding march played stridently out of
key.

Widowers' Houses is Marxist in its condemnation of bourgeois
values, Fabian in its refusal to indulge in "socialist melodrama."[8]
But its subject—slum housing—was the special preoccupation of
East End Anglican parsons, and this, along with the fact that its real
hero (as Shaw calls him) is the off-stage clergyman who protests
against negligent landlords, puts it also in the Christian Socialist

tradition. So does its title, since Christ's scathing condemnation of men who "devour widows' houses" and at the same time go clothed in the "long clothing" of respectability, as Sartorius does, was a favorite text for Christian Socialist sermons.[9] That Shaw, however, should have refused to exploit the pathos of the widow's plight, and instead gives us an icily objective portrait of a rich widower is typical of his whole didactic strategy, which is totally different from the simple moralism of most socialist preachments. His approach is, indeed, that of Swift in "A Modest Proposal." Where Swift argued with cool logic that the starving Irish should cook their babies to alleviate their hunger, Shaw also appears to be setting forth a purely rational proposition on its own merits: since the suffering of the poor is inevitable, let us feed off them as efficiently as we can. The irony is all the more effective because this is simply what laissez faire economists had been saying all along: Eat and keep your eyes shut, since you have no choice. Nor does Shaw give us his own Fabian solution to the problem in his play. Like Swift, he merely leads us syllogistically to a morally intolerable conclusion and leaves us there.

Widowers' Houses shows how a respectable façade may hide a devouring Mammonism. But Mammon, though a god men worship assiduously enough, is rarely worshiped openly. Shaw is more daring in *The Philanderer*,[10] where the gods he attacks are the gods of love and medical science. Shaw had already served notice of his unwillingness to idealize amorous passion in his first play. There, Blanche Sartorius is not the insipid Victorian sweetheart her name conjures up, but a passionately lovesick woman who reacts with flaming violence or chilly reserve to imagined affronts. The effect of love on Julia Craven in *The Philanderer* is, if anything, worse. Though she professes advanced ideals, Julia behaves with the jealousy of a child who has lost a favorite toy when Charteris, disgusted with her scene-making, turns to another woman. In Julia, Shaw is satirizing theatrical standards of conduct. A generation which encouraged every woman who had lost a man's affection to see herself as a tragic Queen Katherine was, Shaw thought, giving too great a rein to feminine sentimentality. Shaw contrasts Julia, the Victorian "womanly" woman, with the self-sufficient Grace Tranfield, who, scorning Julia's tactics, is all too aware that the indulgence and even much of the chivalry men show to women is really a kind of insult, since it implies that in male eyes women are not responsible, self-respecting adults.

In *The Philanderer*, Shaw's naturalism is based not on official bluebooks, but on his own experiences with his first mistress, the tempestuous Mrs. Jenny Patterson, and Florence Farr, the actress who supplanted her. The latter had challenged him to "expose his soul"[11] in a play, and his response was to draw a self-portrait in Leonard Charteris, the "Ibsenist philosopher," who heartlessly refuses to find in love anything more than a recreative pastime. Charteris' wit and penchant for comedic anticlimax makes *The Philanderer* more like later Shaw than either of the other plays in the *Unpleasant* cycle. So does the delicate irony in the satiric treatment of the retired soldier, Craven, and the drama critic, Cuthbertson, when we compare Shaw's treatment of them with the crude guying of the egregious Cokane in *Widowers' Houses*. Craven is presented as an amiable philistine, wholly uncritical of the values of the society in which he lives, who, having no ego of his own, but determined to pick up moral credit where he may, plays in turn the sportsmanlike loser in love, the doomed patient, and the righteous vegetarian, in each case making a heroic merit out of necessity. Cuthbertson, on the other hand, is a self-conscious defender of the theatrical virtues of "manliness" and "womanliness," who prides himself on living "among scenes of suffering nobly endured and sacrifices willingly rendered"—in the theater!—and champions, against Charteris' libertarianism, the ideal of indissoluble marriage, despite his complete failure to come to any workable domestic arrangement with his own wife.

The Philanderer also satirizes a medical researcher who is bent on proving the existence of a new disease he believes he has discovered. In *Middlemarch* George Eliot had given the world a picture of a doctor who was a fool about women and a scholar who was a futile pedant. But why, asked Shaw, assume that all doctors are gifted with scientific intelligence? Could not a man be as infatuated with feminine beauty as Lydgate and as absurd in his researches as Mr. Casaubon? Shaw represents Dr. Paramore as such a man, the difference being that Casaubon worked with manuscripts, while

Paramore, in his blind frenzy to justify himself intellectually, mutilates living animals. Yet Shaw's Charteris is enough of a philosopher to ask whether he is not himself as guilty of causing pain as Paramore. As a satirist given to telling home truths and a philanderer addicted to playing with women to observe their reactions, he pleads guilty to Julia's accusation that he is the crueler vivisector of the two, his defense being only that he is an intelligent man who learns from his experiments, while Paramore is a merely stupid one.

The last of the three *Unpleasant Plays* deals once more with the effect of economics on human lives. In his Fabian essays Shaw had rejected Marx's labor theory of value in favor of Stanley Jevons' contention that prices are set by supply and demand and that an oversupply drives the price of any article toward zero. *Mrs. Warren's Profession* asks what happens when human wages come under this law and the commodity in excess happens to be women. The nineteenth century, which regarded the economically independent woman as morally suspect, went on the general assumption that, when women worked in stores, restaurants, or factories, they did so to supplement the wages of their fathers or husbands, and used this as an excuse for underpaying the wives and daughters. But what if the woman had no family, or was herself its mainstay? Since the common wage for a salesgirl, waitress, or woman factory worker at the turn of the century amounted to a penny an hour (as compared to sixpence an hour for an ordinary dock worker) the plight of women in such situations may easily be imagined.[12]

The Victorian world was not overly shocked by poverty; indeed, following the classical economists, it regarded wages as the function of a free market with which it would be sacrilege to interfere. It did not, however, affect the same indifference to sexual morality. It was shocked by prostitution and even went so far as to distinguish it as *the* social vice. In the nineties, when the English public discovered a flourishing trade in the sale of young English girls to continental brothels, it was very shocked indeed, and a number of sensational exposés appeared in the press which allowed readers to revel vicariously in the horrors of white slavery.[13] But the proprietors of London restaurants, less nice-minded than the general public, had taken it for granted all along that their waitresses would eke out their pittances

by accommodating well-to-do customers, and factory owners were
quite indifferent to the fact that the only way a girl who did not live
at home could avoid starvation was to sell herself on the streets at
the end of the day. Shaw's thesis in *Mrs. Warren's Profession* was
simply that wide-scale enforced prostitution follows grinding poverty
and underpayment of women as surely as night follows day.

Shaw created Vivie Warren in response to Beatrice Webb's plea
that he write about an emancipated woman as a counteractive to the
sex-mad creatures of *The Philanderer*.[14] Vivie is a "modern un-
romantic hard-working young woman" who has devoted her years at
Cambridge, not to acquiring a dilettante's appreciation of art and
literature, but to preparing herself to earn her living as an actuary.
Her life is not without an element of mystery, however; her mother
is a flirtatious, loudly dressed rowdy of very different tastes and
manners from herself, who has never divulged who Vivie's father is,
but nevertheless behaves with the freedom and self-assurance of a
woman of wealth and power. Unfortunately, her freedom from convention breaks down just where her affections are most deeply
engaged, namely, in her relations with her daughter. Mrs. Warren
adopts a proprietary attitude toward Vivie and expects that she will
in turn pay her a conventional filial deference. Consequently, the
coolness with which Vivie announces that she means to lead an independent existence as a self-supporting businesswoman so discomfits
Mrs. Warren that she utters the vulgar parental retort—"Do you
know who youre speaking to?"—a blunder which allows Vivie to
make the pointed counterquery, "No. Who are you? What are you?"
But despite Mrs. Warren's temporary discomfiture, it is in the end
Vivie who is the more shaken of the two. For, stung by her daughter's
manner, Mrs. Warren now finds the revelation of her long-hidden
past a positive relief: as a girl of the slums whose only other choice
was soul-destroying drudgery under conditions demonstrably worse
than life in a brothel, Mrs. Warren had turned to prostitution as the
more self-respecting alternative.

At this news Vivie does not recoil from her mother. On the contrary, she is deeply touched by her story, and for the first time in her
life is filled with affectionate regard for her. The reason is that Vivie
now realizes that she is, in one important regard, her mother's

daughter. She admires her mother for winning through to the independence and self-respect that are the central necessities of her
own life, and for doing it with the whole weight of conventional
morality thrown in the balance against her. Later, however, when
Sir George Crofts, her mother's business partner, boasts of the
ample profits he and Mrs. Warren make from a chain of private
hotels in Brussels, Ostend, and Vienna, Vivie recoils with intense
aversion from the woman she has just embraced. The reader, un-
prepared for this *volte-face*, may wonder why Vivie can accept, and
even like, a woman who has had promiscuous relations with men for
money, but not a well-to-do and socially presentable madam.

The answer, of course, lies once more in Vivie's central point of
honor, her need for self-respect and freedom. Vivie and Mrs.
Warren agree on the need for self-respect for themselves; but here
they part company, for Vivie's conscience has grown beyond the
merely self-interested, individualistic stage of development and demands self-respect not just for herself alone, but for all women. The
names of Brussels and Ostend, notoriously the centers for the sale of
English girls in Europe, are burning brands on her consciousness. In
her eyes her mother was justified in turning to prostitution to free
herself from abject poverty, but, in cajoling other girls into her
houses for the sake of the profit they bring, she has simply joined the
ranks of those who exploit the poor.

Another crux in understanding the play is Vivie's attitude toward
incest. Ironically, the only consideration that gives Crofts a moment's
pause in his pursuit of self-gratification is his fear that Vivie may be
his daughter. The man who has no social conscience whatsoever is
stopped by a superstitious taboo. Later, piqued by Vivie's turning
him down as a suitor, he drops a false hint that she and her young
admirer, Frank, are brother and sister. When Vivie flees in horror
and disgust to her business offices in London, Frank thinks it is
Crofts's innuendo that has produced her revulsion, but Vivie is not a
Moll Flanders, and has no moral objections to marriage with a
brother from whom she has been separately reared. The real cause of
her feeling of nausea is her knowledge of where the money that has
provided her education has come from; moreover, she now ines-
capably identifies Frank with the typical girl-fancier who makes up

her mother's clientele.[15] In the end, when her mother comes to ask what has spoiled their new sentimental relations, Vivie, firmly rejecting her advances, ignores both her pleas and her stage curses and turns to her actuarial work, much relieved that she is, morally speaking, a free agent, in a position to return to her mother the monthly check from her brothel profits.

Mrs. Warren's Profession is undoubtedly the sternest of all Shaw's dramas. Like Dante's poem, it takes us into an inferno; but the sins it depicts are not the seven deadly sins of tradition, but economic and social crimes: idleness, parasitism, exploitation, and the cultivated sentimentalism that keeps people from dealing with these. At one moment Vivie tells us that she herself feels like one of the "damned," but she is really, in effect, the Rhadamanthus of the piece, across the high tension wires of whose moral conscience the other characters unwittingly stumble and are judged. Max Beerbohm, who claimed Shaw had written an academic debate with no appeal to the heart, thought he should have made the play a harrowing tragedy capable of moving the audience to pity and fear. But Shaw's intention was to sear our conscience, not to play upon our theatrical sensibilities. Beerbohm, for all his wit and intelligence, was still under the spell of the kind of play in which an "erring" woman would dramatize her shame and humiliation (for the audience's pleasure), pathetically lament her separation from her family and respectable society, and then die touchingly in the third act while the spectators sat bathed in tears. Mrs. Warren, by contrast, is shown to be unconvincing only when she pretends to feel shame, quite able to have the society she wants on the terms she wants it, and at the end of the play very much alive and flourishing, the very spirit of the economic system which had at first victimized her, but whose principles she has at last twisted to her own advantage.[16]

Shaw turned the nineteenth century morally upside down by opposing laissez faire principles in economic relations and introducing them into personal morality. As a philosopher, the major problem he faced was to reconcile the libertarian egoism of his ethics with the collectivism of his social thinking. In the *Unpleasant Plays* he does this by showing how concern for one's self eventually becomes part of concern for others, and how totally free men and women will ultimately disdain to profit at others' expense. Today, social conservatives, having taken over the economic creed of nineteenth-century middle-class liberalism, no longer justify private enterprise with the classical argument that man's economic destiny is fixed by iron laws it is folly to try to meddle with, but simply defend capitalism in the name of freedom, presented as an absolute good in itself. But in opposing collectivism, conservatives are rarely prepared to accept moral freedom in and of itself. Shaw, by contrast, was ready to do just that, and a defense of human impulse against the restraints of moral codes is the theme of his next half-dozen full-length dramas.

CHAPTER TWO

Arms and the Man

In his next cycle of dramas, Shaw leaves behind exposés of social crimes for comedies ridiculing what he called "the romantic follies" of mankind. The earlier plays sought to make callous consciences sensitive; in the *Pleasant Plays* Shaw demonstrates to us that conscience may be a bane as well as a boon. The road to utopia has many pitfalls, not the least of which is the danger that we may entrammel ourselves in a false idealism. One antidote to such idealism has always been laughter, and Shaw in these comedies makes ample use of laughter in his fight to lead his audiences to moral freedom, for as Freud has shown in *Wit and Its Relation to the Unconscious*, laughter is a powerful instrument for freeing us from constraints. When we laugh, as one critic has put it, the superego "takes a holiday."[1] In these plays Shaw makes war, partly on law and custom, but more especially on our own self-fears and lack of self-respect. Their lesson is the lesson of *The Quintessence of Ibsenism*—that we must constantly be distrustful and suspicious of rigid moral systems that purport to set inviolable standards for human behavior.

Raina and Sergius, the two idealistic characters in *Arms and the Man*, have enormous superegos. They are in thrall to the high ideals of love and war that were part of the code of Victorian chivalry Scott had fathered and Tennyson brought to fruition. These values were in part a return to feudal ideals of honor as opposed to commercial standards of conduct. But they were also strongly tinctured by the morbid introspectiveness of early nineteenth-century evangelicalism. This was a mixture that had produced, among other phenomena, Byron and his self-scorn. Shaw thought such a morality perverse and dangerous, first, because it advocated a reckless disregard for the consequences of actions on the ground that purity of heart or motive was all in all, and second, because it set unrealizable norms of conduct. The result was that their inevitable failure to live up to them cost men their self-respect. To attack these ideas Shaw uses the classical technique for deflating high-toned pretentiousness, the technique of bathos. In *Arms and the Man* repeated descents from the sublime to the ridiculous surprise us into bursts of laughter which are both an emotional and a moral release.

This is a common enough literary device and may result in nothing more than crude burlesque. But what is unique is the brilliantly original way in which Shaw plays the game. Most comedies, as Bergson saw, are socially and morally conservative, and aim at no more than laughing the eccentric back into conformity with his fellows; critically speaking, the audience's emotions and its level of thought may be no higher than those of a lynch mob. But Shaw's strategy is either to invite the unwary members of the audience to identify themselves with some character on the stage and then show his behavior to be preposterous, or else, alternatively, to present us with some idea we are tempted to reject out of hand and then demonstrate its logical necessity. The effect is that of a man who suddenly declares that everyone is out of step but him, and means it. It was this unorthodox refusal to go along with either common literary conventions or moral assumptions that caused so much confusion at the first performance of *Arms and the Man*. Yeats has recorded the anger with which those spectators who sympathized with Raina's romanticism turned on those who first burst out laughing. But this confusion beset not only the members of the audience who might have been expected to be hostile to Shaw's satire, but also those who ought to have responded favorably to it. Even William Archer, the self-constituted high priest of stage realism, complained petulantly in his review that "the author . . . is always jumping from key to key, without an attempt at modulation, and nine times out of ten he does not himself know what key he is writing in." [2] Indeed, Archer's review is of particular interest, not only in showing how much difficulty one of Shaw's close acquaintances had in understanding him, but because it raises directly three central points which have continued to bedevil critics—whether Shaw's moral point of view in the play is any different from Gilbertian topsy-turvyism, whether the Bulgarian setting is to be taken seriously, and whether the love psychology which makes Raina drop Sergius for Bluntschli and mates Sergius with Louka is a whit less arbitrary than the pairings in Elizabethan comedies.

The first peculiarity of Shavian comedy is that Shaw expects us to use our critical intellects while we are laughing. Half of mankind's serious views and moods Shaw regarded as absurd, and wanted to puncture with satire. But Shaw was, if anything, even more aware of the opposite danger. Idle laughter for its own sake disgusted him, and he reserved his most withering scorn for cynics of the "when-in-doubt-laugh" breed. Thus Shaw found heartless farce even more offensive than solemnity parading as wisdom. Over and over again in his theater reviews he protests against galvanic comedy and Gilbertism. Shaw's critics have often made the mistake of trying to relate him to the tradition of Restoration wit. But it is not putting the case too strongly to say that Shaw positively hated Congreve and Wycherley, and that he would find the current tendency to perform his plays in the style of artificial comedy obtuse and offensive. Shaw's avowed preferences, most people will be surprised to learn, were not for the Restoration playwrights at all, but for the eighteenth-century sentimental reaction against them. This is an alignment he makes abundantly clear in his criticism. Consequently, he abominated *The Way of the World* but highly admired a Victorian stage version of *The Vicar of Wakefield*. And far from hailing *The Importance of Being Earnest* as Wilde's masterpiece, he took strong exception to its artificialities, comparing it quite unfavorably in point of feeling and sentiment with Wilde's earlier works:

> Unless comedy touches me as well as amuses me, it leaves me with a sense of having wasted my evening. I go to the theatre to be moved to laughter, not to be tickled or bustled into it; and that is why, though I laugh as much as anybody at a farcical comedy, I am out of spirits before the end of the second act, and out of temper before the end of the third, my miserable mechanical laughter intensifying these symptoms at every outburst. If the public ever becomes intelligent enough to know when it is really enjoying itself and when it is not, there will be an end of farcical comedy. Now in The Importance of Being Earnest there is plenty of this rib-tickling: for instance, the lies, the deceptions, the cross

purposes, the sham mourning, the christening of the two grown-
up men, the muffin eating, and so forth. These could only have
been raised from the farcical plane by making them occur to
characters who had, like Don Quixote, convinced us of their
reality and obtained some hold on our sympathy. But that unfortunate . . . Gilbertism breaks our belief in the humanity of the
play.[3]

This explains why Shaw, in the preface to the *Pleasant Plays*, can
make statements so apparently un-Shavian as the following: "When
a comedy is performed, it is nothing to me that the spectators laugh:
any fool can make an audience laugh. I want to see how many of
them, laughing or grave, are in the melting mood."[4] Shaw is sincere
in this declaration to the extent that half the difficulty in understanding a Shavian comedy is to grasp the serious feelings of his
characters and the serious import of the situations. Edward VII,
who was by no means an unintelligent man, is said to have been
indignant over *Arms and the Man* and to have broken his chair laughing at *John Bull's Other Island*, presumably at the pig episode. There
is no doubt that Shaw would have complimented him on his per-
ceptiveness in the first case and regarded him as among the damned
in the second.

But it is not only the characters and sentiments in *Arms and the
Man* that have puzzled people. Shaw's choice of setting has, if anything, been even more completely misunderstood. Archer thought
that Bulgaria provided an arbitrary and fantastic background which
Shaw had no real knowledge of and no real interest in, and modern
critics have generally followed him in looking on Shaw's Bulgaria as
a kind of light-operatic prevision of Graustark and Ruritania.[5] But
those Bulgarian students who rioted in Vienna during the performance of the play, though no more sophisticated than the Irish
audiences who regarded Synge's *Playboy* as a slur on the national
honor, were nevertheless nearer the mark. Shaw admitted that he had
worked out the basic idea of the play before he picked his war and
country, but he has testified to his later concern for authentic detail.[6]
Indeed, Shaw's picture of Bulgarian realities does not differ markedly
from Edward Dicey's analysis in *The Peasant State*, a study published

in 1894 which likens the level of Bulgarian culture, quite unro-
mantically, to that of western Illinois in the same period.

But we will not understand Shaw's play unless we grasp the fact
that his program heading, "Bulgaria, 1885," was charged with very
strong and definite emotional overtones for English audiences. Nor
were these the connotations of a romantic fairyland. First, the
English mind had been inflamed by Gladstone's evangelical, anti-
Mohammedan account of Turkish atrocities in his *Bulgarian Horrors*
of 1879. Gladstone's preoccupation of the electorate with "the
eastern question" in the early eighties Shaw deprecated strongly as
distracting attention from pressing social problems at home. Secondly, the Servo-Bulgarian War of 1885 had been highly gratifying to
English popular sentiment. King Milan of Servia, jealous of Bulgaria's recent acquisition of Turkish territory, had peremptorily
invaded the country, and been roundly beaten by Prince Alexander
at Slivnitza just two weeks later. On this account, it seemed morally a
wholly satisfactory war, with the aggressor punished and the under-
dog nation triumphant. Audiences in 1894 must have been as much
surprised by Shaw's satire as audiences of today would be if the
Ethiopians had beaten Mussolini in 1935 and someone had then
written a play making fun of the Ethiopians. The point is that Shaw
is not a romantic nationalist of the Liberal ilk with a sentimental
prejudice in favor of small nations. Throughout his lifetime Shaw's
criterion for judging wars was simply, Which side represents the
higher level of civilization? not Which is the littler? This approach
made him not only anti-Prussian in Europe but anti-Boer in Africa
and anti-Confederacy in America. Indeed, the very success of the
Bulgarians must have struck him as giving romantic nationalism an
added dangerous allure.[7]

The satire of *Arms and the Man*, however, is not directed primarily
against nationalism, but against the poetic views of love and war,
those *beaux idéals* of the nineteenth century. Specifically, the play
deals with the disillusionment of Raina and Sergius. Raina, Shaw's
heroine, is enthusiastically entranced with quixotic ideals of gal-
lantry, both amorous and military.[8] In her character we see Shaw's
theory of the seriocomic concretely realized. Shaw wants the audience

to smile at Raina but not to regard her as a creature of farcical burlesque. This complex response, however, demanded a sophistication of mind and emotions both Shaw's audience and the performers found beyond them. Hence Shaw's famous curtain speech after the *succès fou* of the opening night, in which he said he agreed with the one man who booed. Hence also his lively expostulation to Alma Murray, who had played Raina with intense seriousness on this occasion, but modified her interpretation in the direction of farce a few weeks later:

> What—oh what has become of my Raina? How could you have the heart to play that way for me—to lacerate every fibre in my being? Where's the poetry gone—the tenderness—the sincerity of the noble attitude and the thrilling voice? Where is the beauty of the dream about Sergius, the genuine heart stir and sympathy of the attempt to encourage the strange man when he breaks down? Have you turned cynic, or have you been reading the papers and believing in them instead of believing in your part?[9]

Shaw felt a particular exasperation with the critics who interpreted *Arms and the Man* cynically, since the whole point of the satire is that Shaw is exploding idealism not to plunge us into cynicism, but to save us from it. He does not, like Hemingway, reject the slogans of idealistic militarist rhetoric only to fall into nihilism. His indictment of idealism, in essence, is just that it inevitably leads to this kind of despair and collapse of morale. For Shaw, the Hamlet-like hero of Tennyson's *Maud* and Lieutenant Frederic Henry in *A Farewell to Arms* are really fraternal twins, opposite sides of the same coin. The true antithesis to Tennyson's romantic youth who goes off to the Crimea with a conviction that he will find glory and redemption through sacrifice is not Hemingway's disillusioned soldier, but Shaw's practical and sanguine Bluntschli.[10]

This is the lesson Raina has to learn. We first see her caught up in the excitement of the invasion. She is not, however, a vulgar fire-eater like her mother, convinced that all Serbs are devils and rejoicing in victory the way a schoolgirl might cheer a sports team. Her idealism is of a nobler sort, and she is genuinely horrified at the senseless and vindictive slaughter she fears will accompany the Serbian rout. This genuine elevation of mind has not failed to impress Raina's family and servants, who, even if they have not understood her feelings, have still paid her the homage the uncomprehending philistine pays to distinction even if he does not understand it.

But such homage has carried its own temptation. Raina, having a touch of the actress in her, has found it absurdly easy on trivial occasions when she has been in the wrong to cover small deceits by adopting the same noble air and mounting a moral high horse. At the same time her faith in a world glorious "for women who can see its glory and men who can act its romance" is shaken by awful doubts. What if Sergius, the swashbuckling young officer whose superior, patronizing manner and disdain for commonness match her own, is not the hero of her dreams but just another such actor as she is, whose pretensions to unsullied honor and unflinching bravery are also half sham? It is thus with a sense of triumphant relief that she hears how her betrothed has led a near-suicidal cavalry charge against the Serbs and won.

The play's first critics, assuming that *Arms and the Man* must be either a romance with an ideal sentimental heroine, or a farce with a fraudulently hypocritical one, found Raina all but unintelligible. So great was the confusion with respect to the psychology of the play and its treatment of morals and military life that Shaw felt constrained to explain his intentions in detail in a long essay published in the *New Review* under the title "A Dramatic Realist to His Critics." Here he attempts to render intellectual first aid:

> In the play of mine which is most in evidence in London just now, the heroine has been classified by critics as a minx, a liar, and a *poseuse*. I have nothing to do with that: the only moral question for me is, does she do good or harm? If you admit that she does good, that she generously saves a man's life and wisely extricates herself from a false position with another man, then you may classify her as you please—brave, generous, and affectionate; or artful, dangerous, faithless—it is all one to me: you can [not] prejudice me for or against her by such artificial categorizing....[11]

What Shaw is doing here is throwing overboard the whole of Victorian moral rhetoric, with its roots in introspective, absolutist standards, for a utilitarian, naturalistic ethic. Raina, like most of us, is a mixture and not categorizable. One side of her is a woman who assumes the style of a stage queen, the other a sensible, sympathetic person. When Bluntschli staggers into her room, she chivalrously tries to protect him. Compared to her exalted attitude toward Sergius, her feelings for Bluntschli are what she might have for a household pet. The difference is that she does not expect a pet dog to criticize her hero. When the Swiss actually laughs at the cavalry charge and refuses to take Sergius' soldiering seriously, she rebukes him coldly as someone incapable of appreciating honor and courage, though the man's self-assurance and professional knowledge once more raise in her mind the nagging question, Is the romantic Sergius the real Sergius?

Raina, when she comes to know herself—and Sergius—better, eventually finds it possible, and even a relief, to step down from her pedestal. Sergius is not so fortunate. To the eye he is everything a romantic could ask for, a devastatingly handsome man with the style of a Dumas musketeer, possessed of the loftiest conceptions of love and fighting. Psychologically, he is the quintessential aristocrat. In the British Museum manuscript, Shaw makes him boast that he is the last of "a race of 500 boyards." [12] Nevertheless, when it comes to the battlefield, the traditional testing ground of the aristocrat, he finds that though cavalry charges may thrill naïve spectators, modern wars are in the long run won by efficient planning and organization, not by deeds of high chivalry. That Bluntschli, a man "bourgeois to his boots," should be a successful soldier only proves to Sergius that soldiering is a coward's art fit only for hotelkeepers' sons. Major Petkoff protests that it is a trade like any other trade, but Sergius answers with the contempt of a feudal landowner that he has "no ambition to succeed as a tradesman."

But Sergius is a very special brand of aristocrat. Though he is violently and contemptuously antibourgeois he is not antiplebeian, nor even a snob. It is not lack of aristocratic blood he despises in others, but lack of aristocratic spirit. In short, he is an aristocrat, not of the order of a Chesterfield or a Wellington, but of a Byron or a Shelley, with all their radical hatred of oppression and their keen contempt for the pusillanimity of the average man in countenancing indignities. When Sergius is asked by Raina's servant, Louka, if the

poor fought less valiantly at Slivnitza than the wealthy, he replies
bitterly:

> Not a bit. They all slashed and cursed and yelled like heroes.
> Psha! the courage to rage and kill is cheap. I have an English bull
> terrier who has as much of that sort of courage as the whole
> Bulgarian nation, and the whole Russian nation at its back. But
> he lets my groom thrash him, all the same. Thats your soldier all
> over! No, Louka: your poor men can cut throats; but they are
> afraid of their officers; they put up with insults and blows; they
> stand by and see one another punished like children: aye, and
> help to do it when they are ordered. And the officers!!! Well
> [*with a short harsh laugh*] I am an officer. Oh, [*fervently*] give me
> the man who will defy to the death any power on earth or in heaven
> that sets itself up against his own will and conscience: he alone is
> the brave man.[13]

Shaw is here using Sergius as his mouthpiece; he would agree with
him that flogging is degrading and docile submission to it ignominious. But the difference is that while the emotional Bulgarian
indulges his scorn and admires defiance for defiance's sake, Shaw's
temperament is that of the practical reformer who distrusts mere
emotion and wants positive action. Thus his own deliberate response
to the problem of military discipline was his article "Civilization and
the Soldier," published in the *Humane Review*[14] seven years later,
which advocated a mundane military Bill of Rights to give the en-
listed man the same legal protection and privileges as the civilian.

Shaw based the character of Sergius on the Scottish revolutionary
socialist Robert Bontine Cunninghame Graham. Cunninghame
Graham was in every way a remarkable, not to say all but incredible,
personality. A nobleman claiming descent from a thirteenth-century
king of Scotland (hence the "race of 500 boyards"), he looked as
dashingly handsome and impressive as a Spanish grandee in a
Velázquez portrait. At sixteen he ran off to the Argentine pampas,
won fame as a gaucho horseman, had a town named after him, ran a
fencing academy in Mexico City, and later became the toast of salons
in Paris for his literary talents. Eventually his sympathy for the
poor led him to enter the British parliament, where he championed
their rights so obstreperously that he won the epithet "Don Quixote."
It was during his parliamentary career that he uttered his famous

defiance of the House—"I never withdraw"—which Shaw put into
the mouth of Sergius. Naturally, so flamboyant and self-dramatizing
a man was likely to evoke radically different responses from others.
Joseph Conrad, like Shaw, was fascinated by him, and, indeed,
Cunninghame Graham's romanticism makes him look at moments
like a character out of one of Conrad's own novels. "You are a most
hopeless idealist," Conrad wrote him, "your ideals are irrealisable."
Conrad called Cunninghame Graham's outlook on humanity "the
philosophy of unutterable scorn," and warned him, "Into the noblest
of causes men put something of their baseness; and sometimes, when
I think of you here, quietly, you seem to me tragic with your courage,
with your beliefs and your hopes." [15] On less imaginative and sympathetic people Cunninghame Graham understandably made a
much less favorable impression. Beatrice Webb, looking at him not
with the eye of a novelist, but as a sober Fabian, was merely exasperated at his flamboyance and his unwillingness to compromise.
On one occasion she engaged him in political discussion at a break-
fast meeting; later she wrote in her diary:

> Cunninghame Graham is a cross between an aristocrat and a
> barber's block. He is a *poseur*, but also an enthusiast, an unmiti-
> gated fool in politics . . . . "I have a letter from Kropotkin," [he]
> whispers to me; "he says, and I agree with him, if Burns with
> 80,000 men behind him does not make a revolution, it is because
> he is afraid of having his head cut off." [16]

Cunninghame Graham, for his part, never joined the Fabians and
would have found such a humdrum body with its passion for statistics
and its belief in slow progress completely out of harmony with his
swashbuckling. It was entirely appropriate, then, that Shaw should
have chosen as his model for Bluntschli, Sergius' foil, the Fabian of
Fabians, Sidney Webb. In striking contrast to Cunninghame
Graham, Webb came from the dullest of middle-class backgrounds,
his forebears being innkeepers and petty tradesmen. Even his adoring
wife had to admit that he was "undistinguished and unimpressive in
appearance" and totally lacking in any capacity for self-dramatiza-
tion. Where Cunninghame Graham, the believer in the *beau geste*,
had distinguished himself in the annals of British socialism by leading
a charge against the police in Trafalgar Square on Bloody Sunday,

November 13, 1887, Webb scoffed at such impossibilism, preached permeation, and filled his books on socialism not with fiery rhetoric, but with arithmetical tables in support of schemes for better hospitals and housing and cheaper gas and water. To Cunninghame Graham he must have looked like the perfect bourgeois pedant.

Webb's prosaic efficiency and phenomenal industry appear in Bluntschli's quartermasterlike talents, his disdain for heroics in his objections to the mad cavalry charge, and his self-possession in his anticlimactic repartee and his cool ability to make quick reappraisals of situations. The Sergius-Bluntschli contrast in *Arms and the Man* is thus a dramatization of the conflict in the British socialist movement between the so-called barricade socialists, who reincarnated the spirit of the Paris Commune, and the new gradualists, who deplored the uprising as a futile gesture led by naïve souls lacking in even elementary administrative ability. These are, of course, the two eternally opposed elements found in any reform group—the angry firebrands with an outraged sense of justice, and the patient plodders who try to set things right by degrees and seek to avoid dramatic confrontations. Not surprisingly, it was Webb who proved to have the greater staying power and made the significant mark in British politics: Cunninghame Graham eventually withdrew from socialist agitation, just as Sergius threw up his commission, in contempt. Webb, on the other hand, might have boasted like Bluntschli that he was at heart an "incurable romantic," since for all his practicality he had nevertheless chosen to fight battles as a social reformer when he might simply have trusted to his remarkable talents to carry him to the top as a civil servant.

Yet the fact that Shaw based the two principal male characters in his play on politicians should not be taken to indicate that he did not have an abiding, and informed, interest in the psychology of warfare on real battlefields. Just as Shakespeare in *Henry IV* raises the question, What is true courage? when he shows us the military emotions of Hotspur, Prince Hal, and Falstaff,[17] so Shaw is interested in critically analyzing the responses to danger not only of Sergius and Bluntschli, but also of Raina and her mother. Shaw's thinking on these matters was stimulated by two essays published in 1888. The first was an article entitled "Courage," by General Viscount

Wolseley, which appeared in the *Fortnightly Review*.[18] Wolseley, a British commander-in-chief and a veteran of the Crimean and Sudan campaigns, is an example of the hysterical-absolutist military temperament Shaw is satirizing in his play. He begins by assuming that "courage is a high virtue and cowardice a dastardly vice," and then proceeds to recommend that any officer even suspected of the least failure of nerve had "better end his days at once by his own hand." In "A Dramatic Realist" Shaw does not even bother to expose Wolseley's absurdities; he merely shows that even the quixotic Wolseley makes a number of candid admissions on the subject of military courage profoundly shocking to the romantically minded theatergoer. The second essay, "The Philosophy of Courage" by Horace Porter, contrasts amusingly with the first. Porter, who was a distinguished general in the Civil War, has something of Mark Twain's debunking spirit about him. Unlike Wolseley, Porter has a distinct suspicion of the courage born of the heat of passion; he freely admits that though green officers may pose for effect, seasoned leaders are more circumspect, and that after several days of battle, "courage, like everything else, wears out." What must have delighted Shaw especially, however, was Porter's commonsensical definition of an army not as a company of heroes, but as "an intelligent machine moving methodically, under perfect control and not guided by incompetency."[19] In brief, while Wolseley's schoolboyish ideas of bravery are close to Sergius', Porter's are markedly Bluntschlian.

In reading the reviews of the first production of *Arms and the Man*, Shaw was irked that critics regularly mistook his carefully documented episodes illustrating the grotesqueries and ironies of war for mere Shavian whimsy. To refute the charge that he had written an extravaganza, he cited his authorities for the episodes of his play in "A Dramatic Realist." Bluntschli's unheroic description of a typical cavalry charge, Shaw explains, was based almost verbatim on an account given "a friend of mine by an officer who served in the Franco-Prussian war," and the story of Stolz's death by burning on General Marbot's narrative of the Battle of Wagram. As a counteractive to Tennyson's dramatization of the famous charge at Balaclava, he quotes from the eighth volume of Alexander Kinglake's

Invasion of the Crimea (1887). Finally, Shaw had also drawn on Zola's recently published *La Débâcle* (1892), which dramatically revealed how France's swaggering, chauvinstic, enthusiastic, and unstable officer corps had been overwhelmed at Sedan by the phlegmatic but efficient Germans.

In *Arms and the Man*, Sergius' wild exploit at first looks nobly brave, and Bluntschli's desperate bid for survival in Raina's room unheroic in the extreme. Yet on reflection Bluntschli's act becomes human and intelligible, while the more we know of Sergius, the more his charge takes on the air of a suicidal gesture. As we shall see, Shaw thought the entire European aristocratic tradition with its code of "death or honor" and its tradition of dueling and daring on the battlefield was imbued by a powerful death wish. But Sergius, who is in every way nobler and more sensitive than the average member of the upper classes, suffers from a very special brand of this particular malady. Shaw calls Sergius both a latter-day Byron and a Hamlet whose plight has been transposed into a comic key. In the first connection he wants us to think of the self-dramatizing Manfred and of Byron's courting of death at Missolonghi. On the other hand, Sergius is Hamlet in his contempt for existence, in his cruel play with Louka, and in his propensity to fall into Hamlet's "O-what-a-rogue-and-peasant-slave-am-I" vein. He goes to embrace "the blood-red blossom of war" and "the doom assign'd" because, like Hamlet and the hero of *Maud*, he is disgusted with human nature itself.

In a broader sense, the disease from which Sergius suffers is one that Shaw thought afflicted all Europe: sickliness of conscience. Like Nietzsche and Samuel Butler, Shaw traced this morbidity of spirit to the introspective side of evangelicalism, with its cultivation of guilt feelings and its queasiness as to human motives. As such he sees it as the arch-foe of human self-respect and the parent of a debilitating pessimism. In reaction to such a philosophy, Shaw, in "A Dramatic Realist," demands "respect, interest, affection for human nature as it is," and offers us himself as an example of moral health and sanity:

> I am not a pessimist at all. It does not concern me that, according to certain ethical systems, all human beings fall into classes labelled liar, coward, thief, and so on. I am myself, according to

these systems, a liar, a coward, a thief, and a sensualist; and it is
my deliberate, cheerful, and entirely self-respecting intention to
continue to the end of my life deceiving people, avoiding danger,
making my bargains with publishers and managers on principles
of supply and demand instead of abstract justice, and indulging all
my appetites, whenever circumstances commend such actions to
my judgment.[20]

Sergius holds the world in contempt for its failure to appreciate
his quixotic ideals of military valor. His contempt for himself, by
contrast, springs mainly from his inability to live up to his ideals of
romantic love. He has made Raina the queen of an imaginary kingdom in which all lovers are always perfectly truthful and candid,
unfailingly noble in their sentiments and unchanging in their affections, and quite free from any sexual susceptibility to others. Unfortunately, no sooner has he formulated this code than he finds, like
Goldsmith's hero, that the kitchen is a more sexually exciting place
than the salon and Raina's maid more to his taste than her mistress.
But just to the degree that he is shocked by the unworthiness of his
own behavior he is all the more desperately intent on believing that
Raina belongs to a pure world above his, where her worst thoughts
are of an ineffably higher order than her maid's best ones.

When Louka reveals, that, far from being the goddess Sergius
imagines, Raina tells lies, play-acts, and has become affectionately
interested in another man, he recoils with horrified half-incredulity.
More, he taunts Louka with having "the soul of a servant" because
she has spied on her mistress in flagrant violation of his own chivalric
code. But alas, he immediately compromises himself as deeply as
Louka in this regard, since his jealousy leads him immediately to
demand who his rival is, and even by asking the question, he is
implicitly condoning her acts, a fact which he is too candid to hide
from himself. The result is that his self-contempt is still further fed
by his entirely natural behavior.

In the end Sergius discovers the truth of Louka's assertions and
challenges Bluntschli to a duel, which, however, the Swiss accepts so
matter-of-factly that the Bulgarian gives up, declaring that he cannot
fight a "machine." Finally, Sergius marries not Raina but Louka, a
development that led Max Beerbohm to protest that he had cudgeled
his wits to find some meaning in this "strange conjunction."[21] But

this is to miss the psychology of the relationship. Despite her peasant birth, Louka's most marked trait is her compulsive defiance of others. She is in fact exactly Sergius' ideal—the mutinous recruit of his polemic, and her spitfire temperament excites him as Raina's does not. The scheme by which she makes him marry her, however idiotic, is also perfectly in keeping with their personalities. She puts the question to him in the form of a dare: if he compromises himself by making further advances to her, will he have the courage to defy public opinion by making her his wife? In this sense his cavalry charge and his betrothal are of a piece, the insane gestures of a man desperate to prove that though all the rest of the world is cowardly, he is not.

Sergius' opposite as a military strategist is Bluntschli; his opposite as a lover is the servant, Nicola. Everything Sergius does is based on his aristocratic code of honor. Everything Nicola does is the result of his commercialism. As a servant he succeeds by achieving perfect servility, but his real aspiration in life is to enter the shop-keeping class and to rise in it. When he sees that Louka might make a good customer and be less discontented as Sergius' bride, he coolly surrenders her to him.[22] Sergius, trying to apply his own ethical system to this turn of events, is at a loss to decide whether Nicola's act is one of noble self-sacrifice or crass self-interest. But the whole point of the play is the inadequacy of such systems in judging human conduct, and Bluntschli, for whom the meaning of a moral act lies not in its motives but its consequences, cuts the Gordian knot with the simple advice "Never mind." In the end Raina, delighted to subside into a more comfortable relation after the strain play-acting with Sergius has imposed on her, accepts Bluntschli as her new fiancé, and her parents, overwhelmed by the inventory of his hotels, ardently approve her choice.[23]

Arms and the Man is not in the first rank of Shaw's comic master-pieces. Later he himself came to have some doubts about it, calling it a "flimsy," "fantastic," and "unsafe" piece of work.[24] Certainly there are some farcical contrivances—the coat episode, for instance—that Shaw would never allow himself again. Yet *Arms and the Man* cannot be simply dismissed as a spoof of outdated ideals of love and war. True, Raina's pretty airs are as much a thing of the past as the affectations of *Les Précieuses ridicules*, and the Victorian stage attitudes to war died in 1914 with the slaughter of the Sergiuses. But where Victorian manners and the Victorian theater are dead, the psychology of the hypersensitive idealist is still familiar to us all. Most often he turns up as the would-be reformer, who, not realizing that compromise and a willingness to work patiently at abolishing abuses are part of effective action, recoils in disillusionment, denouncing his more realistic colleagues as hypocrites and frauds. And anyone who thinks the battle against Victorian morals in favor of human self-respect is won has only to consider our attitudes toward mankind's sex impulses, from which we still recoil in embarrassed horror and cowardly evasion. William Irvine has contended that *Arms and the Man* is a sour and cynical play because Shaw was engaged in the uncongenial task of turning out a potboiler.[25] This seems to me absurdly wide of the mark. There is more truth in Beerbohm's charge that, from the point of view of his work as a whole, it is a narrow play. Shaw, who was the heir of both the utilitarian and the transcendentalist traditions, is far more of a Benthamite in this play than anywhere else, the humor being of exactly the cool, benign, quizzical, deflating sort that peeps through the dry surface of Bentham's treatises. But before we write off *Arms and the Man* as mere good-natured philistinism spiked with a dash of Nietzsche, we should remember Shaw's caution in his book on Ibsen that, though Don Quixote is a nobler man than his servant, we had better lend an ear to Sancho Panza as a corrective against the Don's madness. It is also important to grasp the exact place of the play in Shaw's didactic enterprise. After all, courage and honor are not merely high Shavian virtues; they are at the very center of his moral philosophy. Here we can profitably compare Shaw's strategy as a playwright-thinker with Ibsen's. Ibsen believed in truth and outspokenness beyond all else, yet he followed *Ghosts* and *An Enemy of the People* with *The Wild Duck* as a warning against making these virtues into absolutes. In Shaw's case the *Pleasant Plays* provide us with a searching look at kinds of false heroism before Shaw shows us his own heroic exemplars in the *Plays for Puritans*. Nor is it remarkable that he gives us the qualifications first, since, as he warns us again and again, it is just the highest ideals that are open to the most dangerous perversions.

CHAPTER THREE

Candida

G. K. Chesterton once remarked pertinently that Shaw's objections to love and war were not, like Tolstoy's, objections to love and war per se, but only to "love songs" and "war songs." Like Bacon and Bentham, Shaw distrusted the poetic faculty for its illusory misrepresentations of the world, and like Plato he feared its power to glamorize socially pernicious behavior. Yet Chaucer, Goethe, Blake, Shelley, and Wagner, to go no further, were all poets who commanded his respect and even his enthusiasm. Clearly, Shaw believed that the "magic glass" of the poet, however dangerously it might distort facts or exalt dubious emotions, could also on occasion reveal significant new visions. If the *Pleasant Plays* were written to demonstrate the necessity of founding morals on "scientific natural history," this did not preclude letting a poet have his say. *Candida* is in fact a resolutely naturalistic play in which Shaw for the first time attempts to give poetry its due.[1]

Of all the poets of the nineties, it was William Butler Yeats whose literary creed challenged Shaw most sharply. Yeats, the young romantic, regarded Ibsen as the arch-enemy, Ibsen's stern realism, his middle-class settings, and what Yeats regarded as his perversion of art into an instrument of social criticism being all antipathetic to him. Shaw, the leading Ibsenite of the London theater, was for the same reasons equally anathema. The buoyant energy of Shaw's utilitarian prose grated on the nerves of the aesthete who cultivated Pater's languorous rhythms for their hypnotic effect. Even when their enthusiasms ran parallel (as they frequently did), they managed to admire the same painters and writers for opposite reasons. Only when Shaw turned his formidable rhetoric against common foes did Yeats feel exhilarated, but Shaw had a way of raking the ranks of the aesthetes as devastatingly as those of the philistines. That he did it all with the greatest good humor only compounded the offense, so that Yeats in comical exasperation finally derided Shaw as a "smiling sewing machine." It is therefore one of the remarkable ironies of literary history that Shaw's *Arms and the Man* should have made its debut on a double bill with a delicate fantasy by Yeats.

This one-act play, which bore the title *The Land of Heart's Desire*,[2] had very little success on the stage (though Shaw compliments Yeats prettily in his preface) and is not a well-known piece. In it a young wife rebels against the drudgery of cleaning pots and pans, and finally escapes, through death, to a happier existence in a fairyland where "nobody gets old and godly and grave." Yeats must have felt that Shaw's debunking satire, following upon this piece of romantic escapism, was a stab at his very vitals. At any rate, he tells us in his autobiography how he hotly defended his anti-Shavianism to Florence Farr, the producer. In making another housewife, whom a poet regards as trapped in a life of dull domesticity, the center of *Candida*, Shaw, in turn, was presumably reacting to Yeats's play, and, indeed, using it as a point of departure for a much more complex drama.

The complexity enters through Shaw's willingness to grant, in part, Yeats's claim that the poet may on occasion soar above the naturalist to glean truth from "the half lights that glimmer from symbol to symbol."[3] Here again the situation has a paradoxical side, for it seems to have been the arch-realist Ibsen who suggested to Shaw how he might combine mundane surface verisimilitude with a subtle and elaborate poetic symbolism. In the same year that Shaw published *The Quintessence of Ibsenism*, Ibsen had himself broken new ground with a play which, though written in prose, is markedly poetic in substance when compared to the social dramas which preceded it. It is the imagery of this new work, *The Master Builder*, Shaw had in mind when he wrote in the preface to the *Pleasant Plays*:

> Let Ibsen explain, if he can, why the building of churches and happy homes is not the ultimate destiny of Man, and why, to thrill the unsatisfied younger generations, he must mount beyond it to heights that now seem unspeakably giddy and dreadful to him, and from which the first climbers must fall and dash themselves to

pieces. He cannot explain it: he can only show it to you as a vision in the magic glass of his artwork; so that you may catch his presentiment and make what you can of it. And this is the function that raises dramatic art above imposture and pleasure hunting, and enables the playwright to be something more than a skilled liar and pandar.[4]

Shaw later interpreted the story of master builder Solness (to which he is obliquely alluding here) as an allegory of Ibsen's own career—Solness' churches and homes corresponding to Ibsen's early verse plays and social dramas, and his mounting of the tower to Ibsen's own attempt to respond to youth's "knock at the door" by attempting the kind of symbolist drama younger writers were turning to in reaction against naturalism. We can even carry the analogy a step further and say that in *Candida* Shaw stands in relation to Yeats as Solness does to the challenge of young Hilda Wrangel, and Ibsen to the new poetic drama. Now, adding poetry to his social realism, Shaw takes us, through the character of Eugene Marchbanks, to the poet's lonely tower to show us visions on the horizon invisible to the multitude below.

Shaw conceived of *Candida* as a Hegelian drama, showing the conflict of two systems of ideals, each inadequate in itself, but both having a claim to our interest and respect. We can perhaps best grasp what these are if we look for a moment at the historical background of the opposing life-views. The first ideal is Morell's Christian Socialism. The Christian Socialist movement began in the fateful year 1848 under the auspices of two Broad Church Anglican clergymen, F. D. Maurice and Charles Kingsley. Like Marxism, it was concerned with the problem of poverty, but unlike Marxism, it did not advocate revolutionary methods or develop a scientific economic theory. Instead, Christian Socialist ministers, as we have noted, devoted themselves to pastoral problems, such as slum housing or sweated labor. At first they were opposed not only by evangelicals, with their emphasis on salvation and piety, but also by Anglo-Catholicism with its dogma and ritual. In the generation after Maurice, however, there was a new development: Anglo-Catholic priests, who had from the start been sympathetic to medievalism for doctrinal reasons, now came to react also against modern capitalism

in favor of medieval social values just as Ruskin (who had begun as
a critic of medieval art) had done before them. In the nineties Shaw
noted that the Church of England slum parishes of East London
were manned almost exclusively by Anglo-Catholic socialists, who
were ardent sacramentalists and made much of the cult of the Virgin.[5]
It is this particular mixture of High Church morality and lively social
sympathies that Shaw means to show us in the Reverend James
Morell, the minister of St. Dominic's.

In opposition to all this, Eugene Marchbanks represents the poet-
aesthetes of the nineties with their strong hostility to literature with
a social purpose. Like Yeats, he worships love and beauty and holds
political reformers in contempt; as his name indicates, he is an
aristocrat who has a fiercely burning contempt for middle-class
manners, art, and morals. Shaw deliberately loads his speeches with
the romantic imagery of late Victorian poetry in the Pre-Raphaelite
tradition. The dream picture of the never-never land to which he
proposes that he and Candida shall flee together is a Morrisian-
Yeatsian fantasy. In brief, Eugene stands for poetry, romance, and
the "land of heart's desire," as against prose, naturalism, social
reform, and the bourgeois kitchen. Or to use the analogy that Shaw
himself deliberately introduces into his play, he stands for the
shadowy world of "Night"—the night of the lovers in the second
act of Wagner's *Tristan and Isolde*, with its freedom and super-
mundane ecstasies—as opposed to the clear, unambiguous "Day"
world with its domestic chores, wearying routine, and dull practical
effort.

Shaw's way of saying this in his preface is somewhat more obscure:
there he calls *Candida* an attempt to "distil the quintessential drama"
from Pre-Raphaelitism and to show Pre-Raphaelitism formulating
"its own revolt against itself as it develops into something higher."
This is Hegelianizing with a vengeance. What these cryptic statements mean will become intelligible to the reader if he realizes that
Shaw is using the term "Pre-Raphaelite" as synonymous with
"neomedieval" and that he deliberately lumps together under this
one term not only the art movement usually designated by it but
also such varied social and religious phenomena as Christian
Socialism and Anglo-Catholicism. But what has Shaw in mind when

he speaks of Pre-Raphaelitism formulating "its own revolt against itself"? This can be seen most clearly if we look for the moment at the history of Pre-Raphaelitism on its artistic side.

The Pre-Raphaelite movement, like Christian Socialism, began in 1848. At its inception it was a protest against the effete neoclassicism of English academic art. In reaction to the ideals of classicism it strove both for a new scientific accuracy in the depiction of natural detail and for a new imaginative suggestiveness. Though these tendencies may strike us now as, in a sense, logical opposites, the new movement managed in its first uncritical stage to endorse both at once by invoking the example of Gothic religious art. Then, as the movement came under the influence of Ruskin, it developed a new social as well as a new artistic conscience. It thus promoted at once a realistic consideration of contemporary problems and an ultra-romantic art based on Dante, Malory, and the Nibelungenlied in which Beatrice, Isolde, and Brunhild replaced the nymphs and goddesses of neoclassicism. Consequently, paintings as different as Ford Madox Brown's "Work," in which Carlyle and F. D. Maurice are shown overlooking a group of street laborers in Hampstead, and Rossetti's "The Boat of Love," where two lovers embark on a magical voyage with an angel helmsman, both go by the term "Pre-Raphaelite," though one shows an extreme of didactic naturalism and the other of romantic escapism. The way in which the movement had bifurcated can also be shown by contrasting the relation of Shaw and Yeats to William Morris, the leading figure in its second generation.[6] Both had a near-worshipful respect for the older man, but Shaw admired the social revolutionary, while Yeats deplored Morris's political interests and was attracted exclusively by "the idle singer of an empty day." Thus by 1894 we have the striking phenomenon of two men, the one preaching Ibsenism and social change, the other aestheticism and antirealism, both claiming to be the true heirs of the Pre-Raphaelite Brotherhood.

Candida opens with a long description of the minister's home and its environs. Shaw's naturalism here spares us nothing, not even the "ugly iron urinals" of Hackney, which symbolize conscientious civic effort at its most homely. The extent to which Shaw is determined to bring both sides of Pre-Raphaelitism together is shown by the

counterbalancing romantic image of the Titian's "Virgin."[7] This
latter represents Eugene's poetic ideal of womanhood, and demonstrates the distance of his world from that of the reforming parson.
Similarly, Victoria Park, which, with all its imperfections, is still for
the clergyman an earnest of the New Jerusalem, remains for the boy
poet, used to the idyllic country parks of the gentry, only another
aspect of the dreary middle-class milieu in which his adored Candida
is imprisoned.

The Reverend James Morell, whom we first meet at his morning's
routine, is a handsome, hearty, high-spirited preacher and orator
with some of Browning's optimism and breezy affability. He is a
particular favorite of the women of his congregation, whose devotion
he somewhat naïvely ascribes to their enthusiasm for the mixture of
socialism and Anglo-Catholic sacramentalism he preaches. Since he
has made himself an apostle, not to the wealthy and influential, but
to small and insignificant radical groups, most of them with a strongly
antireligious bias, we may assume that he is in love with his job and
performs it neither as a boring duty nor with an eye to personal
advancement, but out of real faith in his mission of establishing "the
Kingdom of Heaven on earth."[8] For this he has won the respect of
his secretary, Prossy, who is in love with him, and Lexy, his curate,
who idolizes him as a reformer. Prossy has been carefully selected
by Candida as sufficiently gone on Morell to help with the general
housework, and at the same time neither pretty nor clever enough
to attract him seriously. But both husband and wife are in effect
equally unscrupulous about using their personal attractions for
ulterior ends, Morell having conscripted the callow but doting Lexy
with no greater compunction as to the effect of this radical apprenticeship on his future advancement than his wife has shown for the
secretary's sentimental yearnings.

Morell is soon interrupted by someone a good deal less sympathetic, namely, his father-in-law, Burgess.[9] The collision of the
two men's outlooks provides us with an amusing interlude of intellectual comedy. Morell had earlier denounced his father-in-law
publicly as a scoundrel because his less-than-subsistence wages had
driven his girl workers to prostitution; but Burgess, who thinks he
has only done what any other provident employer would have done,

that is, bought his labor as cheaply as possible, finds this attack quite incomprehensible in terms of his own bourgeois ethic. Burgess had indignantly broken with Morell, but now that he has discovered that Socialist clergymen, far from remaining pariahs, are gaining influence in the church, he has decided to resume relations for the sake of possible profitable future connections. But when, after he has been forced into avowing his motive, Morell not only once more hails him as a scoundrel but then shakes his hand and congratulates him on his open scoundrelism, the sweater is completely dumfounded. The point is that Morell refuses to confuse social with moral judgments. Though he will fight vigorously against Morell's employment practices and might even vote for his liquidation in a socialist republic as a profiteer, he does not adopt a disdainful tone or act self-righteously. In this he is an authentic Shavian, and no more condemns Burgess morally than he would condemn a pig for greedily shoving its way to a feed trough.

Burgess is doubly sure of Morell's derangement, when, far from resenting the epithet, "fool," which Burgess has bestowed on him, the clergyman accepts it with cheerful equanimity. Indeed, "fool" is a word Shaw uses in his comedy almost as freely as Shakespeare does in *Twelfth Night*. But where Shakespeare's characters make fools of themselves for sentimental or amorous reasons, "folly" in *Candida* has a religious as well as a secular meaning. In the course of the play Morell, Lexy, Eugene, Prossy, and even Burgess all redeem themselves from unamiability by making fools of themselves over others, but the first two also rise above this level and make fools of themselves, as Paul would say, "for Christ's sake." So sure was Shaw that a willingness to appear as a fool in the world's eyes was a condition of nobility of spirit that he wrote to Ellen Terry: "You boast that you are a fool—it is at bottom, oh, such a tremendous boast: do you know that in Wagner's last drama, 'Parsifal,' the redeemer is 'der reine Thor,' 'the pure fool'?"[10]

So far, Morell has seemed the almost perfect champion of his cause —generous, vigorous, popular, and efficient. The sublime folly of his devotion to Christian Socialism does not prevent him from handling his personal relations very adroitly; he treats Prossy and Lexy with humorous tact, and even rises to witty eloquence in dealing with a

man like Burgess, whom he despises. But his very virtues as a crusading preacher—readiness of tongue and rough energy—carry with
them their own dangers, for Morell is one of those men who give
themselves up wholeheartedly to worthy causes but lack the subtlety
to gauge the effect of their efforts on their more sophisticated hearers.
Such men may be towers of strength to a religious or social movement
at the same time that their banality of mind and uncritical self-
intoxication may appall the unsympathetic. One may even argue that
banality in such cases may be as much an advantage as a weakness,
since the average man is usually incapable of taking in more than
one original view at a time, and is happily reassured if his unorthodoxy on one point is justified by as much traditional moral rhetoric
as possible, no matter how stale, flat, and offensive it may seem to
more thoughtful people. Clergymen, whose congregations are not
usually in the position to contradict even the most heart-wearying
platitude, are particularly susceptible to this hazard. Fortunately,
such men are most usually blessed with intellectually unventuresome
wives. But though this may be counted on as the case nineteen times
out of twenty, there is always the twentieth chance that the crusading
minister may be married not to a mentally numb wife, but to a woman
who winces inwardly every time he sprinkles his conversation with
the clichés of popular pulpit oratory, quite aware that the divine
foolishness of the saint has been temporarily eclipsed by the stupidity
of the ordinary mortal.[11]

In Shaw's play, Candida is just such a woman, though Morell does
not realize it. Carried away by his enthusiasm for socialism, and
reassured by the admiration of his congregation and her own solici-
tous care of him, Morell is too blind to see to what extent he is
separated from his wife morally and intellectually. Eugene, however,
has no such blindness. The young poet's Pre-Raphaelitism has led
him not to embrace social reform, but to sharpen his aesthetic
responses and to develop his sensitivity to the feelings of beautiful
and intelligent women. When Morell launches on his favorite subject
of marital bliss and rhapsodizes on his own marriage,[12] Eugene does
not listen with either Lexy's complacency or Prossy's frustrated
jealousy. Instead, he turns on him with the shrill vehemence of a
young Shelley, denouncing him as an obtuse windbag who has made

life a mockery for a woman with a "great soul." Morell is taken aback, but manages at first to stand his ground. After all, Lexy is just such another effeminate youth as Eugene; he has been able to win him over with manly warmth and good humor, and he thinks Eugene's unaccountable fit of nerves will yield to the same treatment.

He is even astute enough to appeal to Eugene's obvious idealism and to mix in some clever flattery: the poet and preacher, he tells him, are, after all, cofighters in the wars of humanity and Eugene may even be the "pioneer" or "master builder" who will one day complete Morell's mission, or achieve a greater one.[13] But Eugene, with the fierceness of the weak and the mercilessness of the young, rejects these blandishments with scorn as "sermons, stale perorations, mere rhetoric." What Candida wants, he declares, is "reality, truth, and freedom," the truth in this case being the truth about her marriage, and the freedom, freedom from the bond that ties her to her moralizing husband. Then he looses his most wounding arrow with as little compunction as the boy Parsifal shows in shooting the swan at the beginning of Wagner's opera; Morell thinks Candida worships him as a public speaker like his other woman parishioners, but when she sees him performing in public she despises him in her heart, as King David's wife despised her husband's drunken dancing. Thoroughly aroused, the clergyman attacks the "snivelling whelp" of a poet physically, and suffers the further humiliation of realizing he has so far lost his temper as to stoop to an act of jealous violence. When Candida comes in, all unaware of the altercation, and straightens Eugene's collar, the man who had earlier boasted of his happiness now feels himself to be the wretchedest of mortals.

Eugene's philosophy is one of love as the parson's philosophy is one of social action. It is also aristocratic in its disdain for manual labor, which Eugene regards as socially degrading. His horror on discovering that Candida does her share of the dirtiest and most menial household tasks is akin to what Tristan might have felt if he had come upon Isolde serving as a scullery maid. He indignantly tells her she must have no more to do with scrubbing brushes or ill-smelling lamps, and offers her instead "a tiny shallop to sail away in, far from the world, where the marble floors are washed by the rain and dried by the sun" and "where the lamps are stars." This is, of course, the romantic escapism of Morris's *The Earthly Paradise* and Yeats's early poetry. Its prettiness appeals to the sentimental Burgess, who, dazzled by the glamor of a real, live aristocrat, plays Bottom to Eugene's Ariel. Morell, on the other hand, is incensed, finding in Eugene's exaggerated revulsion an implied contempt for those who do the unpleasant, necessary, routine work of the world. He hotly denounces Eugene's paradise as "idle, selfish, and useless." But Eugene, inflamed by what he regards as the oppression of a beautiful woman by an insensitive man, gives as good as he receives, and Morell finds himself bested even as a debater.

Candida is immediately aware of Morell's loss of assurance but mistakes its cause. Thinking he is merely suffering from overwork, she tries to force him to take a more detached view of his duties. Her strategy is to tease him into self-awareness by warning him, in a half-serious, half-joking fashion, that his hold over the feminine half of his audiences rests, at least in part, on the same basis as any matinee idol's. The clergyman, however, is not only shocked but profoundly upset by this revelation. To Morell the Victorian moralist, the idea that the religious and social enthusiasm of his followers owes anything to so crude a force as sexual feeling, instead of being merely a simple fact of natural history neither in itself good or evil, is intolerable. He recoils from what he calls Candida's "soul-destroying cynicism." In the end Candida's attack proves even more unsettling than she had intended. Having lost his balance, he does what people in a state of shock often do—he clings all the more desperately to the spar that has given way. At least, he tells his wife, he trusts in *her* "purity." But this last stroke of naïveté is too much for Candida, who now reveals the simple truth—unlike him, she does not regard a marriage vow as indissoluble or the sexual act as materially sinful. There is nothing in her formal pledge to him which would restrain her if she loved another man and felt he needed her more than her husband did. Coming on top of Eugene's allegations of the morning, this merely confirms for Morell the poet's claim to understand and appreciate Candida better than her husband does.[14] He realizes that Eugene, through his exclusive preoccupation with the sentimental side of human nature, has been able to grasp a fact beyond his own ken, namely, that when a modern emancipated woman loses sympathy with her husband and wishes to leave him, no traditional theological or moral considerations can possibly force her to stay at home.

Pre-Raphaelitism, which had in earliest days fostered the Victorian piety of a Holman Hunt, had, by the nineties, developed a romantic, rebellious side, which, mingling with the libertarian ideals of Blake and Shelley, produced the antinomianism of the aesthetic revolt. It is this tradition to which Eugene belongs and to whose cry for sexual freedom he lends his voice. Morell, as orthodox in matters of sex as he is radical in his social ideals, is a million miles from all this, and even if he understood these ideas would be in no frame of mind to regard them philosophically. To him the overwhelming reality is the danger of losing his beloved wife. But Candida, who does not know of Eugene's attack, is made impatient by her husband's long face, and ascribing it to mere prudishness, accuses him with teasing scorn of reneging on his own encouragement to her to be not just his wife and parishioner, but a woman with a mind of her own. Then Eugene comes in, only to behave very differently than he had in the morning. A smug Morell was one thing; the presently suffering Morell is another. The element of compassion in his temperament makes him recoil from what he takes to be Candida's deliberate tormenting of her husband. His hand goes to his breast, and he feels Morell's pain in his own heart as sharply as Parsifal feels the pain of the wounded Amfortas in Wagner's opera. Like Parsifal, taught by pity ("durch Mitleid wissend"), he chides the woman he loves for hurting the man he now realizes loves her.[15] Morell, in turn, having realized that if Candida elects to leave him nothing he can or wants to do will prevent her, faces the inevitable crisis with his old manly courage, by inviting Eugene to stay alone with Candida while he goes out to preach.

Eugene is at once struck by the heroism of Morell's action, this being exactly the kind of gesture his own idealism can appreciate. He reads Candida poem after poem to stave off any intimate disclosures, while pretending to himself that he is a latter-day Siegfried who has placed a drawn sword between himself and his Brunhild as a pledge of chastity. Only once does his resolution break down. When Candida (whose mind is not on the poems but on her absent husband) begs for relief, Eugene, in his simplicity, tries to play the conventional gallant. Candida, treating his amorous passion neither with a pretense at indignation nor with affected confusion, simply punctures his pose by asking him to say what he honestly feels. In response he utters her name in a kind of rapturous prayer, as Dante might have addressed Beatrice or Tannhäuser Elizabeth, declaring that this for him is happiness and heaven.

When Morell returns and asks what has happened, the poet replies that Candida did not repulse him, but that an angel with "a flaming sword"[16] stood in the way, by which he means that in the crucial test he could not in his absence make advances to the wife of a man he now regards as a friend. Morell, however, cannot grasp his meaning. He is merely incensed when Eugene tells him that far from playing the virtuous wife, Candida offered him "her shawl, her wings, the wreath of stars on her head" and "the crescent moon beneath her feet." Failing to understand that these are the accoutrements not of some siren, but of the transfigured Virgin of medieval art, he attacks Eugene in a second jealous fit, which on this occasion "the pure fool, through pity made wise" does not shrink from but bears good-naturedly. But Morell, now the more clearheaded of the two, knows that in a marriage of personal sentiment like his own there is no room for a second man, and insists that Candida must choose between them.[17]

The "choosing" scene is, of course, the scène à faire in any play or novel involving a love triangle. Eric Bentley has aptly pointed out the contrast between Candida and the conventional conservative or romantic treatment of the subject. In the conservative drama, the lover would be exposed as a cad and the wife would stick with her magnanimous husband. In the romantic one, the husband would be painted as a dismal tyrant and the wife's elopement with her lover justified on this ground. There is even a third alternative Mr. Bentley does not consider: if the writer is both romantic and conventional (a favorite combination since it gratifies two common human instincts), he can have his cake and eat it too by simply killing off the husband, as George Eliot does in Middlemarch. Shaw's originality lies in refusing to allow any such evasion of the moral issues. He makes both husband and interloper equally sympathetic and shows us an open struggle between the two men, neither of whom is a brute or a seducer.

In the confrontation scene Morell concedes that Eugene had been right earlier about Candida's view of marriage. Now he demands to know if Eugene is also right in believing she is in love with him. He calls Candida his "greatest treasure," and announces, "We have agreed—he and I—that you shall choose between us now." Once more Candida is chilled, both by the stupidity of a man who addresses her as if she were a public meeting and by the word "treasure," which implies that he is unconsciously thinking of her as a possession. She demands to know what each man will bid for her. This coldness so afflicts the by now desperate clergyman that, though it is the frail poet who bids his "weakness, desolation, and heart's need" against Morell's conventional offer of his strength and protection, the latter's every word and gesture reveal the truth behind the manly façade—that he is the one who most needs her affectionate care. Candida is thus able to declare with no hesitation that she chooses her husband as the weaker of the two men.

That is to say, Candida affects to choose Morell. But once again Shaw departs from the conventional formula, for Candida is by no means the typical anguished wife of sentimental melodrama who must either put up with an impossible husband or indulge a guilty passion. The drama of the last act consists in a series of discoveries made by the two men, not in a conflict in the mind of Candida. She does not really choose as, say, a heroine in a play by Corneille or Sartre might choose, by weighing the rational alternatives on their merits. She simply affirms what she has desired all along. The point is that neither of the men has really understood her or her relation to him. To Morell, Candida has seemed merely the dutiful wife and mother who has shared his own Anglo-Catholic view of marriage. The social reformer had, in short, been content to regard his marriage as a Victorian domestic idyll, with himself as his dependent wife's prop and protector.

For Morell, Candida is a "Madonna of the Hearth"—the kind of conventionally pious figure one might find on a religious calendar. To Eugene, on the other hand, Candida is the Virgin as Titian represents her in his famous painting, a transfigured "Virgin of the

Assumption," ready to take flight from the world of mundane reality. Yet though she is not the kind of Virgin either man imagines, Shaw was quite serious in calling *Candida* his "Virgin Mother" play and in ascribing a positive religious significance to his heroine.[18] Reacting against the prejudices of his Irish Protestant upbringing, Shaw regarded the cult of Mary as one of the glories of Catholic Christendom, both for its softening effect on the lives of the masses and as the inspiration of so much magnificent religious art. In his opening stage directions he tells us that Candida does indeed resemble the Titian Madonna over the mantel, a creation Shaw once hailed as the most perfect union of flesh and spirit in Italian painting, appealing at once to the devotional and the voluptuous sides of man's nature.[19]

Candida, as a "Virgin Mother," is neither a conventional moralistic housewife nor a figure in the clouds. If the higher synthesis toward which Shaw sees Pre-Raphaelitism evolving includes both Morell's social concern and Eugene's libertarian views on love, Candida stands above both men by sharing something of the vision of each. Shaw in his letter to James Huneker calls her "immoral" and "as unscrupulous as Siegfried."[20] This, however, is praise for her unconventionality and her freedom from false sentimentality, and is not an attack, as has been mistakenly assumed. Shaw, after all, approved of Siegfried's lack of scruples. Candida's unscrupulousness, as we have seen, comes in her willingness to exploit other people's sentimental feelings in order to further the practical management of the household; in other words she is least scrupulous where Eugene is most so, simply because she does not regard such attachments *au sérieux*. She does not, like the poet, look on a tongue-tied lover as an object of infinite pathos or think of a broken heart as the world's greatest tragedy. Instead, she responds to the boy poet's love with maternal indulgence and regards heartbreak as one of the inevitable —and healthy—experiences of adolescence. Nor does her lack of scruples about her marriage vows matter. As Shaw puts it, Candida is "straight for natural reasons, not for conventional ethical ones."

Eugene's departure at the end of the play has also been widely misunderstood. Many people have concluded, since Candida stays with Morell and Eugene leaves, that Shaw, when the chips were down, simply lacked the courage of his convictions about freedom in marriage. Shaw remarked sardonically to Huneker that no doubt young girls in America would weep at the ending and suppose that Eugene had to leave "to save the proprieties of New England Puritanism." But the real reason for his going is his vocation as a poet. Once he realizes that Candida is the protective mother, a born helpmate and not a glamorous figure out of romance, and that the kind of paradise she has to offer is specifically a paradise of the hearth, he flees from the parsonage into the night, that is, as Shaw explained, into the "holy night" of Wagner's Cornwall and Shakespeare's Venice, "the true realm of the poet."

Freed from illusions, Eugene can now surrender Candida to Morell, glad that the latter has filled the heart of the woman he formerly loved. The secret in his own heart mysteriously hinted at in Shaw's final stage direction was, Shaw explained to a group of Rugby schoolboys who had written him their own conjectures,

> very obvious after all—provided you know what a poet is. What business has a man with the great destiny of a poet with the small beer of domestic cuddling and petting at the apron-string of some dear nice woman? Morell cannot do without it: it is the making of him; without it he would be utterly miserable and perhaps go to the devil. To Eugene, the stronger of the two, the daily routine of it is nursery slavery, swaddling clothes, mere happiness instead of exaltation—an atmosphere in which great poetry dies. To choose it would be like Swinburne choosing Putney. When Candida brings him squarely face to face with it, his heaven rolls up like a scroll; and he goes out proudly into the majestic and beautiful kingdom of the starry night.[21]

Eugene's poetic relation to Candida could no more survive domesticity than Dante's idealization of Beatrice, Petrarch's passion for Laura, or Yeats's worship of Maud Gonne could have persisted after marriage. "He is really a god going back to his heaven, proud, unspeakably contemptuous of the 'happiness' he envied in the days of his blindness."[22] Thus, having shed its illuminating ray of truth, terrifying enough, into the soul of the journeyman minister, the spirit of poetry passes on and the play ends.

Shaw subtitled *Candida* a "Mystery." The mystery celebrated in the play is, of course, the sacrament of marriage. But what makes marriage sacred in Shaw's eyes is not the legal tie or sexual purity

but the nature of the life the couple lead together. Shaw is defending
marriage not on ecclesiastical but on natural grounds. Most radical
plays on the subject of marriage end as Maugham's *The Circle* does,
with a bond dissolved. But Shaw rejects such a solution as either
sentimental or melodramatic and as conceding too much to orthodox
alarmists. Just as his answer to those who believe in punitive justice
was to show men like Caesar and women like Lady Cicely getting
along without it, so *Candida* is an answer to those who believe that
to do away with legal ties is to invite chaos. Shaw's play is intended
to show the absurdity of such an assumption. What he is saying in
Candida is that if marriage were regarded simply as a contract
revocable through mutual consent, though some couples would
escape from unpleasant households immediately, the great majority
would remain together for the same reason they had in the past—
because they *want* to. Candida rejects the idea of sexual purity as
morbid and the notion of marital vows as stultifying, but marriage
on poetic terms is just as little to her taste. Eugene may feel, like
Shelley, that

> The hour is come:—the destined Star has risen
> Which shall descend upon a vacant prison,

but what he discovers is that the scrubbing brush is not an emblem
of Candida's servitude, but of her freely willed vocation.

CHAPTER FOUR

The Devil's Disciple

The first thing to strike the reader of the *Three Plays for Puritans* is the new, larger-than-life quality of their central figures. The *Unpleasant Plays* dealt with social criminals, the *Pleasant Plays* with people who are tragicomically deluded. But the latter may also be regarded, as we have seen, as heroes and heroines *manqués*. Raina and Sergius in *Arms and the Man* and Morell in *Candida* are individuals of character and intelligence whose illusions put them in false positions. The next step for Shaw was to write plays about men and women who, by contrast, would be neither divided by self-doubt nor misled by self-deception—in other words, the kind of persons who, through their strength of will and wholeness of purpose, could lay claim to the title of saint or hero. This was what Shaw tried to do in his third cycle of dramas.

Where the earlier plays scourged the iniquities of the social system or laid bare the complexities and contradictions of human character, the *Plays for Puritans* touch on more fundamental matters which can only be called "religious." But in approaching them as religious plays concerned with basic questions of faith and morals, the reader must not be misled. They are not penitential rituals adorned with poetry more splendidly seductive than any church liturgy, in which the author tries to win us over to ecclesiasticism, as Eliot does in *Murder in the Cathedral*. Rather, they are genuine attempts to revive the spirit of religion in our social lives. Like the early Christian church and the Puritan church of the seventeenth century, Shaw's church is one of rebels. Its prophets are not members of an established priesthood, but such scorners of established faiths as Voltaire, Paine, Blake, Shelley, Carlyle, Bakunin, Wagner, and Tolstoy. For all its rejection of ecclesiastical authority, supernaturalism, and dogmatic creeds, it is, however, no less what Shaw repeatedly calls it in his writings—a true church or "Communion of Saints."

In form the *Plays for Puritans* are melodramas. Unlike the plays of the first and second cycles, they were written neither for coteries of advanced thinkers nor for audiences in fashionable West End theaters. They are popular plays for popular audiences written in the most popular of all dramatic forms. Nor would they ever have seen the light of day if Shaw had not been forced to earn his bread as a critic of the popular stage in the nineties. This experience left him both appalled and intrigued. In his weekly columns he had constantly to come to terms with successful popular melodramas and to assay their significance. The result was a confirmed contempt for their mechanical reliance on stock incidents—fights, rescues, and trials— to the exclusion of any serious moral ideas. Nor was their conventional approach to characterization any more to his taste. He denounced the typical "beautiful, pure, ladylike, innocent, blue-eyed, golden-haired" heroines in which this genre abounded as intolerably insipid and stupid, and the stereotyped "manly" heroes as blackguardly scamps with puerile codes of honor whose ultimate redemption through the power of love left him unconvinced.[1]

But Shaw's fundamental objection to popular melodrama touched something deeper than its conventions of plot and character: it was the religious premises underlying the plays that most dismayed him. Specifically, melodrama was tainted by two ideals of Old Testament morality he regarded as wholly repulsive, namely, the ideal of tribal (or racial) solidarity and the ideal of vengeance. These ideals, which Shaw denounced as antithetic to all that is highest and noblest in the Gospels, have, of course, been the staples of melodrama throughout history. Jingoist melodrama in every age has pitted a hero of the audience's own country, color, or class against a member of a group to which it is hostile. In the mid-twentieth century, melodrama is more peculiarly the province of television and the motion picture industry than of the stage. But our foreign-spy movies, television westerns, and crime thrillers—not to mention most newsreel, radio, and news magazine reporting of the activities of nations with which we are at odds—rest as much as ever on hypocritical self-righteousness and nurture the same passionate desire for retaliation, whether the audience thrills at the threat of subversion, applauds the man-hunters who shoot the criminal down in the streets, or stirs indignantly at tales of enemy atrocities.[2]

In the nineties the British public was terrified by the growth of German sea power which threatened England's traditional naval supremacy. In military melodrama, a British victory, usually effected by a timely arrival of the fleet, was *de rigueur*. Consequently, imported American melodrama, popular because of its impressive stage machinery, often ran counter to the sensibilities of British audiences, who could not be expected to respond to American patriotic rhetoric or to recoil at insults offered to the Stars and Stripes.[3] For this reason, Shaw ironically affected to praise American producers for beginning the education of unreflecting theater mobs who were now required to think about their reactions to such fare. The *Plays for Puritans* were intended to further this educational process. Each of them challenges British jingoist bias at some point: *The Devil's Disciple* ends in a British defeat, the only Briton in *Caesar and Cleopatra* chooses to remain a slave of his country's conqueror, and the rescue operation in *Captain Brassbound's Conversion*, absurd as it is, is undertaken by a contingent of American marines.

But Shaw's attitude toward melodrama was far from being wholly negative. Its very popularity made it appear to him as an ideal medium for the moral re-education of the masses. His aim was to introduce a new kind of melodrama, purging it of its jingoist and Yahwist side, while keeping the harmless and engrossing elements of excitement and suspense. After all, Shaw contended, *Lear*, *Don Giovanni*, and *Faust* were simply melodramas raised above the popular level. In one of his weekly theater columns he gave a recipe for a good melodrama:

> It should be a simple and sincere drama of action and feeling, kept well within that vast tract of passion and motive which is common to the philosopher and the laborer, relieved by plenty of fun, and depending for variety of human character, not on the high comedy idiosyncrasies which individualize people in spite of the closest similarity of age, sex, and circumstances, but on broad contrasts between types of youth and age, sympathy and selfishness, the masculine and the feminine, the serious and the frivolous,

the sublime and the ridiculous, and so on. The whole character of
the piece must be allegorical, idealistic, full of generalizations and
moral lessons; and it must represent conduct as producing swiftly
and certainly on the individual the results which in actual life it
only produces on the race in the course of many centuries.[4]

The *Plays for Puritans* fulfill Shaw's requirement that melodrama
should be allegorical in both theme and characterization. Moreover,
their principal figures have a generalized poetic quality which can
only be called archetypal, the literary progenitors of Dick Dudgeon,
Caesar, Cleopatra, Brassbound, and Lady Cicely being, respectively,
the demonic youthful rebels of Blake's poems and satires, Wagner's
Siegfried, the sinister and alluring *femme fatale* of romantic tales and
ballads, Byron's glowering misanthropes, and Shelley's beneficent
"Witch of Atlas."

As melodramas, they are full of violence, threats of sudden death,
and hairsbreadth last-minute escapes. Each reaches its climax in
what was a common feature of the form—a trial scene. On the
popular stage such scenes were handled with such deadly predict-
ability that Shaw was led to denounce them as "the last resource of
a barren melodramatist,"[5] little anticipating that some half-dozen
trial scenes were to be among the glories of his own as yet unwritten
dramas. It is, indeed, just at this point, where the popular dramatist
becomes least interesting, that Shaw makes a searching attack on
some of the basic premises of what we call civilization. No more than
Shakespeare in *Measure for Measure* does Shaw believe in the so-
called sanctity of the law. All his trial scenes end as judgments of
judges. In these plays Shaw, who had earlier complained that "the
deepest sayings recorded in the gospels are now nothing but eccentric
paradoxes to most of those who reject the supernatural view of
Christ's divinity,"[6] takes his place with Tolstoy as a Christian
anarchist arraigning our whole system of penal justice on the basis
of the one of those gospel paradoxes, "Judge not, that you be not
judged."

The Devil's Disciple takes place in the spiritually dead world of
late eighteenth-century New England.[7] This society, as Shaw portrays it, is sunk in the formalism of a moribund Puritanism, which,
no longer prompting men to attack ecclesiastical tyranny or to follow

their inner light against the world, has become a mere instrument for extinguishing joy and vitality. In this decadent phase its most potent voice in the town of Websterbridge, New Hampshire, had for many years been the Reverend Eli Hawkins. Hawkins is now dead, but his influence lingers on in the life and personality of Mrs. Timothy Dudgeon, who as a young girl had originally loved the town reprobate, until Hawkins, warning her that "the heart of man is deceitful above all things" and advocating self-mortification as her paramount duty on earth, persuaded her to enter into a more respectable but loveless marriage with the reprobate's brother. The experience has left Mrs. Dudgeon a soured and embittered wife whose situation parallels Mrs. Alving's in *Ghosts*, with the difference that where Mrs. Alving found consolation for her unhappy marriage in her love for her son, Mrs. Dudgeon is even more at odds with her children than with her husband. For Mrs. Dudgeon has converted her talent for unhappiness into a means of moral tyranny by railing at anyone who shows any emotion apart from an abject fear of the being she purports to worship as God, though this God is in reality nothing but a devil of her own creation.

Her religious terrorism has turned one son into a "good" man, too cowed to revolt against his mother's rule. He is the stupidest of conventional "Christians," his unmanning being mocked by his family nickname of "Christy." His elder brother is, by contrast, a man of entirely different mettle. Dick Dudgeon has rejected the family's creed *in toto*. Having been tyrannized over as a child, he reacts against any and all bullying of the weak with a violence which is itself brutally savage. Having found nothing but repressive Grundyism in respectability, he has turned to outlawry. But most significant of all, he has recognized the really diabolical nature of his mother's God; and, like John Stuart Mill repudiating a heaven ruled over by an Almighty Torturer, he has chosen "Hell" as his natural home, and its ruler, the traditional antagonist of God, as the master to whom he owes his own allegiance. This diabolonian response to middle-class American morality will be familiar to readers who recall Huckleberry Finn's decision to embrace damnation when he decides to rescue his Negro friend. Shaw's immediate inspiration for Dick's diabolonianism, however, came neither from

Mill nor from Twain, but from a long narrative poem by a minor
Victorian man of letters, Robert Buchanan. Buchanan, who called
his poem *The Devil's Case*, takes as his spokesman a devil who, like
Dick Dudgeon, mixes scorn and pity in his speeches, cursing the God
of the orthodox for his cruelty and defending those who rebel against
him:

> Whoso eats that fruit forbidden
> Knows himself and finds salvation,
> Stands erect before his Maker,
> Claims his birth-right and is free.[8]

Like Prometheus, Buchanan's Christ-Satan, "the gentle Prince of
Pity," has been the declared enemy of the churches, the inspirer of
intellectual and civil freedom, and, like all true messiahs, a thoroughly
"immoral person."

The original inspiration of both Shaw and Buchanan, the perceptive reader will by now have realized, is Blake's *Marriage of
Heaven and Hell*. Blake's satire reverses the usual meaning of
"angel" and "devil"; the devils in the *Marriage* are the religious
prophets whose new insights affront the conventionally minded, and
the angels the men of pretended hypocritical virtue. Shaw plays
ironically on the words "good" and "bad" in the same way. The
"angels," or "good" people, of *The Devil's Disciple* are Mrs.
Dudgeon; Judith Anderson, the minister's wife; and the sheepish
uncles and aunts who arrive to hear the reading of Timothy Dudgeon's will. As against these, Dick represents the spirit of reviving
religion and hence the spirit of immorality, for Shaw, like the
Methodists of Wesley's age, makes belief in morality the opposite of
religious faith. As Shaw contended in his defense of Bunyan's anti-
formalism, "All religions begin with a revolt against morality, and
perish when morality conquers them and stamps out such words as
grace and sin."[9]

Mrs. Anderson gives us what might be called the Sunday school
conception of badness when she cautions Dick's young cousin Essie
against him:

> You must not ask questions about him, Essie. You are too young
> to know what it is to be a bad man. But he is a smuggler; and he
> lives with gypsies; and he has no love for his mother and his

family; and he wrestles and plays games on Sunday instead of going to church. Never let him into your presence, if you can help it, Essie; and try to keep yourself and all womanhood unspotted by contact with such men.[10]

After this sermon and a touch of Mrs. Dudgeon's discipline, it is not surprising that Essie turns to Dick as naturally as a flower turns to the sun. Dick's ruling passion, Shaw tells us, is pity. This links him with Shaw's conception of Christ as a sensitive humanitarian, a parallel which is further underlined by his disreputable associates and his generally poor standing with the pious. Indeed, the words Shaw has Christ speak about himself in *The Black Girl in Search of God* fit Dick exactly:

I too have not been righteous overmuch. I have been called a gluttonous man and a winebibber. I have not fasted. I have broken the sabbath. I have been kind to women who were no better than they should be. I have been unkind to my mother and shunned my family; for a man's true household is that in which God is the father and we are all his children.[11]

Obviously Dick is not far from the Christ of Blake's "Everlasting Gospel," who breaks all the Ten Commandments, declaring that no virtue can exist without such an act of iconoclasm, or the Christ of Luke, who tells his hearers: "If any man come to me, and hate not his father, and mother, and wife, and children, and brethren, and sisters, yea, and his own life also, he cannot be my disciple."

Most eighteenth-century rebels thought of themselves not as religious prophets, but as rationalist deists. Blake, however, denied that Voltaire and Paine were mere "Reasoners," and considered them to be teachers in a reforming religious tradition. Shaw, too, saw them in this light and even regarded such men as precursors of the best and most enlightened late nineteenth-century dissenting clergy. The symbolic transformation of Dick into a preacher at the end of the play foreshadows that particular historical development. Here we may recall Shaw's remark about the development of characters in allegorical melodrama telescoping centuries of human moral progress.

Shaw's notion of an American revolutionist who was a social outcast and a theological radical may strike some readers as a wild

piece of fantasy. Yet the astonishing fact is that in most of his salient
features Dick Dudgeon closely resembles a man who actually did live
and fight and argue theological points in New Hampshire in the
1770's. This man was none other than Ethan Allen, the notorious
leader of the outlaw band called the Green Mountain Boys. Allen,
who cut just such a scandalous figure as Dick in the eyes of the godly
citizens of Bennington, had led a similar Robin Hood existence in the
New Hampshire Grants. After his storming of Fort Ticonderoga in
the Revolutionary War, he was captured by the British and nar-
rowly escaped hanging at their hands.[12] But what is most striking of
all is his aggressive unorthodoxy in matters of religion. In 1784
Allen horrified New England by publishing *Reason the Only Oracle
of Man*, a long and impassioned theological treatise attacking
Calvinist theories of sin, punishment, and human depravity, thus
anticipating Paine's *Age of Reason* by about a decade. Like Dudgeon,
he seems also to have possessed a temperament which combined
scornful derision with an ardent humaneness. If, as appears to be the
case, Shaw created the hero of *The Devil's Disciple* without any
knowledge of Allen's military and literary exploits, then his play is a
remarkable case of a playwright's dramatic imagination intuiting the
facts of history unawares.

Traditionally, melodrama presents the audience with someone to
admire, someone to hate, and someone to pity. In Dick Dudgeon and
Anthony Anderson, Shaw has created not one but two contrasting
heroes. He did not, however, consider it necessary to provide his
play with a villain. Like Hegel, Shaw held that abstract evil was of no
philosophical or dramatic interest. In Shaw's eyes, placing a villain
on the stage merely gave the audience a scapegoat on which to vent
its feelings, thus allowing them to escape from any realization of their
own moral responsibility. Nor did he think the elimination of the
traditional melodramatic villain meant any diminution of suspense;
obviously, respectable society, which, with the best of intentions had
killed Socrates, Christ, and Joan of Arc, had shown itself quite
dangerous enough. Here Shaw's natural philosophical disposition
was encouraged by the success on the English stage of a villainless
American play, William Gillette's *Held by the Enemy*, in which the
hero's life is jeopardized, not by evil machinations, but simply

through his being captured behind Southern lines in the Civil War.[13]

On the other hand, Shaw includes a pitiable, much tried heroine in his play. This he did partly as a way of building up tension through her hysteria, and partly because the introduction of such a character gave him a chance to criticize the popular ideals it embodied. Judith Anderson is all too clearly the stereotyped heroine of conventional melodrama. Like that other stock figure, the good-natured reprobate, this sort of frail, insipid, anxious heroine descends from eighteenth-century fiction. Thackeray's Amelia in *Vanity Fair* is an excellent example of the type as it persisted in the Victorian novel. Military dramatists, playing on sentimental feelings for "the girl I left behind," took such creatures at face value, so to speak, and idealized their piety, their purity, and their clinging-vine dependence on the male. Shaw did not deny the existence in real life of such women—after such qualities had been praised for a century or so he thought them only too common—but his measure of contempt for them is indicated in his warning to an actress who aspired to play Judith that she would first have to have her brains cut out and her face boiled soft.

Judith begins by expressing only horror of Dick. But her self-conscious shrinking reveals an underlying attraction, just as a person's fascination with a work of erotic art or literature is often shown by his professed horror of it. When she is alone with her husband she is still under Dick's spell. "Is it wrong to hate a blasphemer and a villain?" she asks, and then adds naïvely, "I cant get him out of my mind." This vehemence reveals a neurotic conflict which Anderson accurately diagnoses as love-hate. The fact is that Judith, though she likes and respects her husband, has never yet really been in love with him. Like Mrs. Dudgeon, she is bound by her sense of duty to one man while a powerful natural force draws her to another. Unlike the older woman, however, she cannot even acknowledge the conflict, so far does it lie from her preconceived notion of propriety. Only after Dick makes what she thinks to be a heroic sacrifice for her sake does she come face to face with her true feelings for him, though this new awareness, coupled with her fears for his safety, brings her no strength, but merely hysterical impotence.[14]

Martin Meisel has shown how late-Victorian audiences had the chance to witness more than half a dozen "Sydney-Carton" plays in which men made such sacrifices out of love for some woman and a conviction of their own worthlessness. But Dick's action, Shaw makes it emphatically clear, is not based on such sentimental feelings. In *The Quintessence of Ibsenism*, Shaw rejects in turn theological absolutes, utilitarian hedonism, the "greatest happiness" principle, duty, Kant's categorical imperative, and Comtian altruism as really significant ethical motives. Man, in his best moments, is for Shaw in the grip of a transcendent racial will which has the force of moral necessity. As we have seen in the case of *Candida*, this psychology of ethics is the opposite of either classical or existentialist rationalism: instead, it is close to a kind of religious determinism, conceived in Hegelian terms, by which the agent becomes, in a phrase Shaw adapted from Wagner, "the Freewiller of Necessity." This makes individual acts a function of a man's character, which in turn is indicative of his "salvation" or "damnation." Dick is simply not the sort of man who can save himself by endangering Anderson. In this crisis, like Luther, "he can do no other." In his preface, Shaw draws an analogy with the man who rushes into a burning house to save someone whom he may not even know. Shaw sees his own ethic of egoistic individualism as finding its ultimate fulfillment in such gestures of human solidarity. As he puts it in his essay on Ibsen, "When a man is at last brought face to face with himself by a brave Individualism, he finds himself face to face, not with an individual, but with a species, and knows that to save himself he must save the race." [15]

Like Christian in *Pilgrim's Progress*, Dick Dudgeon is forced to withstand a series of temptations or trials. The first of them, the temptation to pious conformity, is not, for a man of his temperament, a very serious one. There is more danger in his falling prey to sentimental love, since love is at least akin to his ruling passion of pity, but his Puritan distrust of sentimental impulses saves him from this pitfall. The final and most serious temptation occurs at the military court-martial and is embodied in the person of General Burgoyne. Most readers and audiences have been so charmed and amused by the witty repartees between Dick and Burgoyne in the trial scene that they have failed to penetrate to Shaw's real intention in writing it. The point is that civilized men, when performing the most nefarious deeds, usually manage to put a pleasant and comforting face on them. This is done not out of any real hypocrisy, but out of the all but universal desire of sensitive people to disguise the real nature of their acts by persuading themselves that they are actually kindly folk with a sincere desire to spare their victims undue suffering, though in the mind of the victim—and of any objective social philosopher who has the clarity of vision not to be taken in by mere forms—such "kind consideration" invariably takes on an aspect of the hollowest mockery.

Shaw, like Tolstoy, regarded all our legal institutions, civil and military together, as monstrous in intention and diabolical in effect. But he goes out of his way to emphasize that the machinery of this so-called justice (really, in his eyes a mere instrument of vengeance and terrorism) is most often operated not by inhuman monsters, but by conscientious, cultivated, and even likable men. General Burgoyne is a good instance of this. In many respects he was a markedly attractive personality. Though Shaw thought his aristocratic snobbery laughable and his military powers limited by his histrionic bent —"Burgoyne," Shaw wrote, "fought until his sense of dramatic effect was satisfied and then capitulated"[16]—he strongly objected to his being made a scapegoat for the loss of America by the British War Office, admired him as an officer who despised Prussianism and opposed the flogging and dehumanization of the common soldier, and was genuinely delighted with his wit and comedic talents.

Shaw projects Burgoyne's charm strongly in his play and underscores his urbanity by emphasizing his Anglicanism. Charm and urbanity have always been Anglicanism's long suits, and its apologists from Hooker down to Arnold have regularly wooed Puritan dissenters with soft words based on the tacit assumption that conformity is, after all, the more gentlemanly choice. But Puritan prophets, from George Fox to Carlyle, have rejected such blandishments and sternly insisted in reply that there are realities decorum cannot gloss over. In this case, the brute fact is that Burgoyne's gallows have taken their place beside the pillory and whipping post in the village square, and for all his charm of manner Burgoyne is now the military representative of Yahweh as the town authorities have been his civil and religious representatives. Shaw put this succinctly in a letter to Ellen Terry:

> Burgoyne is a gentleman; and that is the whole meaning of [the third act]. It is not enough, for the instruction of this generation, that Richard should be superior to religion & morality as typified by his mother and his home, or to love as typified by Judith. He must also be superior to gentility—that is, to the whole ideal of modern society. . . . Burgoyne pleads all through for softening and easing the trial by reciprocal politeness and consideration between all the parties, and for ignoring the villainy of his gallows, the unworthiness of his cause, and the murderousness of his profession.[17]

Worse, Burgoyne purports to punish the rebellious colonists in the interests of Christianity. In his notorious "Proclamation," which Shaw had read in De Fonblanque's biography, Burgoyne had represented his army as "the messengers of judgment and of wrath" who were "acquitted in the eyes of God and men in denouncing and executing the vengeance of the State" against the Americans, the latter being willful outcasts who had now laid themselves open to "devastation, famine, and every concomitant horror that a reluctant but indispensable prosecution of military duty must occasion."[18]

Thus Burgoyne is emulating those prelates and proconsuls whom Shaw scourges in the *Black Girl* for taking "Caiaphas and Pontius Pilate as their models in the name of their despised and rejected victim." Dick, though a man easily touched by generosity, remains intransigently unwilling to be reconciled by mere courtesy to death and tyranny. Judith's hysterical terror is also an essential element of the scene, intentionally underlined in order to keep in our minds the real horror that lies behind the brilliant word-fencing of the two men. Dick's obstreperous behavior, on the other hand, looks diabolical to the officers of the court, but is in essence an *imitatio Christi*, the Christ that he imitates being not the "meek and mild" Jesus of the Sunday school hymn, but the Christ of Blake's "Everlasting Gospel":

> Was Jesus gentle, or did he
> Give any marks of gentility? . . .

He did not die with Christian Ease,
Asking pardon of his Enemies:
If he had, Caiaphas would forgive;
Sneaking submission can always live.
He had only to say that God was the Devil
And the devil was God, like a Christian civil.[19]

Through the person of Dick Dudgeon Shaw pays his respects to
the ideals of Christianity. Yet though he thinks a religion of pity and
passive suffering is noble, he does not think it is an adequate answer
to political problems. The crude realities of power still remain. This
is the meaning of Parson Anderson's role in Shaw's allegory. At the
end of *The Devil's Disciple* it is Anderson, the clergyman turned
warrior, who has to rally the troops to save the scapegrace turned
saint. Desmond MacCarthy puts the case neatly when he says that
Shaw was determined not "to permit us to exalt martyrdom above
effective service in a cause."[20] Thus Shaw's attitude toward Dick is
not unlike the attitude he ascribes to Mahomet vis à vis Christ:
admiration tempered by some hardheaded reservations. It may be—
and to Shaw it undoubtedly was—a damning criticism of the world
that its Christs and Tolstoys do not prevail, but until the world
progresses to the point where mankind's passion for tyranny,
retaliation, and coercion have disappeared, men of good will must
inevitably take up Mahomet's sword. Unless the biggest battalions
are on the side of God, our most godlike aspirations will always
stand in danger of defeat. The liberal's fear and distrust of power will
simply deliver him into the hands of the illiberals.

Anderson is at least honest about the new faith he has adopted in
his moment of trial. He does not, like Brudenell, preach Christ and
wear the robes of his priesthood while sanctioning the dirtiest deeds
of Mars. If Dick's symbolic assumption of clerical garb represents
the transformation of the diabolonianism of Voltaire and Blake into
the liberal theology of the twentieth century, Anderson's shedding
of the mantle of the Prince of Peace for the uniform of a warrior is a
tacit acknowledgment that "the Christian god is not yet."[21] When
Anderson rides home as the conqueror and liberator, Judith turns
to him with joy and a new affection. She makes Dick promise never
to tell; by this she refers not to her love of the would-be martyr

(for which she feels no shame), but to her weak and foolish lack of
faith in the husband she now finds she can love wholeheartedly. As
for the Devil's Disciple, domestic love, with its tenderness, comforts,
and constraints (not to mention its disappointments and murders),
far from being the inmost need of his soul, is merely an indulgence
which, like Paul, he is willing to allow to others.[22]

CHAPTER FIVE

Caesar and Cleopatra

Caesar and Cleopatra is the second panel in the triptych made up by the *Three Plays for Puritans*. Like *The Devil's Disciple* and *Captain Brassbound's Conversion*, it is a military melodrama that asks us to think more deeply than usual about violence and justice. Like them, too, it is a religious allegory dramatizing the conflict between Old Testament and New Testament morality. Even its exotic setting is part of a pattern: where the *Unpleasant Plays* conjure up the gloom of city slums, and the *Pleasant Plays* the sunshine of snow-capped peaks, park lands, and the seashore, the *Plays for Puritans* all take place on remote imperial frontiers where what passes for civilization clashes with what is conventionally regarded as barbarism. In *Caesar and Cleopatra*, Egypt under the Roman occupation becomes, like Revolutionary America and contemporary Morocco, a proving ground for a conflict between subhuman and superhuman elements in man's nature.

Throughout these three plays Shaw attempts to define his idea of heroism. In the second he puts on the stage an actual historical figure, Julius Caesar. This choice will inevitably seem perverse to most English-speaking people. Despite the re-evaluations of nineteenth-century historiography, the popular view of Caesar in Anglo-Saxon countries is still a hostile one. That is to say, Caesar is still regarded as a usurping tyrant who seized political power for selfish ends. To the man on the street whose knowledge of history is limited to Shakespeare and Plutarch, the pro-Caesarism of Goethe, Mommsen, and Froude is wholly unintelligible, and Dante's decision to make Brutus share with Judas the place of honor in hell in the very jaws of Satan remains a curious vagary. If we want to understand Shaw's attitude toward Caesar, we must first understand why he rejected the common estimate of him.

59

The view of Caesar as the great subversive who plotted from his
cradle to overthrow the Republic derives, of course, from Plutarch's
and Suetonius' *Lives*. But most readers of these biographies are unaware that Plutarch writes primarily as a staunch moral conservative
and Suetonius as a constitutionalist who sympathized with the Senatorial faction in the Roman Civil War. Still, for all their moral and
political bias both biographers make Caesar a great man. It is not
until we come to Shakespeare's play that we find a picture of Caesar
that reduces him to a mere petty self-glorifier. *Julius Caesar* gives us
Plutarch's Caesar diminished in stature so that he is nothing more
than an Elizabethan stage-tyrant[1] who, as Shaw complained, utters
no speech even up to the level of a Tammany boss:

> It is when we turn to Julius Caesar, the most splendidly written
> political melodrama we possess, that we realize the apparently
> immortal author of Hamlet as a man, not for all time, but for an
> age only, and that, too, in all solidly wise and heroic aspects, the
> most despicable of all the ages in our history. It is impossible for
> even the most judicially minded critic to look without a revulsion
> of indignant contempt at this travestying of a great man as a silly
> braggart. . . . As far as sonority, imagery, wit, humor, energy of
> imagination, power over language, and a whimsically keen eye for
> idiosyncrasies can make a dramatist, Shakespear was the king
> of dramatists. Unfortunately, a man may have them all, and yet
> conceive high affairs of state exactly as Simon Tappertit did.[2]

Instead, Shakespeare exalts Brutus at Caesar's expense. But Brutus-
worship logically involves Senate-worship and the endorsement of a
republicanism that was antipopular at the same time that it was
antimonarchical. The Roman Republic under the Senate was a narrow oligarchy based on aristocratic privilege. The roots of its power
lay in the ownership of land and slaves and in the exploitation of
the overseas provinces. In these respects it had much in common,
say, with eighteenth-century England or with the ante bellum
American South, so that John Wilkes Booth, looking at Lincoln
through the eyes of another ruined oligarchy, could easily idealize
himself as Brutus' successor.

Ultimately, of course, it is simply a question of what meaning we
give to the word republican. A republic may be either a popular

democracy or a kingless oligarchy. Throughout his life Shaw called himself a republican—meaning by this that he preferred the American and French systems of government to the feudalism of prewar Russia, Germany, and Austria. If we keep these two meanings of the word in mind, then Caesar's remark in the play—"Were Rome a true Republic, then were Caesar the first of Republicans"—becomes perfectly intelligible, and we will be able to see how Shaw's admiration for Caesar is not at odds with his democratic socialism, but part and parcel of it. Indeed, Caesar's championing of the populace against the patricians in the Roman class war made him anathema to such writers as Lucan, Suetonius, and Shakespeare. On the other hand, nineteenth-century historiography, reacting against aristocratic feudalism, hailed Caesar as the long overdue reformer of an outmoded constitution.[3] Hence the admiration that Caesar awakened in such men as Goethe, Niebuhr, Hegel, Mommsen, Victor Duruy, James Froude, and Warde Fowler.

Of all these it is Mommsen who sets forth the pro-Caesar side with the greatest cogency. As a German liberal of the revolution of 1848, he seems to have looked on the erudite volumes of his monumental *History of Rome* as a series of tracts for the times. He clearly associated the Roman Senatorial party with the defenders of the *ancien régime* in Europe; in his vision, Rome's Catos, Ciceros, and Pompeys are the classical counterparts of the Bourbons, Metternichs, and Castlereaghs of his own day. His Caesar is the heir of the Gracchi and Marius, and the embodiment of an impulse to social reform which had been germinating in Roman society for a hundred years. In opposition to a recalcitrant, selfish, and backward-looking Senate, Caesar made himself the leader of the democratic party which was striving to enlarge the franchise, open overseas possessions to colonists, and remodel the political, military, and financial life of the state. Thus, far from finding Caesar a tyrannical autocrat, Mommsen considered his career "so little at variance with democracy," that democracy only attained its fulfillment in it.[4]

Shaw's play is permeated with Mommsen's antiaristocratic and anticonstitutional point of view. The soldiers' prologue ridicules the snobbish pretensions of the Royal Guard, whose class prejudices and chivalric code hopelessly limit their effectiveness as fighters. The Ra prologue, in its devastating judgment of Pompey, echoes the scorn upon scorn Mommsen pours on the legalism and political myopia of Caesar's rival.[5] Shaw further extends this antiaristocratic criticism to Egypt's rulers, scourging the flunkeyism of the court and the playboy extravagances most spectacularly evident in the reign of Cleopatra's father, Ptolemy Auletes, "the Flute-Blower." In so doing Shaw presumably had in mind the wastrelism of the nineteenth-century khedives, who set a pattern familiar to the twentieth century in the person of King Farouk.

British historians who read Mommsen were naturally keenly sensitive to the analogies between Caesar's Rome and imperialist England. James Anthony Froude found in the collapse of the Roman Republic an object lesson for the British aristocracy, which had also amassed great wealth at the expense of the proletariat and failed to take its social duties seriously. Froude regarded Caesar not as a dangerous revolutionary, but as a man whom an age of sham and cant forced into his role as a reconstituter of the state.[6] But though he read Froude's *Caesar: A Sketch* (1879), Shaw does not mention it among the sources for the play. He does, however, refer to another book, Warde Fowler's *Julius Caesar and the Foundation of the Roman Imperial System*, which is in the same vein. Published four years after Victoria's Golden Jubilee, this book extends Froude's analysis to show how Roman capitalism had, by Caesar's day, spread from Italy to the whole Mediterranean world. For Warde Fowler, Caesar's greatest achievement was the replacement of a self-seeking city oligarchy by a genuine imperial system: "Julius Caesar, personifying the principle of intelligent government by a single man, had made it possible for the Roman dominion, then on the point of breaking up, to grow into a great political union, and eventually to provide a material foundation for modern civilisation."[7] Clearly it is Warde Fowler's reading of Roman-English parallels that lies behind the Ra prologue of 1912. The Egyptian god, who here represents the *Zeitgeist*, or spirit of history, castigates modern Britain for following the way of Rome at home and abroad, and hails Caesar as the one man who has risen above the level of the exploiters to grasp the necessity for change.

Undoubtedly, part of the attraction Caesar held for Shaw lay in the role he played in Roman history. Yet, though this is an essential element of Shaw's play, it is not central to it. As we have indicated, *Caesar and Cleopatra* is primarily a religious rather than a political drama. Shaw's Caesar is not the reformer of codes, but the man who has outgrown them. He stands for progress, not in the political or social, but in the evolutionary sense. He is a new breed of animal born with sounder instincts than the average man. Being biologically more advanced, he is without the burden of original sin which finds expression in resentment and vindictiveness on the one hand and a respect for moral systems on the other. His ethic is not the creation of any formal ethical system, but of the developed will which has identified its ends with those of the race; Caesar is the libertarian egoist who in doing exactly what he wants to do serves humanity. As Shaw puts it "Having virtue, he has no need of goodness." This is a conception Shaw discovered first in Wagner and then in Nietzsche. In Wagner's philosophy the idea of the triumph of the individual will over the constricting trammels of Church and State finds its clearest expression in Siegfried, and, indeed, Shaw's remarks on the hero of the *Ring* in *The Perfect Wagnerite* can quite appropriately be applied to his own Caesar. Siegfried, Shaw declared, was "the type of the healthy man raised to a perfect confidence in his own impulses by an intense vitality which is above fear, sickliness of conscience, malice, and the make shifts and moral crutches of law and order which accompany them."[8]

Shaw is in effect warning us against trying to apply ordinary moral standards to Caesar at all. Given any code of ethics, it is always possible to trump up a telling indictment against anyone we have a mind to vilify. Macaulay's essays, in which statesmen and generals he sympathizes with politically are praised for their lofty conduct and ones he dislikes excoriated in the same high-toned fashion, are a good example of this mechanically concocted moral rhetoric, and mutual recriminations among nations in the cold war continue the tradition *ad nauseam*. Shaw is quite aware that his Caesar might be called a brutal plunderer, a destroyer of national freedom, a tyrant, a condoner of incest, a conscienceless sensualist, a reveler, a hypocrite, a vain dandy, and (in the library-burning episode) a soldier callously indifferent to literature and history. On these

64   Shaw the Dramatist

grounds anyone could interpret Caesar as a type of anti-Christ. But it would be equally easy, on the basis of his paternal kindness, his freedom from resentment, his insouciance, his horror of treachery and political assassination, his devotion to his followers, and the paraphrase of the Sermon on the Mount Shaw has him deliver at the climax of the play, to make him out a type of Christ. Shaw's aim is not to establish one or the other as the true Caesar, but to show that this kind of moralizing is mere childish name-calling whose categories any clever writer can invert at will.

Shaw had developed his own moral antinomianism before reading Nietzsche, and differed from him radically by remaining all his life an ardent socialist and humanitarian. Nevertheless, his Caesar does bear a strong resemblance to the "Great Man" as Nietzsche characterizes him in *The Will to Power*. Like Nietzsche's hero, Shaw's Caesar has a "loneliness within his heart which neither praise nor blame can reach" and possesses "courage even for unholy means."[9] The loneliness is expressed in Caesar's opening soliloquy, one of Shaw's most elaborate pieces of prose poetry. Its wistfulness is meant to come as a shock to those whose experience of Shakespeare has led them to expect a ranting Caesar. Its style is surprisingly Pateresque, and it is full of antinomian and erotic overtones. Those critics who, like MacCarthy, have accused Shaw of denying the sexual side of Caesar have missed the point. Shaw does not, as Froude does, discount the stories of Caesar's sexual exploits as mere malicious gossip concocted by his political enemies. He accepted Suetonius' description of Caesar as "every woman's husband and every man's wife," and declared that he meant his Caesar to be as susceptible to women as Mahomet was, with one important provision:

> As to my alleged failure to present the erotic Caesar, that is a matter almost too delicate for discussion. But it seems to me that the very first consideration that must occur to any English dramatic expert in this connection is that Caesar was not Antony. Yet it is precisely because Caesar in my play is not Antony that I am told he is not Caesar. Mr. MacCarthy says that Caesar stayed too long in Alexandria for Cleopatra's sake. But the fact remains that Caesar did not think it too long, and that, as the upshot proved, he was right. Antony let Cleopatra disgrace and ruin him: when he left her he came back to her like the needle to the magnet. She

influenced Caesar's affairs so little that few people know that he ever met her; and when he left her she had to go after him to Rome to get hold of him again. Antony was Cleopatra's slave: Julius was "every woman's husband."[10]

Where the question uppermost in the mind of the man in the street will be whether or not Cleopatra has become Caesar's mistress, and where the sentimentalist will be ready to condone the sexual relation provided Caesar is in love with her, Shaw thinks that the lack of any such emotional bond is the important thing. Given this, it is to him a matter of indifference whether their relation is or is not a sexual one.

Since Shaw was not concerned primarily with Caesar the politician, we can understand why he did not write a "Caesar and Pompey" or a "Caesar and Cato." But, we may still ask, why a "Caesar and Cleopatra"? If Caesar is to be shown in conflict, not with political institutions of his day, by with the very idea of moral law itself, would it not have been more logical to have made his antagonist some representative of what Shaw frequently refers to as "the Nonconformist Conscience"?[11] This element is not entirely lacking from the play; it is represented by Britannus, who either opposes Caesar with moral clichés when he is scandalized by him or defends him with the same clichés when he is pleased. But the tone of the play in dealing with such moralizing is simply one of good-natured amusement. Instead of opposing Caesar to Mrs. Grundy, Shaw adopts a much bolder plan, and accepts the challenge of the conventional moralist in its most trenchant form. For, asks the conventional man, if one abrogates the traditional social restraints, will not society become, as Britannus puts it, "an arena full of wild beasts tearing one another to pieces"? Shaw's reply is, in effect, to present us with human nature in its most dangerously violent form and to show us his hero facing it fearlessly without any of the common moral or judicial sanctions.

In Shaw's play, Caesar stands for humanity in its highest development, Cleopatra for untamed natural passion. To underline the distance between Caesar and those Romans and Egyptians who share the stage with him, Shaw uses an allegorial device unique to this play. He identifies the aggressive, greedy Romans with bull-like and doglike animals—a wolf-headed Roman war tuba opens the play

with a "Minotaur bellow"; Rufio calls himself a dog at Caesar's
heels; and the Egyptianized general, Achillas, is described as looking
like a curled poodle. In contrast, the feminine and treacherous
Egyptians are given catlike and snakelike qualities—Cleopatra is
compared to a kitten and a serpent, Theodotus to a viper, Ftatateeta
to a tiger and a crocodile. Caesar is kind to Romans and Egyptians
alike; but, as Cleopatra comes to realize, the kindness he bestows on
others is not the result of sentimentality, as she at first supposes, but
is the sort of kindness one might show to an animal of another
species, free alike from passionate attachment and moral indignation.

Shaw's Caesar and Shakespeare's are simply two different men.
By contrast, their Cleopatras are recognizably the same woman.
Shaw's girl-queen has the winsomeness, the grace, the impertinence,
the caprice, the petulance, the cowardice, the treachery, the histrionic
bent, and the cruel anger of Shakespeare's Cleopatra, together with
her inability to conceive of any approach to men which is not mere
imperiousness, babyish wheedling, or languorous seduction. That
one is sixteen and the other forty Shaw considers an irrelevance, his
point being that the Cleopatra temperament is fully formed at the
earlier age, since it is in fact a kind of arrested development. Shaw
admired Shakespeare's Cleopatra as an artistic achievement. Where
he thought the older playwright had "made a mess of Caesar under
the influence of Plutarch," he considered the role of Cleopatra "so
consummate that the part reduced the best actresses to absurdity."[12]
But though their conceptions of Cleopatra's character are identical,
the judgments the two playwrights render are totally different. In
the end Shaw accuses Shakespeare of having lent a false glamor and
"spurious heroism" to someone he regarded as embodying only
"the genius of worthlessness."[13]

Where Shaw does go significantly beyond Shakespeare is in emphasizing Cleopatra's murderous and sadistic side. This is a result
of Shaw's attempt to present what might be called the dynastic view
of Cleopatra. Historically, the Ptolemaic kings and queens of Egypt
had shown a remarkable brutality in disposing of relatives close to
the throne, evincing, in their willingness to connive at the murder of
parents, children, brothers, and sisters, a ruthlessness resembling
that of the later Ottoman sultans. Shaw seems to have thought of

Cleopatra as very much a typical Ptolemy in this sense. He replied to Gilbert Murray's charge that he had "overdone Cleopatra's ferocity," by declaring that "if she had been an educated lady of the time," he should have "made her quite respectable and civilized," but that what he was "able to gather about her father, the convivial Flute Blower, and other members of the household, joined with considerations of the petulance of royalty" had led him to draw her as he did.[14] Here Shaw seems to have been following the lead of the Irish historian John Pentland Mahaffy, whose book *The Empire of the Ptolemies* (1895) makes Cleopatra hereditarily fratricidal and recognizably akin in "beauty, talent, daring, and cruelty," to the six earlier Cleopatras who had preceded her on the throne of Egypt.[15]

Half of the fascination of Shaw's play lies in the way in which we are invited to watch the Cleopatra of history and literature develop from the panic-stricken hoyden of the Sphinx scene. At first she is childishly naïve on the subject of kingship. "My father was King of Egypt; and he never worked," she tells Caesar, to which Caesar replies dryly that there may have been some connection between her father's negligence and his political and financial difficulties. Six months later, she manages to sound more sophisticated. At this point Cleopatra can mouth Caesarisms in order to impress others with what she conceives to be her new maturity: "Now that Caesar has made me wise, it is no use my liking or disliking: I do what must be done, and have no time to attend to myself. That is not happiness; but it is greatness." But in reality nothing but her external manner has changed. In a deeper sense Caesar's example has not influenced her at all, and she remains profoundly ambivalent in her feelings toward him. Part of her, the affectionate and sentimentally dependent child, wants his fatherly approval and is achingly jealous of any attention he pays to others, while the other part, the passionate woman, longs to be free of his paternal surveillance. When Pothinus accuses her of secretly desiring Caesar's death, Cleopatra, who does not understand herself at all, is thrown into a murderous fit of rage, hatred, and chagrin, all the more bitter because the eunuch has come so close to the truth. Caesar, who understands her perfectly, calls her behavior natural and makes no attempt to alter her conduct beyond providing the lessons in deportment which are the most her nature can absorb.

In his interpretation of *The Ring of the Nibelungs* Shaw divides the actors in Wagner's allegory into four categories: the predatory, lustful, greedy people; the dull, patient plodders; the "gods" or lawgivers who invent the religious, moral, and legal codes society is bound by; and finally, the heroes who free men from the rule of the "gods" when their codes become obsolescent. Clearly, Cleopatra belongs to the first of these categories as Caesar belongs to the last. Of Caesar's two servants in the play, Rufio is loyal and affectionate as a dog is loyal and affectionate, but Britannus stands on a level of development beyond Cleopatra's naïve passionateness or Rufio's simple devotion. He is a man of the third class, a moralist, a legalist, and a rhetorician, shocked when Caesar challenges the "gods" by sanctioning the incestuous royal marriage, careful to restate Caesar's blunt demand for money in legal terms, and appalled at his not bothering to punish those who are plotting against him. What makes his character comical, of course, is his trick of translating all his enthusiasms and antipathies into resounding moral imperatives. Britannus cannot conceive of a world without punishment or "justice," as he calls retaliation. To him, Caesar's anarchist vision of a society without punitive laws or deterrents is unthinkable and frightening. But to Shaw as to Wagner, it is exactly the highest developments of civilization that stand directly in the way of further advance through their moral prestige; and law and order as presently incorporated in Church and State are merely swaddling bands humanity has wrapped itself in until it is ready to burst them and proceed a stage onward.

The result is that Caesar must, like Dick Dudgeon, appear to the morally hidebound as another sort of "devil's disciple"; the embryonic superman will usually impress others as shockingly immoral. The difference is that where Dick is always attended by a faint smell of sulphur, Caesar commits his impieties with Olympian serenity. This debonair quality of its hero is one of the sources of the play's remarkable charm. Another is what we may call its "musicality." From the delicate rhythms of Caesar's prose-poem soliloquy onward, *Caesar and Cleopatra* has about it a happy air of improvisation, so that its mood reminds us of one of the freer musical forms, say a fantasia or a divertimento. In this it contrasts strongly with the more closely knit, but rather mechanical, structure of the other two *Plays for Puritans*.

Yet these musical and poetic qualities should not blind us to the fact that *Caesar and Cleopatra* is also a melodrama. It is, for Shaw, a remarkably violent play. Two murders actually take place in the course of the action, and we are implicitly asked to judge three others. This is an almost Shakespearean quota of deaths, but, unlike Shakespeare, Shaw is not interested in the dramatic poetry of murder either on the sensational, theatrical side or from the point of view of what Samuel Johnson would call poetic justice. Rather, Shaw wants us to think critically about the moral and social significance of killing. Hence each of the five violent deaths has a distinctly different context and meaning. First we have the cold-blooded murder of Pompey by Septimius at the behest of the Egyptians, who have ordered the death of the defenseless refugee in the hope of winning political favor with Caesar. Shaw's Caesar reacts to this cold-blooded butchery of his enemy and rival with all the horror that Plutarch and Appian ascribe to him. Then follows the discussion of the judicial murder of Vercingetorix, which Caesar now repudiates as mere terrorism parading as statecraft. In the play itself we are all but spectators at the murders of Pothinus and Ftatateeta. And finally, we learn of the impending assassination of Caesar on his return to Rome, an act which Shaw regarded as a particularly outrageous blunder on the part of well-intentioned political idealists.

As we have already seen, melodrama has its roots in certain moral religious feelings of which Shaw strongly disapproved. Though a critic as civilized as A. C. Bradley found it consoling that *Hamlet* and *King Lear* vindicated retributive justice in their gory endings, Shaw would have pointed out that this is a feature they share with any movie or television western in which the audience feels gratification when the villain gets his thrashing. Once again, as in *The Devil's Disciple*, Shaw is trying to draw our attention to the contradiction in popular Christianity, which illogically mixes Yahweh-worship with the Sermon on the Mount without any sense of their incongruity. It is exactly this endorsement of Christianity on its Tolstoyan, and

repudiation of it on its Pauline side that underlies the banquet scene
which is the climax of *Caesar and Cleopatra*. Here Ftatateeta, goaded
on by Cleopatra, vows vengeance on Pothinus for his betrayal of the
queen, and shortly after, kills him.

At this point it is interesting to compare Shaw with the one other
major dramatist who has dramatized Caesar's relation to Cleopatra.
Corneille, in *La Mort de Pompée*, wrote a typical revenge melodrama,
the theme of the play being the struggle of Pompey's widow, Cornelia,
to avenge her husband's death, and its denouement the overwhelming
of Pothinus, Ptolemy, and the others who had connived at it. Shaw
turns Corneille's ethic upside down. Cleopatra, still smarting from
Pothinus' accusation, thinks her honor has been vindicated by his
death and appeals haughtily to Lucius Septimius, Britannus, and
Apollodorus to justify her. Each man gives an answer in keeping
with his life-philosophy: Septimius discreetly equivocates, calling
the murder just but unwise (since it will not please Caesar); Britannus
applauds it as a moral deterrent to others; and Apollodorus regrets
that he was not allowed to kill the man in a chivalrous duel. Only
Caesar disagrees:

> If one man in all the world can be found, now or forever, to
> know that you did wrong, that man will either have to conquer
> the world as I have, or be crucified by it. [*The uproar in the streets
> again reaches them.*] Do you hear? These knockers at your gate
> are also believers in vengeance and in stabbing. You have slain
> their leader: it is right that they shall slay you. If you doubt it, ask
> your four counsellors here. And in the name of that right [*he
> emphasizes the word with great scorn*] shall I not slay them for
> murdering their Queen, and be slain in my turn by their country-
> men as the invader of their fatherland? Can Rome do less then
> than slay these slayers, too, to shew the world *how Rome avenges
> her sons and her honor*. [Italics added.] And so, to the end of history,
> murder shall breed murder, always in the name of right and honor
> and peace, until the gods are tired of blood and create a race that
> can understand.[16]

This "trial" of Cleopatra corresponds, by analogy, to the other trial
scenes in Shaw's melodramas, and ends like them, not with justice
triumphant, but with justice repudiated. But Caesar's speech was, of
course, much more than a rebuke to Cleopatra. It was, among other

things, a criticism of the English, who, having waged war in the Anglo-Egyptian Sudan to revenge their national honor and the death of Gordon, had at its conclusion dug up and mutilated the body of the dead Mahdi, an act of public policy which Shaw thought revealed how little English mentality was removed from the outlook of the barbarous tribesmen they were fighting.

At the end of the scene Cleopatra sees Ftatateeta's red blood streaming over the white altar of the god she worshiped. In response to a murder done out of spite, Rufio has added another death. What, Shaw now asks, are we to make of this new killing? It is a measure of the hardheadedness that goes with his humanitarianism that he has Caesar justify the slaughter of Ftatateeta. In his essay on prisons Shaw denounces the idea of punishment relentlessly, but argues for the social necessity of killing irremediably dangerous people as one might kill dangerous animals, without malice or any pretense of moral superiority. In reply to Desmond MacCarthy's charge that he had made Caesar overly squeamish, Shaw wrote:

> To confess the truth, if there is a point in the play on which I pride myself more than another, it is the way in which I have shewn how this readiness to kill tigers, and blackguards, and obstructive idealogues (Napoleon's word) is part of the same character that abhors waste and murder, and is, in the most accurate sense of the word, a kind character.[17]

Like Christ's "I came not to send peace but a sword," this is a hard saying, but one that will bear pondering by those who, while objecting to the death penalty, think that half a century of incarceration is a humane alternative.

It is now possible to see further into the significance of the animal symbolism in *Caesar and Cleopatra*. Morally, Shaw's refusal to draw a line between men and animals, which has its roots in eighteenth-century humanitarianism and nineteenth-century biological science, is fraught with all sorts of radical consequences. If we look at the animal-human world from Shaw's perspective, we arrive at a drastic transvaluation of values. No one pretends to be morally superior to an animal he has decided to destroy, or hopes that its death will encourage other animals to refrain from manslaughter or depredations. Nor does one speak of its crimes against society, or ask it to

pay for its deeds, or cage it as a punishment for its sins or under the
pretense that this will reform its character. Instead we accept animal
nature for what it is, and act accordingly. In so doing, Shaw would
argue, we treat animals far more sensibly and kindly than we do
human beings. But on the other hand, we do not speak of the sacredness of animal life or hesitate to kill dangerous animals or suffering
and neglected ones. Caesar, who looks at men and women from the
Shavian vantage point, regards human beings in the same way that the
keeper of the Humane Society pound looks at its inmates. As the
new animal toward which nature is evolving,[18] Caesar is as free of
malice toward, or passionate regard for, Cleopatra and the other
people in the play as the ordinary man is toward monkeys in a zoo. It
is in a mood of profound irony that Shaw has the devil in *Man and
Superman* warn us: "Beware the pursuit of the Superhuman: it
leads to an indiscriminate contempt for the Human. To a man, horses
and dogs and cats are mere species, outside the moral world. Well,
to the Superman, men and women are a mere species too."[19] But if
Shaw disagreed with his cynical-sentimental devil, neither did he
share the philosophy of Carlyle, who regarded the finding of the
ablest poundkeeper as the solution to the political problem. Rather,
Shaw counts on the race as a whole leaving Yahoodom behind; as he
puts it in the preface to his next play, he wants his mob to be "all
Caesars."[20] Thus *Caesar and Cleopatra* is not a glorification of
Caesar as a hero we should worship, but as a goal we should strive
toward.

These are the currents that run through the depths of Shaw's play.
But the surface is covered with gay ripples, and the mood of Caesar's
final leave-taking is that of a festival. So little is Caesar enamored of
Cleopatra that he forgets all about her in the press of business. When
she does appear, she demonstrates that she has learned nothing since
they met but poise and histrionic effectiveness. Acting the grand
tragedienne, she demands vengeance for the death of Ftatateeta. But
Caesar simply refuses to play the scene in this key. Napoleon once
remarked that the difference between tragedy and comedy was the
difference between standing up and sitting down, and told how, when
the Queen of Prussia appeared before him "à la Chimène," he simply
offered her a chair. Caesar similarly reduces a tragic pose to farce by

stuttering over the dead nurse's name, and then coaxes Cleopatra out of her sulks by promising to send Mark Anthony. The Siegfried motif swells buoyantly in the background: Caesar has subdued the Egyptians and will conquer three or four more armies on the way home. He goes lightheartedly to Rome and his death, as Cleopatra, childishly enraptured, awaits the coming of her demigod—and Shakespeare's.

CHAPTER SIX

Man and Superman

With *Man and Superman* Shaw leaves behind such popular forms as melodrama and domestic comedy to enter into a kingdom peculiarly his own. This play, with the two that follow—*John Bull's Other Island* and *Major Barbara*—shows his wit at its most brilliant, his speculations at their boldest, and his purview broadened to encompass what he has called "the destiny of nations." Together the three plays make up a trilogy as closely linked in subject and form as the *Unpleasant*, *Pleasant*, and Puritan plays, though they were not published in one volume. Undoubtedly, it was only the unusual length of *Man and Superman* that prevented this. Had it been practicable, Shaw would in all likelihood have preferred to issue them together under some such heading as "Comedies of Religion and Science," the comprehensive title he suggested to Trebitsch for the German edition.[1]

Each play of this new genre—the only appropriate name for which is "philosophical comedy"—begins as a Molièresque satire on a liberal reformer and then develops into a full-fledged Platonic dialogue. Such a radical fusion of opposites has repeatedly puzzled and exasperated Shaw's critics. *Man and Superman*, for example, has been denounced as an "amorphous monster" and a "Frankenstein."[2] But Shaw's strategy has an inescapable logic of its own, once we have sufficiently recovered from our amazement to see each play as a whole. What he does is to present us first with some high-minded idealist who regards himself as an enlightened crusader, well in advance of the benighted masses. This character is then made the butt of a comedy in the style of Molière,[3] not in order to unmask him as a hypocrite, but to expose in comic fashion the inherent contradictions in his ideas and temperament and to demonstrate

75

the outmodedness of his social or political thinking. By this means
Shaw reveals the bankruptcy of nineteenth-century liberalism in the
face of the brute facts of sex, nationalism, and economics. Then, as
the problems raised at first in a comicosatirical vein are examined in
a more and more serious light, the audience, which had originally
settled down for an evening of fun, finds it must transform itself from
a group of idle pleasure-seekers to a "pit of philosophers," or founder
hopelessly in the dialectic of the dream sequence of *Man and Superman* or the last-act discussions of *John Bull's Other Island* and *Major
Barbara*. An impossible procedure, you may complain, to mix
spirited farce and serious philosophy in such a fashion. But not,
Shaw would reply, to a man who believes that "every jest is an
earnest in the womb of time," and that the prophet who does not
make his audience laugh may suffer, at worst, the fate of Socrates
and Christ, and, at best, that of Spinoza and Tom Paine.

The idealistic liberals who are the butts of Shaw's satire are
Roebuck Ramsden in *Man and Superman*, Tom Broadbent in *John
Bull's Other Island*, and Lady Britomart Undershaft in *Major
Barbara*. Since our subject here is the first of these plays, let us look
at Ramsden as a representative of his species. Ramsden is named
after John Arthur Roebuck, the mid-Victorian Radical member of
parliament whose outspokenness had won him a reputation for
stern integrity in early life, but who, by failing to bring his Radicalism
up to date, finally alienated his more progressive contemporaries.
In *Man and Superman*, Ramsden is specifically the man whose bold
skepticism on the subject of religion and the British constitution has
not been matched by any corresponding advance in his thinking
about sex and morals. This typical Victorian tendency to combine
theological and political radicalism with moral conservatism was in
some degree a strategy of prudence. The unreflecting public was prone
to find blatant immorality lurking behind any rejection of church
dogma and Biblical literalism; and many intellectuals, leary of
fighting on too many fronts, tried to avoid sounding heterodox on
morals as well as faith. But for the most part, their conservatism was
perfectly sincere. Having abjured orthodoxy and one set of sanctions,
many emancipated Victorians clung all the more determinedly to
the signposts remaining. Such men were usually convinced that

traditional sexual morality was sound and would only have to be removed from the area of religious dogma to that of philosophical principle to become intellectually respectable. The moral horror Shelley inspired in Matthew Arnold was therefore quite genuine, even though the modern reader may be startled that so sophisticated a man should sound so much like Mr. Pecksniff on the issue of divorce. Sometimes, also—as with Arnold—a note of mild hysteria intrudes into questions of love and marriage which suggests that the writer's own susceptibility has heightened his anxieties. In Ramsden's case we may assume that all these considerations are present, so that we are treated to the comedy of a professional dissenter recoiling in horror from a reputedly immoral book on sex without having read a page of it, his reaction to Jack Tanner's "Revolutionist's Handbook" being hardly distinguishable, for all his professions of liberalism, from that of a Legion of Decency member of a generation ago.

Shaw's comedy opens ironically with Ramsden consoling his young friend, Octavius Robinson, on the death of a common acquaintance. The deadly banality of the clichés of condolence the two men exchange reveals Shaw's quizzical attitude toward mourning. But more trials still are in store for them. Ramsden's first shock is to find that he has been named coguardian of the dead man's daughter with the "immoral" Tanner. He has barely recovered from this blow when another discovery sends both men reeling: Violet, Octavius' sister, has just visited a strange doctor and is apparently expecting a child out of wedlock. The reactions of Ramsden, Octavius, and Tanner to this news provide an amusing study of temperamental idiosyncrasies. To begin with, Shaw's audience would have been acutely aware of the Victorian dramatic convention which dealt with such crises neatly and summarily by killing the woman off, the law of the stage being that no fallen female should survive the last curtain. Shaw satirizes this kind of response through Octavius, whose quivering poetic sensibility reacts to the news with shame and embarrassment. This is, of course, nothing more nor less than a kind of masochistic enjoyment of the situation, and Shaw means here to reveal the real psychological basis for the literary convention. Ramsden's good sense preserves him from any such histrionics, but there is just enough embarrassed shuffling in his manner to provoke from Tanner an impassioned defense of illicit pregnancies.

In order to understand Jack's vehemence it is necessary to know something about radical views of love and marriage in the eighties and nineties. The two main attacks on the conventional idea of matrimony earlier in the century might be called the sentimental and the economic. The sentimental call for reform aimed at protecting women against the calculated brutalities of unsympathetic husbands and, to this end, attempted to secure the property rights of married women. Such a program was a primary concern of John Stuart Mill's *The Subjection of Women*. But as Belfort Bax put it, "Many good men who have abandoned the dogmas of the Church, cling to 'social purity' as to a living rock."[4] This was especially true of the Positivists, who wrote strong rhetorical defenses of marriage and idealized women as the upholders of morality in society. Marxist critics, on the other hand, usually regarded marriage as simply a social contract which reflected bourgeois property relations and would undergo radical changes as society advanced. Bax, who was the most outspoken of this school, and Edward Carpenter, who approached reform from the sentimental-Shelleyan side, were friends of Shaw's, while two other "advanced" sociologists—Havelock Ellis and Grant Allen—influenced him through their writings.[5] All accepted the position that with the growing economic independence of women, the state regulation of marriage would vanish and be replaced with simple registration, and the doctrine of the indissolubility of marriage give way to divorce by mutual consent.

By the end of the century social thinkers had already begun to evaluate marriage customs from yet a third perspective, that of modern biological science. In the age of Ricardo and Mill, the neo-Malthusians argued that reproduction had a social side to it, and that unchecked increases in population directly worsened the living conditions of the lower classes. After the middle of the century, marriage also came to be looked at in relation to the evolutionary process, and a new question was raised: Does modern monogamous marriage as practiced in Western Europe foster or retard the development of the race? Some men, like Grant Allen, objected that it did retard it, and that, in particular, class barriers stood in the way of marriages that were highly desirable on eugenic grounds. Pondering these new ideas, Shaw came to a radical conclusion of his own, namely, that sentimental love, marriage, and reproduction, far from being necessarily related, as they seemed to the conventionally minded, might better each be treated on its own merit as a separate phenomenon: the kind of love sung by poets was more effectively a source of inspiration if it was unconsummated; marriage as cohabitation might be mainly a matter of domestic convenience (as in his own case); procreation, on the other hand, though of crucial significance in regard to the race, need not be connected with either. Shaw seems in the end to have agreed with Bax that the latter might best be provided for by the kind of group marriages described in Plato's *Republic* and actually carried into effect by the Perfectionist community at Oneida, New York, in Victorian times. Most reforms of marital customs have been popularly acceptable only when based on ostensibly sentimental considerations. Since Shaw's bold functionalism challenged not only the traditionalists, but also the overwhelming majority of liberals who belonged to the sentimental school, we can see why he should have adopted the evasive ruse of ascribing the ideas of "The Revolutionist's Handbook" (all of which are in fact Shaw's own) to a dramatic character.

This, then, brings us to the question, central to an understanding of Shaw's comedy, of the relation of the sexual reformer to modern society. In earlier ages the chief challenge to the sex mores of society had come from its Don Juans and Casanovas, that is, from the libertine seducers of women. In the preface to *Man and Superman* Shaw connects Tanner with the Don Juan tradition despite the fact that Tanner runs away from the one woman in the play who has a specifically sexual interest in him. For this Shaw was accused by Max Beerbohm of using a dishonest device to "catch the ear that he desires to box."[6] There is a measure of truth in this charge, though Shaw might have reminded Beerbohm that the seventeenth century used the term "libertine" to denote both the woman chaser and the freethinker. What he does instead is to give us a piece of cultural history. Shaw argues that the amorist and skeptic who was once the antagonist of a god threatening hell-fire is now menaced instead by the purely mundane, but no less impressive force of middle-class public opinion. Faced with this new threat, he has changed his tactics. Instead of *grands amants* and Restoration rakes, we have austerely scholarly men like Francis Galton, Ernest Westermarck, and Sigmund Freud penning, not erotic verses or memoirs, but essays on eugenics with titles like "The Possible Improvement of the Human Breed Under Existing Conditions of Law and Sentiment," anthropological surveys of the history of human marriage, and studies in the psychology of sex. And in our own day, to complete the tale, we have the most powerful plea yet voiced for the freedom of the human sex instincts coming not from a Frank Harris or a Porfirio Rubirosa, but from a professor at a midwestern state university, whose arguments take the form of tables of cold statistics. Obviously, men doing serious scientific work of this sort, whatever their philandering instincts, are more likely to barricade their doors against ardent female admirers (as Shaw did in the case of Mrs. Patterson) than to scale garden walls. Thus we end with the paradox of the libertine moralist in the position of the pursued instead of the pursuer.

This brings us to another of the play's apparent paradoxes. Tanner, who is the spokesman for Shaw's economic and biological criticism, wins all the intellectual battles but makes a hopeless fool of himself in matters of practical judgment. Because we are expected to laugh at Shaw's spokesman in the play, some readers have concluded that *Man and Superman* is a piece of self-satire or a sign of disillusionment. But this erroneous view is based on too narrow a conception of Shaw's comic art. Traditionally, of course, most comic writers who have landed their characters in absurd situations have wanted to convince us that they held false ideas. Cervantes' knight, Molière's megalomaniacs, and Jane Austen's heroines are all presented to us as intrinsically wrongheaded individuals. The laughter they evoke is Bergsonian laughter, intended to bring the nonconformist back into line. Before *Man and Superman* there is hardly an example in world literature of a writer who puts his choicest speculations and sharpest criticism into the mouth of a man we are supposed to laugh at. But laughter directed at Tanner is not corrective laughter; it is rather what Shaw would call the laughter of "good fellowship," appropriately directed at a man whom we like and respect but whose volatile temperament leads him into awkward predicaments. It is related, though at several removes, to the kind of laughter Goldsmith evokes in *The Vicar of Wakefield,* and was intended by Shaw to promote that "kindly atmosphere" without which he thought his play would inevitably appear "inhuman and repellent" and his revolutionist insufferable.[7]

Shaw's originality lies in his having created in Jack Tanner a comic Prometheus. Ordinarily, Promethean types in literature have been singularly humorless, but Tanner, who, to begin with, looks like Jove and hurls Jovian thunderbolts with wild exuberance, is a fighting Prometheus, not a suffering one. The high-spirited tirades in which he denounces the cruelties, injustices, and stupidities of society not only delight us with their gloriously impassioned rhetoric, but inspirit us at the same time that we smile at the mad-bull element in the speaker's character. Thus the impetuous generosity he brings to Violet's defense wins our admiration even though it turns out to be misplaced, and the insight with which he analyzes Ann's pursuit of a husband remains true and brilliant even though we realize long before he does that Tanner is himself her prey. Shaw saw that the only way in which the thoroughly subversive morality of his play could disarm criticism at the start was through a comic disguise. But the laughter we direct against Tanner is not meant to discredit him. It is merely the result of our perception that we are listening to a philosopher who is right in all his major premises and amusingly wrong as to his minor ones.

Jack Tanner's approach to sex has been shaped by his study of Marx and Francis Galton, and is thus as far as possible removed from middle-class standards. When he sees the others responding theatrically to the news that Violet is to have a baby, he is all the more exasperated, since he had earlier found the Ramsdens, Robinsons, and Whitefields luxuriating in the orgy of grief and sentiment that regularly accompanies funerals in our society. But a civilization that makes a high festival of death and shrinks from an extralegal birth as from a horrible crime strikes Tanner as so perverse that he cannot contain himself, and he strikes out in passionate defense of Violet, praising her for doing the state a service and for fulfilling a woman's highest purpose—"to increase, multiply, and replenish the earth." This application of religious language to what he regards as flagrant immorality calls forth a shocked protest from Ramsden and an indignant denial from Violet, who now reveals her marriage and repudiates Tanner with cutting scorn. Like Don Quixote, Tanner has tried to be chivalrous, only to find that he has committed an outrageous *faux pas*.

Part of the confusion over Shaw's intention in *Man and Superman* springs from the identification of Tanner with Shaw himself. This identification has, it is true, a kind of justification in the stage tradition, going back to the first London production, in which Granville Barker was made up to look like Shaw. Yet anyone who has read the printed description of Tanner's appearance will have been struck by the contrast with Shaw in feature, physique, manner, and social background. In these repects Tanner is very unlike Shaw and very like the man Shaw meant to portray—Henry Mayers Hyndman. Hyndman was the Oxford-educated scion of a wealthy family that had made its fortune in the West Indies. Just as Tanner advertises himself as a "Member of the Idle Rich Class," so Hyndman boasted that he owed his affluence to his descent from a long line of "marauders."[8] He began life as a businessman-playboy-athlete, was converted to Marxism by reading *Das Kapital* on a trip to America, and returned to England to found the violently revolutionary Social Democratic Federation, the rival of Morris's Socialist League and the Fabian Society. In his role as an agitator he amazed West End clubmen and working-class socialists alike by retaining his bourgeois sartorial splendor for his street-corner harangues. Shaw maintained that Hyndman gave the impression of having been born in a frock coat and was as imposing in looks as God in Blake's illustrations to Job.

But the most important difference between Shaw and Hyndman was their style in public controversy. In his preface to Morris's writings, Shaw pays tribute to the amazing fluency of Hyndman's "brilliant conversational performances," and to his majestically Olympian platform manner.[9] In public debate, however, Hyndman's style was what Shaw called the "Marx style," that is, it was virtuperative, impetuous, and flamingly denunciatory, while Shaw, by contrast, cultivated the cool, analytical, ironic tone of the Fabians. In other words, the most characteristic element of Hyndman's temperament, his mad-bull side, is very un-Shavian, and very close to Tanner. Here is Shaw's sympathetic but amused account of Hyndman's failure to master his indignation at a public meeting:

> Social Democracy is not to him merely a state of society in harmony with his intellectual convictions, it is his idol, his darling, his mistress. When it is attacked, all his judgment, his acuteness, his *aplomb*, his knowledge of the world fail him. You can see him inwardly making good resolutions: he will be calm, careful, and considerate, as becomes a thinker and a student; wary, vigilant, and vigorous as becomes a combatant; but never forgetting that, as a gentleman discussing with a gentleman, he must keep his temper. He rises with his coat carefully buttoned, and begins with dignity and fluency in a fine voice, produced, one suspects, in accordance with a carefully matured private theory of elocution. And all this lasts—not two minutes. At the first genuine grapple with the scorner of Social Democracy, dialectics and deportment vanish together; and the real man rages out, vehement, intolerant, jealous, indignant, exacting, unreasonable, everything that a debater ought not to be, everything that a passionate Social Democrat cannot help being when he thinks, not of his immediate business, but of all he knows. . . . Then perish the artistic point of view, and speak out the uppermost invective and the innermost aspiration, though Mrs. Hyndman had received fifty promises of perfect calm, and is visibly concerned as they prove false as dicers' oaths.[10]

This, we cannot help feeling, is how Ann Whitefield will look on Jack Tanner ten years after their marriage.

In *Man and Superman*, Tanner is only secondarily the political revolutionist: he is first and foremost the philosopher of love and sex. Besides its laughable side, comedy has always had its love-interest, which has been the occasion for sentiment, pathos, or cynicism, as the case may be, but never before for the kind of far-ranging critical analysis to which Shaw here subjects it. This is the real distinction of the play, that it offers us a love comedy, which becomes, through Tanner's philosophizing, a critique of love as it usually appears in plays or novels. Shaw elects to make us smile at love in its poetic aspects, to laugh at its passionate follies, and to discount the widely held theory that love in its married form is an invaluable prop to social morality. But these views, though put forth amusingly in the play with an apparently inexhaustible stock of good humor, did not

in themselves leave Shaw satisfied. He could not accept a purely
negative approach to the subject or believe that sex was in the long
run a merely frivolous matter. The problem, clearly, was to discover
a view of love that would steer clear not only of sentimentality, but
also of cynicism, and present the ubiquitous phenomenon of erotic
infatuation in the light of modern natural history.

Shaw thought that he had found such a vantage point in Schopenhauer's famous essay "The Metaphysics of the Love of the Sexes."
Schopenhauer begins by asking whether the apparently obsessive
preoccupation with love in life and literature is not merely the symptom of man's inveterate triviality. On the surface it seems absurd
that such a trifle should so largely monopolize the attention of poets
and dramatists and even disorder the lives of otherwise serious
people. He decides that it can be explained only by the remarkable
imperiousness of the sex impulse, which, he suggests, underlies all,
including the most apparently ethereal expressions, of human love.
Schopenhauer expects that "lofty sentimental souls" will cry out
against his apparently materialistic interpretation of the facts, but
he protests that it is they and not he who will not take love seriously,
for "the ultimate end of all love affairs, whether they are played in
sock or cothurnus is really more important than all the other ends
of human life . . . and is therefore quite worthy of the profound
seriousness with which everyone pursues it."[11] The reason is that
human love preferences settle a matter of great importance—
nothing less, in fact, than "the composition of the next generation."
Such a theory, far from being mere materialism, Schopenhauer
contends, is of the greatest metaphysical significance, since it raises
love far above "the exuberant feelings and supersensible soap
bubbles" of the love poets.

Schopenhauer published his essay on love as a supplement to *The
World as Will and Idea* in 1844. A decade later Darwin gave another
turn to the screw by showing that selective mating was responsible
not only for the composition of each particular generation, but also
for the very development of the human species from the lower animals.
With this new consideration in mind, Shaw chose to re-endorse Schopenhauer's views on the psychology and teleology of love. Psychologically, love is an inspiring and intoxicating illusion created by nature

in the minds of lovers in order to persuade them that their personal happiness lies in the gratification of their erotic instinct. Teleologically, however, it is merely a trick of the life force, which is pursuing a superpersonal, racial aim having nothing to do with mere egoism or private pleasure. Such an approach is, of course, highly paradoxical, since it simultaneously debunks love and invests it with a new transcendental significance. It is also radically conservative in that it depreciates the personal side of love and puts the emphasis on procreation, so that Shaw is able to declare that the love instinct is indeed sacred and holy, as popular writers have maintained, but for eugenic rather than moral or sentimental reasons. In the apparent anarchism of this biological urge Shaw found realized some of the deepest intentions of nature. His radicalism lay in his willingness to give it expression free of the restraints of marriage or cohabitation; hence Tanner's defense of Violet. Hence also Shaw's criticism of theatrical traditions as they bear on comic denouements. For if comedy is not only an exposure of the absurdities of human behavior, but also, through its epithalamiums, a Dionysiac celebration of life, we must in the light of this new theory of sex make its end not the lovers' bliss, but the creation of new life; not the marriage bed, but the cradle. As Shaw foresaw, it was not the moralists but the sentimentalists who felt most affronted by this treatment of sexual psychology. There is surely something very amusing in the fact that it was not a conventional philistine who raised the loudest outcry against *Man and Superman*, but James Huneker, the anarchist firebrand, who attacked the play violently on the grounds that Shaw "despises love, and therefore cannot appeal deeply to mankind."[12]

Throughout *Man and Superman* Tanner proclaims that a woman's real aim in life is to find the man nature tells her is the right father for her children. This is, to put it mildly, not the attitude toward women held by Octavius, Mendoza, and Hector, the three conventional males Shaw includes as foils for Tanner. Each of these three types is satirically contrasted with the others. Octavius is the man who loves poetically and sees his beloved as an image of high romance. In temperament he has a good deal in common with the archetypal poet of the Victorian age, Tennyson. Just as Tennyson mourned Hallam's death, took delight in picturing forsaken women and the

baffled hero of *Maud*, and reveled in Guinevere's humiliation before
Arthur, so Octavius tenderly nurses his sorrow at Mr. Whitefield's
death, his hopeless love for Ann, and his awareness of his sister's
supposed shame. That is, amiable and inoffensive as his character
is, its deepest need is expressed in a morbid desire to suffer. Nevertheless, as Schopenhauer points out, such suffering is above all things
the appropriate stuff of traditional love poetry; it is the frustration
and not the gratification of the love instinct that produces the rhymes
of a Petrarch and a Dante. But if the nightingale must press its
breast against a thorn before it can sing, this compulsion, though
harmless, is still perverse, and Shaw obviously feels something of the
same impatience and contempt for Octavius' lack of vitality that Ann
does.

Mendoza, who has fled to the Sierras to bury the recollection of
the English cook who rejected him, is the frustrated lover in his
passionate as opposed to his poetic guise. He is the kind of man the
Foreign Legion is supposed to have recruited for its ranks, a fact
which, if true, must have made the Legion a very singular military
organization. Shaw spoofs Mendoza's self-dramatizing tendencies
by providing him with the same stereotyped *mise en scène* of wild
mountain landscape and bandit crew that had served as background
for half a hundred "desperado" romances, from Schiller's *The
Robbers* through Verdi's *Ernani* and Bizet's *Carmen* down to Offen-
bach's *Les Brigands*. Indeed, one may, if one wishes, trace the
stereotype back to the opening scene of *Paradise Lost*, where Milton,
according to Shaw, "struck the popular fancy by changing the devil
into a romantic gentleman who was nobody's enemy but his own."[13]
But the seventeenth-century Satan, Shaw would have added, had
at least defied God, while his sentimental Victorian descendants
were usually nothing more impressive than men crossed in love.
Nevertheless, though Mendoza is as foolishly obsessed with his
beloved as Octavius, he is at least more clear-sighted about the object
of his affections. While Octavius' Ann never existed on land or sea,
Mendoza's Louisa is an amusingly real spitfire.[14]

Octavius' and Mendoza's tragedies lie in their losing their inamor-
atas; Hector Malone's tragedy lies in winning his. The first two men
cut poor figures as foiled Romeos, but the latter, as his wife's captive,
is more ignominious still. Shaw treats Octavius' love, the aching

love of lyric poetry, and Mendoza's, the passionate love of operatic melodrama, with humorous detachment; but for Hector's brand of love, the "virtuous" love of the hero of the popular magazine story for the respectable young heroine, Shaw the social critic has nothing but withering scorn. Indeed, the Hector-Violet subplot, if we analyse it carefully, has the acrid flavor the philosophical comedies regularly take on when they touch on economic matters. In this respect it harks back to the mood of *Widowers' Houses*. For in contrast to Ann, who represents the instinct of the race working toward the creation of the next generation, Violet, as the symbol of the dead bird in her hat warns us, is a kind of predator.

Jack's chivalry she regards as a deadly insult which places her on the same level as women who, as Shaw sardonically puts it, are blacklegging in love by failing to take out a union card. She also perceives that his attacks on private property call into question the right to an unearned income she regards as the prerogative of her class. She automatically equates gentility with idleness, and in sincere naïveté asks what is the use of having a husband if he has to work. Where Blanche Sartorius (who bears a similarly innocent name) wished to add gentility to money through marriage, Violet wants to add money to gentility. Hector's absurd moral idealism merely blinds him to the realities of their relationship. He quite seriously believes that "a woman's morl number is higher than a man's," and that marriage must on this account ennoble him. But for all his mouthing of high-flown sentiments, he is for Violet an instrument of no more moral significance than a watch or door key. His schoolboy pose of manliness and his moral muscle-flexing are totally irrelevant gestures which satisfy his need for an ideal of conduct without touching any social realities.

The love of Hector's Irish-American father for his son points to another side of the critical psychology of Shaw's comedy. Shaw ironically contrasts the elder Malone's attachment to Hector with Mrs. Whitefield's maternal feelings. Mrs. Whitefield warmly reciprocates the devotion the Robinson children show her and vastly prefers their company to that of her own daughter, though her conventional belief in the naturalness of family affections makes it impossible for her to admit it, even to herself. Hector Malone senior, in contrast, really does love his son with a passion that is both demanding and protective. But though he plays the strong father in the same fashion that his son plays the manly husband, in the long run his paternal longings also deliver him helpless into Violet's hands, as he comes to realize that only by allying himself with this strong-minded woman can he hope to remain part of his son's life. Thus Shaw looks just as skeptically at familial love in his play as he does at sexual amorism. Indeed, he approves the very hypocrisies of Mrs. White-field as healthier and more socially desirable than the sincere feelings of the elder Malone; so much better, when love is at issue, are the mere pretenses of life to the conventionally approved emotions they appear to mock.

Shaw is not at all censorious of the hypocrisies Ann employs in her pursuit of Jack, though he exploits their comic side. Far from being incommoded by the demands of middle-class respectability, Ann knows she need only appear respectable enough and she will be able to steal every peach in the garden. All the conventions of filial piety and enforced affections which might shackle the ordinary non-vital woman she twists into sanctions for her own whims so that out of her very chains she forges traps for others. But Shaw differs from the traditional moralist in seeing all this pretense and play-acting as justified by its ends. "Women," according to Schopen-hauer, "regard the affairs of the species as more serious than those of the individual. . . . It lies therefore in the nature of woman to regard everything solely as a means to win the man, the interest in anything else being never more than a simulated one, a mere detour." [15] Shaw does not look on such an opinion as a cynical slander; he thinks this single-mindedness is natural and right. Rather than falling below the standard of male romanticism, the woman who is intent on the practical problem of finding a mate has risen above it. Consequently, we are prompted neither to like nor dislike Ann Whitefield. Such idle sentiments are for Shaw beside the point. Instead, she commands the respect, and something of the awe, we might feel for an ineluctable force of nature.

Shaw has not infrequently been accused of writing sexless drama. What this means is that he has not stooped to vulgar titillation or to the absurdity of showing his characters theatrically agonizing over the dilemmas of "guilty" love. But surely no playwright has dramatized the naked power of the sex impulse more directly or with more respect. His own conversion from rationalism to vitalism in his twenties seems to have been based on his realization of the power of the sexual urge: "It was Woman," he makes his alter-ego Don Juan declare in the hell scene, "who taught me to say 'I am; therefore I think,'" that is, will is anterior to reason. He does not have any of the fundamental ambivalence toward sex that Schopenhauer manifests. For the latter, sex is both commendable in its superpersonal aim and evil as a manifestation of the will to live and continue the race. Here the contrast between the respective biases toward rationalism and voluntarism in the two men's philosophies stands out most clearly. In Schopenhauer's ethical system the goal is to use our reason to escape from the world of will into the world of pure knowledge, from the condition of original sin to Nirvana. But Shaw thought this kind of escape was neither possible nor desirable, and regarded man's will, not his rational faculty, as the real instrument of his salvation.

To the comedy of Ann's maneuvers to capture a mate Shaw adds the comedy of Jack's efforts to escape. What is laughable in the first case is the way Ann works behind a façade of bland propriety while she uses all her sexual attractiveness to entice and every social convention to entrap her prey. What is funny in the second is the way the defiant orator and Promethean rebel of the first part of the play becomes the defensive feeble-vehement protester of the second, as his desire to live the free and unconstrained life of a revolutionist comes into conflict with Ann's determination that he shall be her husband. This is nothing less than the classical struggle between the male impulse to think and improve the world and the female desire to propagate the species and be provided for. Ann's advantage in the contest is that all her efforts are bent toward one end—overcoming Jack's resistance for one crucial moment—while his is the purely negative aim of evasion. But not even the depths of the Spanish Sierras are obscure enough to hide him. There, desperately cornered, he fumes, declaims, turns at one moment insulting, at another pleading: Ann is as deaf to his pleas as to his abuse. The philosopher of the life force finds himself hopelessly enmeshed in its toils. Like the canoeist who has gone too close to the brink of Niagara, he is swept willy-nilly along. Here is a description of Tanner's capitulation as Shaw stage-managed it at the first production of *Man and Superman*:

> At the Court we devised a sort of pantomime at the point where Tanner and Ann are left together for the great final scene. Ann was in the centre of the stage; and Tanner took walks which began as resolute attempts to leave the garden by the gate or the terrace, and ended by vacillation, renewals of the attempt more and more feeble, always getting nearer and nearer to Ann. Finally he goes to her as if she were a magnet and he a rather reluctant needle, and stops close to her with a sort of collapse as if his backbone had visibly given way. Barker did this extraordinarily well.[16]

Schopenhauer thought of the child which an erotically attracted couple have it in their power to create as possessing a will of its own, as being, in fact, a kind of Platonic Idea striving to realize itself in the world of phenomena. Naïve lovers anticipate happiness in the consummation of their love; but since nature, in mating men and women, often tries to balance qualities and defects by uniting couples of opposite temperaments, there is always a strong chance of incompatibility in love matches. Hence the irony with which Schopenhauer regards the pleasure a spectator at a comedy takes in the apparently happy ending: "At the conclusion he leaves the victorious lovers quite confidently, because he shares with them the illusion that they have founded their own happiness, while they have rather sacrificed it to the choice of the species."[17] Shaw, adopting the same perspective on marriage, resolutely refuses to sound the "happily-ever-after" note at the end of his comedy. Instead, he makes Ann tell us in a moment of clairvoyance that she will risk her life in childbirth, and has Jack cry out in sympathy, "Is there a father's heart as well as a mother's?" But the philosopher of sex refuses to accept felicitations. His marriage to Ann may or may not be happy, but that is beside the point, since something more important is at stake. Hushing any merry peal of wedding bells, Shaw warns us in effect that "you never can tell"; and on that skeptical note, Jack and Ann, having played out the comedy of courtship, now turn to face the tragicomedy of marriage.

Don Juan in Hell

Despite his elaborate advertisement of *Man and Superman* as a Don Juan play, it is only in the third-act dream fantasy that Shaw enters into direct competition with the dozens of playwrights, novelists, and poets who have written of the famous lover.[18] As we have seen, Tanner is a Don Juan only to the extent that he holds unorthodox views on sex. But even in the dream sequence, where Don Juan appears in his original guise as a seventeenth-century Spanish nobleman in company with other characters from his legend, Shaw's conception of Juan's personality is so much at odds with the popular tradition that one specialist has called the change "the most strange and complete transformation that any character of the stage has ever undergone," and a second has declared that he would not be surprised to learn that Shaw "thought of Don Juan after, rather than before, planning his play."[19] It might at first seem likely, on the basis of the divergence of his Juan from the historical norm, that Shaw's researches into literature concerning the great amorist were merely superficial. Yet this does not seem by any means to have been the case. There is evidence, indeed, that he was familiar not only with the classical treatments of the tale by Tirso de Molina, Molière, Da Ponte, and Byron, but also with such lesser-known versions as the dramatic extravaganza by Dumas *père*, De Musset's poem, and the stories of Hoffmann and Mérimée, and that he consulted essays on the subject by a large number of scholars, including Manuel de la Revilla, Francisco Pí y Margall, Felipe Picatoste, Antoine de Latour, Philarète Chasles, Gustave Larroumet, and Maurice Barrès.[20]

Nevertheless, it must be candidly admitted that Shaw's portrait of the Don is unusual enough to justify the critical bewilderment. The protagonist of Tirso's seventeenth-century religious melodrama, *El Burlador de Sevilla*, is articulate only in wooing women and issuing challenges to duels. No stage figure could be farther from a prophet-thinker. Shaw's Juan shares with him only his dignity and pride, and in the case of Tirso's hero this pride is not the intellectual pride of the critic and philosopher, but the class pride of the dashing *caballero*. Molière's Don Juan, on the other hand, is distinctly closer to Shaw's. The hero of *Le Festin de Pierre* (a play Shaw ranked above *Tartuffe* and *Le Misanthrope*) is a far more sophisticated person than Tirso's reprobate. He is clever and ready-witted in debate, skeptical in matters of faith and religion, and enough of an ironist to relish keenly his perception of the discrepancies between people's pretenses in matters of sex and their actual behavior.

Still, though he certainly takes us closer to Shaw, Molière's Juan
is a sophister and not someone seriously concerned to solve the
world's problems. And, compared to him, the roué Da Ponte created
for Mozart's opera is a much less interesting man. Whatever
Mozart's musical genius, Don Giovanni in the opera is merely a
brave, resourceful scamp, whose mental energies go first of all into
planning his intrigues and then into extricating himself from them.
Where Tirso's amorist is a triumphant seducer who moves from
conquest to conquest, Da Ponte, in adapting the story to the conventions of *opera buffa*, makes the Don a pursued and harassed
husband—an essentially comic figure, more often a fugitive than a
conqueror. But Shaw has carried the notion of the fugitive lover a
good many steps further. As Shaw portrays him in *Man and Superman*,
Don Juan, after a career as a womanizer, has fled his actual and
would-be mistresses, given up love in disgust, and become an austere
contemplative philosopher and social reformer. Indeed, in Shaw's
allegorical dialogue he ends not as Juan the damned but, as Saint
Juan, a member of the heavenly host, forced into the company of
the redeemed by his own vital will and his boredom with the world's
pleasures, amorous and otherwise.

But why ever did Shaw pick Don Juan as his spokesman if he was
going to end, so to speak, by standing him on his head? It is perhaps
not surprising that this riddle has teased literary historians, since the
answer in fact lies outside literary history and in Shaw's own biography. It may seem at first wildly paradoxical that a modern revolutionary of a Puritanical bent should choose as his mask a Renaissance
nobleman-rake. It is not, of course, unprecedented to find a Puritan
arguing for sexual liberty; Milton and Bucer would be early examples,
and the Oneida Perfectionists more recent ones. But a Puritan Casa-
nova is perhaps a degree more unlikely. Yet this is exactly the reputation Shaw himself earned in the eighties among his Fabian friends.
His nickname in this circle, was, indeed, none other than Don Giovanni, an epithet he bore partly for his well-known enthusiasm for
Mozart's opera and partly for his numerous philanderings, carried
on both out of natural curiosity and with an eye to his future career
as a literary psychologist. Shaw himself pointed to the paradox when
he wrote candidly to a French friend, Jules Magny: "As to 'les

séductions de la femme,' I believe opinion is divided between the people who regard me as a saint or a statue, and those who suspect me of being an Irish Don Juan who will eventually compromise Socialism by some outrageous scandal of the Parnell sort."[21]

Eventually, however, Shaw came to feel that his reputation was absurdly in excess of the facts. In 1887 he even adopted an ingenious method of setting the record straight. In a fantastic short story which he entitled "Don Giovanni Explains," Shaw causes the ghost of Mozart's hero to materialize before a girl in a railway carriage and to elaborate on the situations that resulted in his being mistaken for an avid pursuer of women. The explanation is, in effect, nothing more nor less than Shaw's own apology for himself. Giovanni-Shaw admits that his friends considered him "eccentric, wanting in earnestness, and destitute of moral sense."[22] Nevertheless, the ghost protests that he was, in fact, a man "much more highly evolved than most of my contemporaries, who were revengeful, superstitious, ferocious, gluttonous, intensely prejudiced by the traditions of their caste, brutal and incredibly foolish when affected by love, and intellectually dishonest and cowardly." After this riposte, the mock Spaniard goes on to tell how his first mistress conquered his shyness, the details of the episode being apparently those of Shaw's own real-life seduction by Mrs. Jenny Patterson:

At last a widow lady at whose house I sometimes visited, and of whose sentiments towards me I had not the least suspicion, grew desperate at my stupidity, and one evening threw herself into my arms and confessed her passion for me. The surprise, the flattery, my inexperience, and her pretty distress, overwhelmed me. I was incapable of the brutality of repulsing her; and indeed for nearly a month I enjoyed without scruple the pleasure she gave me, and sought her company *whenever I could find nothing better to do*. It was my first consummated love affair; and though for nearly two years the lady had no reason to complain of my fidelity, I found the romantic side of our intercourse, which seemed never to pall on her, tedious, unreasonable, and even forced and insincere except at rare moments, when the power of love made her beautiful, body and soul. Unfortunately, I had no sooner lost my illusions, my timidity, and my boyish curiosity about women, than I began to attract them irresistibly. [Italics added.][23]

After this account of his introduction to sexual intercourse, Giovanni goes on to explain that he had no designs on either Doña Ana or Zerlina, and that Elvira was simply an insanely jealous woman who (like Mrs. Patterson) first invented and then believed absurd tales about him. The Don-Juan-in-hell scene of *Man and Superman*, written more than a decade later, simply carries the cryptobiography a stage further. In it, Juan's history of his education in the arts recapitulates Shaw's career as a critic of painting, music, and drama in the London press; and both the jealous possessiveness Juan finds in his female admirers and his own clear-sightedness about his love-making closely match Shaw's own experience.

But the Don-Juan-in-hell scene is more than just covert autobiography: it is also a statement of Shaw's theology of salvation. The basis of his theology is also to be found in embryonic form in "Don Giovanni Explains." There Giovanni tells of being borne off to a hell made up of "brutish, weak, good-for-nothing people, all well intentioned," who despised heaven-dwellers as "unfeeling, uppish, precise, and frightfully dry in their conversation and amusements."[24] *Man and Superman* develops this allegory with such paradoxical ingenuity that Shaw, finding he had left most of his readers bewildered, provided an analytical program note for the first production in 1907. In this commentary he explained that the "higher theology" rejects the hell of popular religion, holding instead that the world itself "may be made a hell by a society in a state of damnation: that is, a society so lacking in the higher orders of energy that it is given wholly to the pursuit of immediate individual pleasure, and cannot even conceive the passion of the divine will."[25]

Shaw's hell is not the home of thieves, murderers, and ravishers, but of happiness-seekers, despairing cynics, and the self-indulgent. The hellish spirit is the spirit that fosters connoisseurship in art, dilettantism in literature, and sentimental amorism in personal relations. In a word, it is what inspires the whole round of social pleasures and organized amusements our well-to-do middle classes indulge in, from the crude vulgarity of a Las Vegas to the refinements of the Glyndebourne and San Francisco opera. Above all, it smacks of the theater. In hell as Shaw conceives it, everything is make-believe:

any woman may, like an actress in make-up, be any age she likes, and any male may, like a vain actor, parade with a padded figure more statuesque than any nature has provided for him. The hell-dwellers are obsessed with glamor, and with youth, beauty, and love. Those were the preoccupations of the London stage in the nineties, and they remain the preoccupations of Hollywood and television in our own day.

Shaw's devil, like the entrepreneurs of the amusement world, serves up his concoctions with an air of forced good-fellowship and touchily resents critics as carping malcontents who do not know how to enjoy themselves. Seen from this angle, he resembles both the turn-of-the-century impresario and the modern movie producer, with his facile sentiment, his cynicism, and his belief in popularity as a measure of worth. Shaw wanted him to be played by the same actor who played Mendoza, because in Shaw's London, such men were often Jews, though Shaw warns us in the preface to the *Plays for Puritans* that there is little consolation for anti-Semites in this fact, since Jewish tastes in entertainment differed from Gentile tastes only in being more romantic and markedly less coarse.[26]

Shaw's hell is his revenge upon the English theater for the four years of ennui and disgust he suffered as a critic. In the same preface, he indicts the stage for attempting to substitute "sensuous ecstacy" for "intellectual activity and honesty." This he denounces as "the very devil." In the hell scene of *Man and Superman* Shaw gives material form to his metaphor in the shape of a devil who is before all else a hedonist. Now hedonism, of course, was far from being the avowed creed of the late-Victorian middle classes. Consequently the devil is every bit as much at odds with conventional morality as Juan-Shaw is. It is simply that their reactions to it have taken totally different directions. For Shaw's religion of struggle and reform, the devil has substituted a religion of love and beauty. He has made up his creed out of the neopagan lucubrations of men like Swinburne, Symonds, and Wilde in England and Gautier and Anatole France (in his pre-Dreyfusard days) on the Continent. To savor intensely the pleasures of art and the delights of cultivated personal relationships is the whole of his existence. What Pater stands for in a scholarly and intellectual way in his *Studies in the History of the Renaissance*, the devil represents, say, on the level of a relisher of Fitzgerald's translation of the *Rubáiyát*.

Shaw considered happiness not the aim of human existence, but a by-product of useful activity. Like Carlyle, he rejected the hedonistic calculus of pleasures on the ground that the surest way to achieve misery was to seek happiness directly. The literary hedonists of the late Victorian period were, however, for the most part avowed pessimists from the start, their creed being "Let us eat and drink, for tomorrow we shall die." Shaw looked on such men first as denizens of a post-Darwinian world for whom "the alternative to believing silly things about God seemed to be blank materialist Hedonist atheism,"[27] and second, as the latest heirs of a long and distinguished literary tradition stretching back to Ecclesiastes. The devil is thus simultaneously the spokesman for a specifically *fin de siècle* despair and the representative of a line of writers as diverse as Shakespeare, Swift, Thackeray, and Hemingway, all of whom have taken as their text "Vanity of vanities," and been overwhelmed by their sense of the futility and senselessness of the human condition. As a result, the eloquent speeches which Shaw puts into the mouth of the devil are a compliment to the literary distinction of those writers, whose majestic rhetoric and seductive poetry Shaw recognized at the same time that he deplored their will-sapping conclusions.[28]

But how do three people as different as Juan, Doña Ana, and the Commander happen to turn up in the devil's kingdom? Here Shaw indulges his penchant for impish humor. In "Don Giovanni Explains" the Don is sent to hell in error on the recommendation of the Commander, who had mistaken him for a bon vivant on the strength of his reputation—much as if Shaw's fame as a witty scoffer and womanizer had won him an invitation to join an Omar Khayyam club. Ana's arrival in hell, on the other hand, is a satire on conventional piety. Ana, unlike Juan, has rigorously repressed her own natural inclinations and lived by the moral code of her day. She has not sacrificed her desires, however, out of any real passion for virtue, but in hopes of a substantial postmortal reward. When she wakes up in hell she complains that she could have been "so much wickeder" and that all her good deeds were "wasted," thus revealing where her real regrets lie. At first she argues that she has been sent to the wrong place, but it soon turns out that her Christianity has its own "hellish" side. Temporarily wearied by the trials and struggles of life, she had rashly assumed that the eternity of bliss promised by popular religion would be to her liking. In short, Shaw makes Ana a concrete illustration of Nietzsche's caustic remark that the orthodox Christian was a man who carried the Epicurean principle as far as it was possible to carry it.

If Ana is Everywoman in her unreflecting piety, the Commander is Montaigne's *homme moyen sensuel.* As an easygoing philistine he takes his pleasures for granted and is quite content to let the premises of his existence go uncriticized, even to the point of killing other men for doing what he has done himself, simply because he thinks society expects him to. Amiably thickheaded, he enjoys the debate between Juan and the devil as a kind of diverting sporting contest and is only shocked when Juan strips off the sentimental veils he has cast over his own sexual escapades. Unlike his daughter, whose instinctive vitality finally takes her out of the devil's realm in quest of something more than idle amusement, the Commander is one of the truly and naturally damned. His temporary sojourn in heaven is merely the consequence of a pretended interest in serious questions he had feigned for propriety's sake, which he now drops with relief, just as an ordinary man whose wife had dragged him to a community meeting might escape afterward to a bar or nightclub.

The heaven the Commander has left out of tedium Don Juan hails as the home of "the masters of reality," who work and live instead of merely pretending. If Juan's scorn of hell embodies Shaw's animus against the theater, his joy in escaping to heaven expresses the feelings with which Shaw gave up play-reviewing in 1898 to devote himself to work on the St. Pancras Borough Council. There he labored on the health, electric, housing, and drainage committees, even relishing garbage problems when he recalled his enforced theater going. "I love the reality of the Vestry and its dustcarts," he wrote happily, "after the silly visionary fashion-ridden theatre."[29] Shaw's heaven is thus a kind of cross between a Fabian committee room and a town council session. Metaphysically, it is the sum of all true values, social, political, intellectual, and aesthetic. We learn that

Rembrandt arrived there when he could draw an old woman with as much pleasure as a young girl. Mozart has also entered the transcendental regions, presumably through writing *The Magic Flute*, which Shaw regarded as a philosophical prelude to Wagner's *Ring*. As to Wagner himself, Shaw appears to accept Nietzsche's view, expressed in *The Case of Wagner* and *Nietzsche Contra Wagner*, that, having passed through an earlier triumphant phase in *Siegfried*, where he showed the world liberated by a free spirit and immoralist, Wagner then fell into decadence, going over to the devil's side by preaching not affirmation of the will, but Schopenhauerian negation in *Parsifal*. Thus heaven, in so far as it is the home of artists, belongs to those whose art is a stimulus to life, not to the practitioners of an aimless "art for art's sake."

Having brought his cast before us, and having, in the light of his new theology, established the difference between the heavenly and the hellish states, Shaw now begins the great debate between the devil and Don Juan that makes up the core of the dream episode. In form this dialogue is Lucianic-Platonic. The Lucianic element is evident in the use of legendary characters and the comic irreverence that makes it seem as if here Shaw were out to realize dramatically the "gay science" Nietzsche had called for, with its "light feet, wit, fire, grave, grand logic, stellar dancing, and wanton intellectuality."[30] By contrast, the Platonic side appears in the dialectical structure of the dialogue and in the seriousness of the themes Shaw plays with. These are, in brief, first, the relation between creative and destructive forces in human society, and second, the function of women and sex in the universe.

The first inning is the devil's. To Juan's contention that man's mission is to help "Life in its struggle upward," the devil replies that man is not the vitalist Juan makes him, but a mortalist, in love with death. In a long and eloquent speech, parallel in many respects to the diatribe of the King of Brobdingnag in *Gulliver's Travels*, the devil argues that man finds his keenest delight, not in creation, but in funerals, sensational tragedies, and more and more horrendous wars. He is much more willing to spend money on munitions than on improving his squalid living conditions. Bloody victories excite him to enthusiasm, and the whole machinery of the political state is no more than an engine for torture and destruction under the guise of justice, duty, and patriotism. In the light of these grisly facts a man's wisest course is to withdraw from political life entirely in favor of the pursuit of private pleasure, since such an existence is at least relatively harmless.

So forceful and cogent are the devil's arguments that Shaw's interpreters have been seriously confused by them. Why, they have asked, if the devil is wrong, does he speak so many home truths, and ones that sound so much like Shavian truths at that? But this is, after all, no more than asking why Shaw does not make his devil simply a transparent sophist. The answer, of course, is that he rejects so easy a game. The devil, even a dilettante devil, must have his due. Shaw wants to show us not a man of straw, but a real tempter, that is, someone whose arguments might plausibly influence cultivated people who have some real knowledge of the world. The devil's indictment of society is therefore a cogent one, and we must pay this pessimistic cynic the compliment of acknowledging not only that his facts are irrefutable, but that his skeptical hedonism, in detaching him from the mere acceptance of the status quo, gives him the power to see behind social façades as no smugly complacent church-going optimist is likely to do.

But if skeptical hedonism can highlight the world's ills so tellingly, that is not to say that its picture of life is complete or that its answers are acceptable ones. Don Juan admits the devil's evidence but rejects his conclusion that man, socially organized, is simply a dangerous demoniac. This is both too melodramatic and at the same time too flattering an appraisal of human nature. Man's chief sin is not his tendency to violence, but his apathy and abjectness in the face of his social degradation. On the contrary, his willingness to kill is not his greatest failing, but a redeeming feature. Man the coward was willing to fight for religion in the Crusades, for freedom in the English and French Revolutions, and against slavery in the American Civil War. And if religious ideals and a hatred of tyranny and slavery have roused him to action, then even the devil's conventional retort that a generation after Lincoln the white factory worker is worse enslaved than the black field hand may soon lose its force; Juan predicts that the factory worker too will have his day as the result of a series of

social revolutions against which, in the long run, not even mighty
armadas will prevail. In man's sense of social solidarity and in his
willingness to do God's work even in the face of bombs and bayonets,
Juan-Shaw sees his ultimate salvation.

With this, Shaw's debaters now turn from arms and men to the
subject of love and women. For the devil, woman exists solely as an
object of romantic passion. To such a view Juan opposes neither popular moralism nor the philosophical "gynolatry" Comte had made
fashionable among Victorian intellectuals. Instead he turns to contemporary biological speculations, especially those of the American
sociologist Lester Ward. Against the androcentric view of evolution,
which made man the primary and woman the secondary sex, Ward
had argued that it was more logical to regard primitive single-sexed
organisms (like the amoeba) as feminine, since they were endowed
with what is usually regarded as the feminine faculty par excellence,
namely, the ability to reproduce. According to this gynecocentric
theory, the male is only a late innovation in the evolutionary scheme,
a contrivance of the female to gain the advantages of cross-fertiliza-
tion. But the male, though insignificant in relation to the female in
some species, has in the case of *Homo sapiens* undergone an "efflores-
cence" so that he is able to dominate woman by virtue of his greater
strength and mental capacity.[31]

It is in the light of this theory that Juan now looks at love, courtship, and the "sacred" institution of marriage. The Commander,
speaking as a man of the world who desires to enjoy his pleasures
without thought, naïvely begs Juan to regale them with spicy
anecdotes about his adventures with women. But Juan objects that
the purpose of human love-making is not the personal gratification
of men or women, but the eventual creation of a race that will be
godlike in knowledge, in power, and in self-awareness. Scorning the
sentimental haze most people throw over their love escapades, Juan
proceeds to analyze his experiences with all the cold clarity of a
Stendhal or a Schopenhauer. When his education in the arts made
him curious about women, he began to study them at first hand, but
though he was fully aware of the extent to which the real flesh and
blood fell short of his ideal, the experiment soon proved fatal to his
critical detachment: once he had moved into near proximity the

racial urge swept him irresistibly on, propelling him into mating in spite of himself.

When the shocked Ana protests that such conduct is immoral and that men must be held to strict fidelity in their sex relations, Juan, playing the skeptical *philosophe*, retorts that, on the contrary, the life force cares nothing for chastity at all. Ana objects that marriage at least "peoples the world," but Juan, seizing the teleological point he had made earlier—that the end of marriage is the perpetuation and improvement of the species—asks if our present form of Christian monogamous marriage really does it in the most effective way. In taking this position, Shaw no doubt had in mind such convictions as Ward's that "all attempts on the part of society to regulate the relations of the sexes, necessary though they may be to the maintenance of the social order, interfere with the biologic principle of crossing strains and securing the maximum variation, development, and vigor of the stock," [32] as well as warnings like this by Havelock Ellis:

> A cosmic conservatism does not necessarily involve a social conservatism. The wisdom of Man, working through a few centuries or in one corner of the earth, by no means necessarily corresponds to the wisdom of Nature, and may be in flat opposition to it. This is especially the case when the wisdom of Man merely means, as sometimes happens, the experience of our ancestors gained under other conditions, or merely the opinions of one class or one sex. Taking a broad view of the matter, it seems difficult to avoid the conclusion that it is safer to trust to the conservatism of Nature than to the conservatism of Man. We are not at liberty to introduce any artificial sexual barrier into social concerns. [33]

Hence, a woman like Ana, Juan points out, might have done the race an even greater service if she had borne her twelve children not to one but to twelve different husbands.

This is Juan's reply to the conventional moralist. But what significance do these speculations on marriage have for the devil, who, after all, is not a moralist, but only a hedonist who does not want his private pleasures interfered with? The answer is, Shaw thinks, that our present-day marriage arrangements may serve the devil's purposes very well. Modern methods of birth control, by allowing cultivated people to realize the kind of love idyll hitherto

confined to story books, make it possible to turn marriage partner-
ships into a kind of antisocial *égoïsme à deux*. In the eyes of Shaw
the utopian social philosopher, a one-woman harem is a harem still,
and monogamous marriage owes a good deal of its popularity to
the fact that, as Tanner expresses it in "The Revolutionist's Handbook," it "combines the maximum of temptation with the maximum
of opportunity."[34]

But Juan rejects any kind of stasis, even an idyllic-erotic one:

> I tell you that as long as I can conceive something better than
> myself I cannot be easy unless I am striving to bring it into exis-
> tence or clearing the way for it. That is the law of my life. That is
> the working within me of Life's incessant aspiration to higher
> organization, wider, deeper, intenser self-consciousness, and
> clearer self-understanding. It was the supremacy of this purpose
> that reduced love for me to the mere pleasure of a moment, art
> for me to the mere schooling of my faculties, religion for me to a
> mere excuse for laziness, since it had set up a God who looked at
> the world and saw that it was good, against the instinct in me that
> looked through my eyes at the world and saw that it could be
> improved.[35]

Nevertheless, it is one thing to have such aspirations and another
to assume that they correspond to anything in the permanent order
of nature. The devil scoffs at Juan's faith that nature has a purpose.
To adopt such a view is, to him, to follow a false analogy: it is no more
logical to argue that nature must have a purpose because Juan has
one than to argue on the same grounds that nature must have fingers
and toes. Juan's reply is that nature's will and his are not separate,
since the human will itself is simply the highest embodiment of
nature's intention, and that, moreover, nature has, against all
likelihood, actually turned digitless creatures into digited ones in
response to some blindly felt need in man's nonhuman ancestors.
Now, he declares, it is only necessary for man with his newly won
intellectual powers to assume the role of nature's pilot, rather than
drifting like the devil, absorbed in the sterile contemplation of love
and beauty.

Juan's optimism makes the devil laugh with the disillusionment
of the confirmed cynic who believes it is totally futile to seek anything
from life but the delights of the passing hour. Life for him is "an

infinite comedy of illusion," a series of repetitive cycles leading nowhere, the emptiest of vanities. At this point, Juan and the devil have, so to speak, fought their duel to a standstill and arrived at the rock-bottom premises of their respective faith and no-faith. Neither can finally refute the other logically. Only an act of will can resolve an impasse which has its roots in fundamental temperamental differences. Shaw, as we have seen, is theologically a Neo-Calvinist who believes that character is fate and that on this basis individuals are either predestinately damned or saved. The devil enthusiastically embraces his damnation by remaining in hell; Juan instinctively seeks his salvation by leaving it. For either to choose otherwise would be to condemn himself to an eternity of boredom, and this, the most appalling fate of all, Juan refuses to face.

Shaw even has a certain amount of respect for the devil as someone who at least does what he really wants to do and not merely what society thinks he should. By contrast, Ana may look like a naïvely duped victim of social convention. Yet in the final test we discover that she is not, like her father and the devil, among the naturally damned. Dismissing their romantic and sentimental ideals of woman-hood with contempt as phantoms of the male imagination, she stoutly defends flesh-and-blood wives. Ana, Shaw tells us, is "incapable both of the devil's utter damnation and of Don Juan's complete supersensuality." She cannot, "like the male devil, use love as mere sentiment and pleasure," nor can she, "like the male saint, put love aside when it has once done its work as a developing and enlightening experience." [36] But where her circumscribed intellect cannot save her, her womanly procreative instinct can, and it is as Woman Immortal that she pursues Don Juan to heaven, demanding, with the compelling urgency of someone who realizes that her work is not yet done, "a father for the Superman."

I have analyzed Shaw's hell scene in some detail because it has so often been treated as a mere literary *jeu d'esprit*, instead of being recognized for what it is—a classical philosophical dialogue shot through with comedy and wit and an ironic sense of human character. Whether one accepts Shaw's arguments or not will depend, of course, on one's basic attitude toward evolution, revolution, and marriage. It is not likely that Shaw will change the minds of those who think that efforts at social reform are useless, that biological change is somehow or other both a matter of pure chance and absolutely predetermined, and that our modern sentimental-domestic ideal of marriage is immutable. But anyone who is willing to think open-mindedly about these matters will find himself challenged. As to the present-day relevance of Shaw's hell, aesthetic hedonism as an avowed and philosophically held creed is no longer fashionable, and, in the age of the absurdists, influences serious literature so little that its revival would be an interesting novelty. Yet, as a lived rather than a professed way of life, can anyone doubt that it is the real religion of our cultivated middle classes and especially of those university teachers who are not mere philistines? Shaw's dialogue is a profession of faith and a call to action, intended to summon us from the art gallery, the concert hall, the foreign-movie house and the cocktail party to deal with the awkward and difficult problems of the real world.

CHAPTER SEVEN

Major Barbara

The didactic element in *Man and Superman* is, if anything, intensified in *Major Barbara*. This propagandistic purpose has been from the start a bone of contention. It is not by chance that critics holding a formalist position, from Shaw's friend A. B. Walkley down to Francis Fergusson in our own day, have denounced the play as a kind of literary farrago,[1] while philosopher-critics have regarded it as one of the few dramas with anything serious to say on the subject of politics.[2] Indeed, *Major Barbara* raises the central issue of modern aesthetics as squarely as any piece of writing can. The question— putting it in the simplest possible terms—is whether art is to be regarded as autonomous and *sui generis*, or whether it is to be judged in relation to some ulterior standard of reality, that is, as a form of science or knowledge. But even if you accept this second view of the nature of art—which is certainly Shaw's view—you will still have to ask yourself whether your own ulterior reality corresponds to Shaw's. Thus the play presents a double challenge—first to the dominant literary theory of our day, and second, to our political and social ideals.

We have already pointed out that each of the philosophical comedies begins with a satire on an idealistic liberal. In *Major Barbara* the liberal is Lady Britomart, whose character, like most of those in the play, was drawn from a real person. It is a well-known fact that Shaw based Adolphus Cusins, his professor of Greek, on Gilbert Murray, but it is less well known that he based Lady Britomart on Murray's real-life mother-in-law, Lady Rosalind Howard, Countess of Carlisle. (Shaw jokingly told Murray in a letter that he was at work on a play to be called "Murray's Mother-in-law."[3]) The Countess of Carlisle was, like Lady Britomart, a Whig peeress;

her father was the Liberal whip in Parliament, and she was herself a crusading temperance reformer and for eighteen years the leader of the national Women's Liberal Federation. Her husband, the Earl, being more interested in art than in estate management, she ran the extensive family estates like a private fiefdom, attending in minute detail to the farmer's personal welfare—and to their moral characters. Castle Howard and her house in Kensington were salons for the Liberal intelligentsia. Murray himself has paid tribute to her crusading enthusiasm and to the heartening quality of her formidable benevolence.[4] But he was also aware of the "difficult" side of the Countess, what he called her "awful egoism and self-pity, the possessiveness, the jealousy, the inability to forgive or ever to admit that she was wrong, and of course the lack of self-control."[5] All these traits become part of Shaw's characterization.

The clue to Shaw's treatment of the comic contradictions in Lady Britomart's personality may be found in a remark by James Froude, Carlyle's biographer, on the subject of Lady Rosalind. Froude, who disapproved of her politics but admired her character, said that though she professed to be a Liberal, she was by temperament better fitted to be an empress. Hence if Shaw had chosen to make her the central figure of the play, he might have imitated Molière's "Bourgeois Gentleman" to the extent of calling it "The Imperious Liberal." By family tradition and personal conviction Lady Britomart is an avowed believer in free speech and a democratic franchise, but every speech that she utters shows her native aristocratic spirit and natural masterfulness at odds with these ideals. She thinks she is consulting her son Stephen about the family inheritance when she is in fact revealing her own firm convictions. She can no more be said to be consciously bullying Stephen than an avalanche can be accused of intending to obliterate a tree in its path, but the effect is just the same. She declares that her children are her friends and equals but in reality treats them like kindergarten toddlers unable to take care of themselves. If she were not as amiable as she is willful and domineering, she would be an atrocious tyrant; but as her children are as strongminded as she, and, as she is prevented by her affectionateness from acting as peremptorily as she talks, we even end by feeling something like pity for her as a well-intentioned mother balked in the pursuit of her heart's desire and too heroic to play for commiseration. *Major Barbara* has been glibly likened to *The Importance of Being Earnest* for its wit and farce, and there is indeed a superficial resemblance between Lady Britomart and Lady Bracknell in Wilde's play, but nothing could be more unlike Wilde than the stroke by which Shaw has the frustrated Lady Britomart burst into tears at the end of Act One when her children desert her for their father.

But where, if we take Shaw's formula seriously, is the earnest of the particular joke which underlies this brilliant piece of high comedy? We do not have to look far for it. It lies in the fact that Lady Britomart represents the hereditary British governing class in its most enlightened and liberal aspect, but also under its limitations. For, despite all her admirable civic energy, her vision is circumscribed by two ironclad principles—her conventional morality and her belief in the divine right of the aristocracy to rule the country. Behind her reformism is an intense moral fervor, but she does not see that moral tyranny is in itself the most oppressive of all tyrannies and that moral indignation is no substitute for critical thought and action. When Stephen, assuming that she is about to reveal some youthful indiscretion of his father's, shows embarrassment, she chides him: "It is only in the middle classes, Stephen, that people get into a state of dumb helpless horror when they find out that there are wicked people in the world. In our class, we have to decide what is to be done with wicked people; and nothing should disturb our self-possession." But, as we shall see later, "helpless horror" and moral indignation are almost all that Lady Britomart can oppose to the brutal facts of the Undershaft munitions works and the political power of a capitalist class out to realize its profits at whatever cost.[6]

Where Lady Britomart's moralism is not an aristocratic Mrs. Grundyism, a Queen Victoria-ism, so to speak, it is merely a rationalization of her class prejudices and privileges, "right" and "propriety" being whatever furthers the Stevenage family interests, and "wrong" or "impropriety" being whatever conflicts with them. For the central issue of the first act, and indeed of the play as a whole, is who will inherit the armament factory owned by Lady Britomart's husband, Andrew Undershaft.

The question of the Undershaft inheritance has caused a rift between the husband and wife: according to the tradition of the firm, the inheritance must go, not to a son of the owner, but to some promising adopted heir. This condition, utterly at odds with aristocratic belief in birth and blood, so offends Lady Britomart that it is useless for Andrew to argue that the Roman Empire was run successfully on this scheme and that it brought to the throne Marcus Aurelius. She is so used to thinking of the Stevenages as governors by natural right that when Andrew had refused to break the firm's law of succession in favor of his son Stephen, the resulting quarrel led to a legal separation. Lady Britomart's way of putting it is to declare that nothing can bridge fundamental moral disagreement.

We have only to spend two minutes in Stephen's presence to realize the soundness of his father's decision, for Stephen is a conscientious, thoroughly well-intentioned prig and moral pedant, tediously prating about right being right and wrong being wrong; in short, he is ten times the slave of conventional morality his mother is, with her spiritedness all soured into sulky petulance of the most high-toned sort. His sister Sarah lacks his pretentiousness, but also his starchy character, and is, in fact, no more than a fashionable nonentity. Only in their third child, Barbara, has the Undershaft-Stevenage marriage justified itself as an evolutionary experiment in the crossing of types and classes, for Barbara has Lady Britomart's genius for leadership and mothering, with none of her class limitations. So little is she concerned with mere propriety and good form and so intensely does she identify herself with the religious spirit of the race that she has thrown aristocratic prejudice to the winds and demonstrated the family independence of mind by joining the least snobbish of the reforming religious sects of the day, the Salvation Army.

As the play opens we learn that Sarah and Barbara have both become engaged, Sarah to Charles Lomax, an amiable aristocratic noodle as empty-headed as herself, and Barbara to a man as complex and subtle in his moral and intellectual perceptions as Lomax is silly. Shaw shows us in Cusins a representative of the humane conscience in its most tender and perceptive form. In writing to Gilbert Murray, his model for the part, Shaw pointed out that he had taken pains to make his professor "the reverse in every point of the theatrical strong man":

> I want him to go on his quality wholly, and not to make the smallest show of physical robustness or brute determination. His selection by Undershaft should be a standing puzzle to the people who believe in the strong-silent still-waters-run-deep hero of melodrama. The very name Adolphus Cusins is selected to that end.[7]

In choosing Murray as his model, Shaw had in mind a type of Liberal in strong contrast to the active, bustling Lady Britomart. Cusins is the academic, cloistered, sympathetic, skeptical, ironic, super-civilized Liberal who shrinks instinctively from what E. M. Forster has called the world of "telegrams and anger."

Murray's liberalism sprang from several sources—from the radicalism of Castle Howard, from his Irish rebel background, and from a strain of Shelleyan humanitarianism that made him, like Shaw, a vegetarian and a hater of all forms of cruelty. The other side of the picture was his Hellenism.[8] For Murray, Greek literature was a living force having direct bearing on modern politics, morals, and culture. Here is how he writes of Euripides, the Greek playwright to whom he felt especially drawn:

> His contemporary public denounced him as dull, because he tortured them with personal problems; as malignant, because he made them see truths they wished not to see; as blasphemous and foul-minded, because he made demands on their spiritual and religious natures which they could neither satisfy nor overlook.[9]

In short, Murray regarded Euripides as standing in relation to the golden age of Athens as the "New Drama" of Shaw and Ibsen stood in relation to the age of Victoria and Edward VII. Shaw returned the compliment by hailing the production of Murray's translations of Euripides at the Court Theatre as modern masterpieces that had earned their place on the contemporary stage in their own right.

During the Boer campaign of 1899–1901, Murray belonged, with his cousin by marriage, Bertrand Russell,[10] to the small but vocal Liberal minority who opposed the war. No doubt his antiwar sentiments endowed Euripides' *Andromache* and *The Trojan Women*

with particular significance for him; at any rate these were two of
his earliest choices for translation into English verse. In *Major
Barbara*, Shaw makes Undershaft give Cusins the nickname Euripides, thus implying that he looks on human affairs with the same
mixture of ironic pessimism and pity as did his Greek predecessor.[11]
When Cusins is brought face to face with the facts of armament-
making, he tells Undershaft, "There is an abyss of moral horror
between me and your accursed aerial battleships."

When Lady Britomart invites her estranged husband to meet his
prospective sons-in-law in the drawing room of her West End
mansion, her intention is the eminently practical one of extracting
dowries from Andrew, her estimate of the earning power of a feckless
man-about-town and a classics professor being realistically small.
But Lady Britomart's attempt to bring up once more the matter of
the inheritance meets flinty resistance from Undershaft. Indeed, the
family reunion appears headed for a fiasco, and it is only the unexpected interest Undershaft shows in Barbara's novel religious aspirations that saves the meeting from disaster. It is an immense puzzle to
both the naïve and the sophisticated members of the family that
Undershaft should show such a concern with her new faith, particularly since he is resolutely unashamed of his destructive trade and even
seems to glory in it, declaring, "Your Christianity, which enjoins
you to resist not evil, and to turn the other cheek, would make me a
bankrupt. My morality—my religion—must have a place for cannons
and torpedoes in it." Barbara challenges him to maintain his faith
after visiting her East End Salvation Army shelter. Her father accepts
the invitation, and issues a counter-challenge: she shall, in return,
pay a visit to his arms factory and face the temptation offered by a
religion of "money and gunpowder." He warns her that she may end
by giving up the Salvation Army for the sake of the cannons; strong
in her conviction of the impossibility of any such monstrous even-
tuality, she accepts his condition.

The scene at the Salvation Army shelter is a remarkable piece of
low-life melodrama, equalled in English only by the works of O'Casey.
The refugees at the barracks include a cynically smart young man
and an old crone, both posing as redeemed sinners, and an unem-
ployed older man who is brought in in a state of semistarvation.

This man, Peter Shirley by name, has been turned out of his job as overage; he finds the necessity of accepting charity all the more bitter because he holds the faith of a secularist, in contrast to the others, who believe in nothing but their right to bilk and exploit capitalist society as it has bilked and exploited them. Finally Bill Walker enters, a half-drunk, blustering bully in a very mean mood, who bawls angrily for his girl and curses the Army for taking her from him.

It will be seen that this is not a particularly cheerful, amusing, or attractive group of slum-dwellers. Unlike other writers who are sympathetic to the poor, Shaw does not sentimentalize or idealize them, his argument being that if poverty actually did improve people, this would be the strongest reason for making poverty compulsory. Shaw insists rather that poverty is unequivocally *de*moralizing: its fruits are not simple piety, honest rectitude, and altruistic sentiment; they are more likely to be, at best, hypocrisy, cynicism, and shattered self-respect, and, at worst, conscienceless brutality.

Looking into this abyss of hopelessness, Lady Britomart would first of all be shocked at the total lack of respect of the poor for their governors—sincerely shocked, since she would be conscious of having their spiritual and physical welfare at heart. Barbara and Cusins as humanitarians are most appalled by the bitterness and violence of the lives of the poor. Moreover, Christianity itself must assume part of the blame for the moral debasement, for besides teaching humility and acquiescence, it also, through its Pauline theology, first preaches a retaliatory morality, and then allows the blackguard to escape the consequences of his actions through a belief in divine atonement.

Shaw's second act makes this last point through a moral parable in the vein of Tolstoy. Bill Walker, the bully, first strikes the old woman and then a young Salvation Army girl. When the old woman curses him he simply jeers at her, knowing that hard words break no bones and that she is, spiritually speaking, on the same level as himself in her vindictive desire for revenge. The young girl, by contrast, instead of reproaching him prays for him. Her unexpected behavior has the effect of giving his anger time to cool, and then, as he reflects more soberly on his deed, of causing a noticeable twinge of conscience. This sensitivity Barbara exploits skillfully, not scolding him, but keeping the naked fact of his deed inexorably before him. Finally he feels he must somehow make amends, and the way he tries to do it is highly significant. First, he tries to atone by getting himself pummeled by a Salvation Army officer who is a converted boxer; this is the Pauline-Christian method. When this fails, he then fines himself as he has seen other blackguards fined in law courts: this is, of course, only Pauline Christianity as we have institution-alized it with our legal system of penalties and prisons. But Barbara, whose Christianity is not that of Paul, but of Christ—that is, a Christianity which scorns vengeance, retaliation, and punishment—is still inexorable; she will not play the role of Tetzel on any account. Bill Walker cannot buy salvation from the Salvation Army. The only way he can redeem himself is through a growth of conscience that will make it impossible for him to repeat his deed. Under no circumstances must he be encouraged to sin so that grace may abound.

Barbara's fight for Bill's soul comes very near to success and fails only through a stroke of diablerie on the part of her father. The latter frustrates her simply by demonstrating that although the Salvation Army can afford to refuse to sell the blackguard his salvation for twenty shillings, it cannot, no matter how scrupulous it affects to be, refuse to sell the millionaire his for, say, five thousand pounds. Barbara had refused to accept her father's tuppence in the collection plate because the money was earned through the creation of destruc-tive forces far more brutal in their effect than anything the slum ruffian might aspire to. But when Mrs. Baines, the Army commis-sioner, comes to plead for money to carry on the Army's work in a hard winter, she is forced to accept Undershaft's proffer of the afore-mentioned thousands despite his sardonic emphasis on the terrifying nature of his enterprises. The ruffian, when he sees the rich man's gift accepted where his own conscience money was rejected, turns on Barbara with cynical scorn, and Barbara, facing at once the failure of her attempt at salvation and a realization that the Salvation Army, if it is to exist at all, can exist only as the pensioner of the distillery and cannon industries, utters her bitter and heart-rending cry of despair, "My God: why hast thou forsaken me?"

The melodrama of the scene at the Salvation Army barracks thus reaches its climax in a loss of faith. But it is at this point that the play takes the most surprising of its many surprising turns. For at the moment that Barbara's God, the God of evangelical Christianity, appears to have failed her, the professor of Greek hails as a new deity the very man Barbara now fears as anti-Christ, her diabolical-seeming father. Cusins, in a transport of ecstasy, declares himself to be possessed by the spirit of Undershaft, whom he addresses as the new Dionysos. Barbara, in the pain and confusion of her loss, can of course see nothing in this behavior but a piece of perverse irony.

Since the reader or spectator of the play may be left in the same puzzlement as Shaw's West End heiress, it may be well at this point to ask what Shaw means by his idea of a new Dionysos. What has the ancient Greek god to do with modern society? The answer is to be found in the meaning Dionysiac religion had in the Greek world. Historians and philosophers, of whom Nietzsche is the most famous, have repeatedly emphasized the strange disparity between the serene rationalism of Greek society as we usually conceive it and the wild barbarity of the Bacchic cult which entered Greece from Thrace and Macedonia in the tenth century before Christ. Nietzsche traces the birth of dramatic tragedy itself to this irruption of frenzied rites and ecstatic orgies into the calm order and moral rationalism of Greek life, which the new religion challenged with its worship of supernormal psychic energy and its identification of the worshiper both with the new god and with the life processes of the animal and vegetative world.

Cusins had earlier praised the services of the Salvation Army as the "true worship of Dionysos," finding in the Army's ecstasy and enthusiasm (literally, a standing outside oneself and possession by the divine will) an analogue of the uncouth religion that shocked the cultivated Greeks as the Army shocked the conventional Anglicanism of the West End. In its stirring religious music he had seen the primitive dithyramb reborn, the trombones, timbrels, and drums being the antithesis of both the tepid hymns sung in fashionable churches and the salon music of the fashionable drawing room. Even its symbols, blood and fire, Cusins points out, are Dionysiac symbols. Its joy and happiness are those of the god-possessed, as Barbara's later grief is that of the God-forsaken.

Thus Dionysianism is what Bergson calls a "dynamic religion," with its basis not in conventional morality or institutionalism, but in a mystical union with the divine will. It breaks down social barriers, taking the intellectual into University Settlements in the slums, and pitting him actively against evil. It carries its devotees beyond the bounds of logic and reason. Aroused and lacking rational direction, it finds its expression in the frenzy of the revolutionary mob.

Cusins is a sophisticated intellectual who has joined the Army, as Lady Britomart puts it, to worship Barbara (no bad object of worship, Shaw would insist). As a student of comparative religion and a disciple of Sir James Frazer, his view of the Army is, to say the least, not that of a fundamentalist. But Barbara's obvious religious genius attracts him strongly, and her evangelicalism, on its practical side, is not at all incompatible with his own religion of love, pity, and forgiveness. Indeed, for all his sardonic irony, he faces a crisis of his own beliefs at the same moment Barbara faces hers. As we have already seen, Cusins, in his skepticism and humanitarianism, is akin to the young Euripides who cast doubts on the traditional Greek attitudes toward patriotism, religion, women, and slaves.

But the Greek playwright's later development has a strange and unforeseen twist to it. For Euripides, who first turned the Greek drama away from its roots in Dionysiac religion toward a critical and skeptical direction, does return to Dionysos at the end of his career. In what is generally regarded as the last work of his old age, *The Bacchae*, the humanistic and humanitarian playwright does come face to face with the religion in which the drama had its origin. It is probably no exaggeration to say that *The Bacchae* is, by a good margin, the most terrifying, unedifying, and enigmatic of all Greek tragedies. You will recall that in this play Dionysos visits in disguise the city of Thebes, where his rites have been forbidden by the moralistic King Pentheus, and works a horrifying revenge. The problem Euripides' drama poses, put in the briefest terms, is this: What attitude are we to adopt to this new force in society, at once so terrible and so fascinating? Does Dionysos' ghastly triumph over Pentheus signify the rebirth of vital religion, or does the god symbolize some dark, demonic power from which we are to recoil in dread?

Now, like the Greeks of Euripides' day, Cusins has also been brought face to face with a brutal, primitive force of life and death which the cultivated, sensitive side of him recoils from, but which the clearheaded student of society is forced to take into account.[12] This power is the destructive-creative energy of Cusins' prospective father-in-law, the arms maker. And Shaw, to emphasize the fact that he has had the parallel with Euripides' drama in mind all along, has Cusins quote some twenty or thirty lines from the play in what Cusins identifies as his own (that is, Murray's) new translation.[13]

It is no exaggeration to say that Shaw's Undershaft has created the same bafflement in critics as Euripides' Dionysos, whether the critic be as naïve as the *Time* reviewer who accused Shaw of making a "complete about-face" and firing on his own socialist ranks or as sophisticated as Francis Fergusson, who for all his learning and intelligence, denounces *Major Barbara* as based on an "unresolved paradox."[14]

What, then, are we to make of this man who has so puzzled Shaw's commentators? It may perhaps be best to turn first to the living models from whom Shaw may have obtained hints for his millionaire munitions maker. One was suggested by a neighbor at Ayot Saint Lawrence, Charles McEvoy, who told Shaw of his father, a quiet and gentle man who had manufactured torpedoes for the North during the American Civil War.[15] But I should like to suggest that Shaw, in drawing the sardonic side of Undershaft's character, seems to have had in mind the Swedish arms maker Alfred Nobel, the inventor of dynamite. During the closing decades of the nineteenth century, Nobel's success in creating more and more powerful explosives had sent a wave of panic around the world. A leading figure in European business and international finance, Nobel was also a man of intellectual and literary cast. Like Undershaft, he belonged to a munitions dynasty, his father having been an armaments maker before him. In thought and sentiment, Nobel was a Shelleyan radical and humanitarian, but this did not limit has hardheadedness in business, and he sold his patents indiscriminately to autocratic and liberal states alike. (In a manuscript draft of *Major Barbara* Shaw makes Undershaft boast that he has sold a new rifle to the Swedish, Italian, and German governments without any compunctions on the score of politics.[16]) Nobel was very ironic in temperament, and when he gave money to charity, usually did so sardonically. An ardent Social Democrat, the combination of his shy, retiring personality and revolutionary political beliefs earned him the epithet "the gentle Bolshevik." His motto, "My home is where my work is, and my work is everywhere," might well have been Undershaft's. And, of course, one of the last deeds of this complex man was his endowment of the Nobel Peace Prize, which challenged the humanitarian liberals among his personal friends to solve the problems his discoveries had created. The Peace Prize was first awarded in 1901, four years before Shaw began his play.

The foregoing will perhaps explain in part one of the paradoxes of *Major Barbara*—that it is a dealer in lethal weapons who plays the role of Socrates in this socialist drama. But what of Undershaft's peculiar commercial ruthlessness, that specifically cold-blooded side of his personality that has so shocked and baffled the critics and audiences? To unravel the puzzle we must begin by considering his background. Undershaft is an East End slum boy, reared in that wilderness of desolation that was East London in the middle of the nineteenth century. He has, like all members of his dynasty, taken the name of the firm's founder, an abandaned orphan reared in the parish of St. Andrew Undershaft in the City.[17] His early career had resembled in its single-mindedness the careers of the American industrial barons of the post-Civil War period. Determined to escape from the indignities of poverty, he had taken for his own the stern old Scots slogan "Thou shalt starve ere I starve."

Here the second paradox appears, for we expect Shaw, as a Socialist, especially to condemn this spirit. But he condones it and even insists that for a poor person it is indeed the only possible "manly" attitude. (Undershaft's Christian name, Andrew, means "manly.") For Shaw, the great cardinal virtues are courage and self-respect, and he believed that if the poor in a democracy let themselves be exploited, starved, and snubbed, it is only because of their own inveterate abjectness. Hence the cutting remarks which Undershaft, the former slum boy, addresses to Peter Shirley, the downtrodden, long-suffering worker, in the Salvation Army shelter:

> SHIRLEY [*angrily*]. Who made your millions for you? Me and my like. Whats kep us poor? Keepin you rich. I wouldnt have your conscience, not for all your income.

UNDERSHAFT. I wouldnt have your income, not for all your conscience, Mr Shirley.[18]

Undershaft is driving home the point that the play makes over and over again—that a conviction of moral superiority is in itself the hollowest of consolations, the last resource of the weak and cowardly, and the treacherous quagmire in which true worth and manhood are lost.

Honor, justice, and truth are indeed part of Undershaft's religion, but he is firm in pointing out that they can be had only as the "graces and luxuries of a rich, strong, and safe life." Any liberal like Cusins who preaches these virtues to the poor without taking into account economic realities is a fool. Undershaft can even declare that his determinedly ruthless conduct satisfies the Kantian test, since the world would be an immeasurably better place if all the poor behaved exactly as he has. But first we must rid ourselves of the liberal belief that moral virtue by itself is ever capable of becoming a significant force in the world. Shaw puts the point plainly enough in a speech of Undershaft's in the unpublished Derry manuscript of the play:

> Come, come, my young friends: let us live in the real world. Your moral world is a vacuum; nothing is done there, though a good deal is eaten and drunk by the moralists at the expense of the real world. It is nice to live in the vacuum and repeat the fine phrases and edifying sentiments a few literary people have manufactured for you; but you know as well as I do that your morality is tolerated only on the understanding that nothing is to come of it. Your Christmas carols about peace and goodwill to men are very pretty; but you order cannons from me just the same. You ring out the old, ring in the new: that is, you discard muzzleloaders and introduce breachloaders. Barbara converts laborers whose conversion dont matter, because they have no responsibility and no power; but she does not convert the Secretary of State for war. Euripides abhors war, he says; but he will not stop it by Greek verses. It can be stopped only by a mighty power which is not in his class room.[19]

Undershaft soon makes it clear that the "mighty power" is the power of bombs.

Liberal intellectuals frequently distrust power and decry the use of force.[20] In so doing, they blind themselves to the fact that the authority of governments in liberal democracies rests on the police and army as surely as in any authoritarian state. Shaw, speaking through Undershaft, defines a government as a body of men with the courage to kill. Stephen, the conventionally-minded parliamentarian, must himself be as ready to kill his political opponents as Caesar, Cromwell, Washington, Lincoln, and Stalin were to kill theirs. Being a totally conventional young man with his head stuffed full of moral clichés and a conviction of the divinely righteous nature of upper-class British interests, he will kill stupidly and senselessly. How little his high-mindedness represents anything in the way of real scruples we see when the Undershaft party arrives at the factory. Stephen, who has earlier expressed priggish horror at his father's business, is now all admiration for this triumph of industry.

But for the intellectual humanitarian and the former Salvationist, the reconciliation to the factory of death is not so easy. The last scene of the play is at once an intellectual argument and a religious wooing of the souls of Cusins and Barbara by Mephistopheles-Dionysos-Undershaft. Cusins may admit that force is the basis of present-day society and that a capitalist state exists for the sake of protecting the rich man's dividends, just as the Salvation Army inadvertently plays into the hands of the rich by diverting the attention of the poor from revolution. But is the answer perhaps not to use force against force, but to abandon force completely and to appeal for social justice on the grounds of Christianity, love, and mercy? No, Undershaft inexorably insists; government means killing: all political progress (not to mention political conservatism) rests ultimately on the willingness to kill.

Since this is the idea which readers and audiences of *Major Barbara* have found most puzzling and unintelligible, coming as it does in a play by a writer who can by no means be accused of lacking moral sensitivity and compassion, and who otherwise hardly seems to be of the school of Hobbes and Machiavelli, let us see if we can determine exactly what Undershaft means before we raise the cry of "unresolved paradox." I think that Shaw's intention is clear enough if we give full weight to what Undershaft says in the final scene; but since these relatively straightforward statements have been for most people as music to the deaf and sunsets to the blind, we may profitably take another look at the unpublished manuscript version of the play in the British Museum. Here Undershaft does not, I think, depart from any of the positions he maintains in the final version of the play, but he is perhaps more explicit:

UNDERSHAFT (*grimly*). Why do [the poor] starve? Because they have been taught that it is their duty to starve. "Blessed are the poor in spirit"—eh? But now mark my highest claim, my proudest boast. To those who are worth their salt as slaves I give the means of life. But to those who will not or cannot sell their manhood—to those who will not stand tamely and suffer their country to be ravaged by poverty and preyed upon by skulkers and idlers—I give the means of death. Poverty and slavery have stood up for centuries to sermons and Bibles and leading articles and pious platitudes: they will not stand up to my machine guns. Let every English citizen resolve to kill or be killed sooner than tolerate the existence of one poor person or one idler on English soil; and poverty and slavery will vanish tomorrow.
BARBARA. Killing! Is that your remedy?
UNDERSHAFT. It is the final test of conviction, the sole lever strong enough to lift a whole people. It is the right of every man who will stake his own life on his faith. It is the only way of saying Must.[21]

At this point it is perhaps natural to ask whether Shaw, in giving Undershaft these speeches, was expressing his own political philosophy or merely presenting an idea, so to speak, dramatically. Any doubts on this subject may be resolved by consideration of another British Museum manuscript, that which contains Shaw's notes for a lecture on Darwin delivered to the Fabian Society in 1906, the year after the production of *Major Barbara*:

Revolutions, remember, can only be made by men and women with courage enough to meet the ferocity and pugnacity of the common soldier and vanquish it. Do not let us delude ourselves with any dreams of a peaceful evolution of Capitalism into Socialism, of automatic Liberal Progress, of the conciliation of our American bosses, and South African Randlords and British county society and Pall Mall military caste by the Fabian Society. The man

who is not a Socialist is quite prepared to fight for his private
property, or at least to pay someone else to fight for him. He has no
doubt whatever of the necessity and morality of such warfare. . . .
    We must clear our minds from cant and cowardice on this
subject. It is true that the old barricade revolutionists were childishly and romantically wrong in their methods; and the Fabians
were right in making an end of them and formulating constitutional Socialism. But nothing is so constitutional as fighting.
Rents cannot be collected now without force, nor are they socialized—to the small extent to which they are already socialized—
without force.[22]

Shaw is here appealing to history to verify Undershaft's statement
that "the ballot paper that really governs is the paper that has a
bullet wrapped up in it." Above all else it was the ruthless suppression of the Commune of 1871 that had demonstrated to him the
willingness of the proprietorial class to fight for their property rights.
Later in the same Fabian lecture Shaw argues that the classic instance
of nonviolent change, the passage of the Reform Bill of 1832, is
really an instance in favor of his view; for the Reform Bill passed
only when the temper of the English nation reached the point where
it was clearly a choice between passing the bill and facing a revolution.
    Most of those who have found Undershaft unintelligible have
misconceived the meaning of Shaw's Fabianism. Shaw rejected
catastrophic, violent revolution, not because he disapproved of
violence, but because he thought it would be ineffectual, since a
revolution achieved in this fashion would simply collapse for lack of
administrative knowledge and experience on the part of the revolutionists. Shaw remarked that if socialism could have been instituted
by a few days of fighting it would have been well worth the cost in
bloodshed. His gradualism was not based on any moral objection to
force, but on his belief that a process of education was necessary
first. The threat of violence was never renounced; it was merely, so to
speak, held in reserve. Thus it was Shaw who insisted in adding
to the otherwise pacific Fabian "Manifesto" of 1884 a final proviso
that "We had rather face a Civil War than such another century of
suffering as the present one has been."
    I have called the last act a religious wooing of souls. Undershaft,
seeing in Cusins the brains and sensitivity he thinks necessary in

anyone who is to run a factory of death (or let us say, a democratic, or any other kind of state), offers him the management of the munitions works. The intelligentsia is to undertake the responsibilities of political power, that is, the power of life and death over millions. Cusins finds himself in the position of a famous predecessor of academic renown: Mephistopheles has once again put in a bid for a professor's soul; and though Cusins, wiser than Faust, realizes that he has already sold his soul for his professorship, it does not make his dilemma less cruel.

For Barbara's engagement to Cusins is both a love match and something more. That is to say, their marriage is to be a religious marriage in the sense of dedicating them to something beyond themselves, to "larger loves and diviner dreams than the fireside ones." Their understanding is that unless their marriage can foster this religious side of themselves, they are to part and seek other mates, or join the legion of the world's celibate saints and philosophers. If Cusins elects to sell his soul to Undershaft, he thus jeopardizes his relation with Barbara, who is first of all a "salvationist" (in an unsectarian sense) and only secondly a fiancée.[23]

At this point Shaw turns to an episode from real life to solve the dilemma. When an idealistic student of Murray's set out for the Greco-Turkish War in 1897, Murray had given the young man, not a copy of Plato's *Republic*, but a revolver.[24] Shaw ascribes this incident to Cusins, and makes Undershaft seize upon it to demonstrate to the professor that he must, for all his hatred of war, commit himself to the side of the industrialist. When Murray, having read the first draft of Act Three, complained that Shaw had made the triumph of Undershaft over Barbara and Cusins too complete, Shaw replied:

> As to the triumph of Undershaft, that is inevitable because I am in the mind that Undershaft is in the right, and that Barbara and Adolphus, with a great deal of his natural insight and cleverness, are very young, very romantic, very academic, very ignorant of the world. I think it would be unnatural if they were able to cope with him. Cusins averts discomfiture and scores him off by wit & humorous dexterity; but the facts are too much for him; and his strength lies in the fact that he, like Barbara, refuses the impossibilist position (which their circumstances make particularly

easy for them) even when the alternative is the most sensationally anti-moral department of commerce . . . . His choice lies, not in going with Undershaft or not going with him, but between standing on the footplate at work, and merely sitting in a first class carriage reading Ruskin and complaining what a low dog the driver is and how steam is ruining the country.[25]

Cusins in the end chooses the "reality and power" of the factory of death, even if it means losing Barbara.

But Barbara, for all her talk about turning her back on wickedness, can no more turn away from life than can Cusins. Now she will be able to preach to the well-fed, self-respecting men and women in Undershaft's model factory town and know that, when they abandon their snobbishness and selfishness for higher ends, they are not simply being tempted by the bribe of bread. She has regained her faith and courage: the enthusiasm of the new Dionysianism possesses her and she goes "right up into the skies," saved forever from the fate she has most dreaded, the boredom and triviality of the genteel drawing room.

CHAPTER EIGHT

The Doctor's Dilemma

Having scanned far horizons in the great comedies, Shaw adjusted his lens to a much narrower focus in his next plays. *The Doctor's Dilemma, Getting Married,* and *Misalliance* form a cycle[1] dealing, not with the future of the human race, but with such mundane aspects of domestic economy as medicine, marriage laws, and child-rearing. They portray, respectively, doctors in consultation, couples married or contemplating the leap, and parents distracted by unmanageable offspring. In structure these plays resemble group portraits by Rembrandt or Hals, diffusing their interest over a wide range of characters and making their points not through philosophical debate, but by the dramatic interaction of men and women of contrasting temperament responding to specific crises. Their mood, too, is quite different from the genial *élan* that pervades the philosophical comedies; they are, by contrast, ironic and even astringent in tone. Their artistic merit varies markedly. *Getting Married* is hardly more than an animated tract. *Misalliance*, which prefigures *Heartbreak House* in its handling of a large cast of characters, is a much subtler play. But it is *The Doctor's Dilemma*, the most conservative in point of form, which is the minor masterpiece among them.

In this play, Shaw weaves together two radically different threads of interest: a love triangle and a satire on the medical profession. Some critics have objected that love and medicine are themes too diverse to tie together in this way. But such readers have failed to see that Shaw here wants us to look at monomaniacal medical men and victims of amatory infatuation from one and the same point of view. In *The Doctor's Dilemma*, Shaw is interested in examining the psychology of human credulity, whether it relates to scientific

123

theories or to sex. The psychology of belief is, of course, a subject
which also fascinated Shaw's contemporary, William James, and
Shaw addresses himself to the same questions James raises in his
writings. Like James, Shaw wants to know why men and women
adopt certain convictions and reject others, whether belief rests on
logic or on emotion, and whether it is the result of inductive reasoning
from observed facts or actually precedes and vitally influences the
process of investigation itself. Like James again, Shaw is neither a
rationalist (in the tradition of Descartes) nor a logical empiricist (in
the tradition of Mill), but a convinced voluntarist who believes that
willing is anterior not only to thinking, but to seeing as well. All the
answers Shaw gives to the questions rest on the assumption that
emotion rather than ratiocination is the key to understanding the
workings of the human mind. Shaw wrote his dramatic satire to
demonstrate this fact; in it he shows us how men and women under
the spell of a favorite scientific theory, beguiled by the glamor of art,
or simply in love see facts and people, not as they are, but as their
feelings predispose them to see them. With delicate irony he reveals
the will to believe interpreting evidence to fit preordained intellectual formulas and transforming real human beings into creatures
of the imagination.

Shaw's play is thus a scintillating comedy about a dry-as-dust
subject—logic. It is common knowledge that Shaw based Colenso
Ridgeon on the famous immunologist Almroth Wright, who was the
discoverer of the opsonin treatment which figures centrally in the
play. It is also widely known that Wright gave Shaw the idea for his
central situation by asking of a patient, "Is he worth saving?"
There was even some of the same irony surrounding Wright's knighthood as attends Ridgeon's. In 1906 the War Office, wanting to use
Wright's antityphoid injections, first had him knighted and then used
his knighthood as evidence of the unassailability of his theories. In
addition to all this, however, Wright was a keen logician and attracted Shaw's attention by what the latter called his "devouring
interest in, and curiosity about, the pathology of controversial
cerebration."[2] Wright eventually collected his ideas on the subject of
thinking into a systematic treatise called *Alethetropic Logic*. Though
the book was not published till almost half a century after Shaw's

play, its strongly held contentions obviously underlie Wright's lively debates with other medical men and with Shaw himself. A kind of skeptical antithesis to Newman's *Grammar of Assent*, the book is in the tradition of Mill's *System of Logic, Ratiocinative and Inductive*, though Wright is less interested in the canons of inductive reasoning than in the emotional and prelogical bases for what he considers to be the fallacies of popular thinking on religion, politics, and sex.

Wright's rationalism makes his approach to logic the exact opposite of Shaw's. Shaw would have agreed with him on the human tendency to found beliefs on extrarational premises, but he would have rejected out of hand his view that it is possible to abstract wish and will and sentimental preference from human thinking and obtain something like pure reason as a residue. In a fashion closely parallel to James's, Shaw believed that "our passional and volitional nature" lies "at the root of all our convictions,"[3] and that there is always a controlling tendency to believe or disbelieve before we look for evidence. In the search for truth, as elsewhere, reason is only the instrument of the will. It is possible to set up logical rules for thinking, but in the long run, hopes and fears, passion and prejudice, tradition and partisanship settle the matter. In the lecture on Darwin he delivered in the same year he wrote *The Doctor's Dilemma*, Shaw put forth this view quite explicitly:

Do not be deceived by the pretensions of Rationalism to steer a straight course to the truth through the storms of passion. All that reason will do for you is to find out the ways and means to fulfil your will. No doubt, without careful reasoning and investigation of facts, your attempts to fulfil your will are as likely as not to land you in disappointment and destruction . . . . But the reasonable case is always forthcoming when the will is urgent: for the will takes care that we shall see only the facts and arguments that support it, and keeps us at work discovering fresh facts and arguments on the same side.[4]

Nowhere does the will to believe run more wildly rampant than in regard to new medical discoveries. The general public firmly believes in the omniscience of medical practitioners, though they are often jealous of what they regard as doctors' exorbitant incomes. Shaw's concern is exactly the reverse of this. It is the doctor's proneness to hold his medical beliefs uncritically that worries Shaw. When it comes to earnings, Shaw, writing in a different age from ours, is more alarmed by the problem of the overworked and underpaid doctor than he is by medical affluence. Economic considerations underlie his studies of the poverty-stricken Blenkinsop and the Jewish physician Schutzmacher, the two portraits in grey and brown in Shaw's wonderful gallery of doctors. Blenkinsop recommends greengages as a panacea, Schutzmacher phosphates; the difference has nothing to do with the intrinsic merits of these remedies or with medical science at all, but is simply the difference between a bone-poor district and one where people are in slightly less desperate straits. Both doctors believe in their prescriptions even to the point of taking them themselves merely because self-respect leaves them no alternative. Nor is Schutzmacher guilty of the "conscious and deliberate fraud" some critics have accused him of. He attains modest affluence because of the slight economic margin his patients enjoy over Blenkinsop's, and he is genuinely embarrassed that popular credulity forces him to play the cure-monger.[5]

When he comes to show us rich and famous doctors, Shaw no more impugns their motives than he does in the case of poorer men, though his satire takes on a keener edge and his sense of comedy comes ebulliently into play. One might, for instance, imagine an insensitive surgeon who extirpated harmless organs out of mere cupidity.[6] But the ruling passion of Shaw's Cutler Walpole is not avarice but solicitude. Walpole, who lives in a state of acute sympathetic anxiety about other people's health, finds the spectacle of men whose vitality falls below his own level of energetic robustness an agony. Since he is convinced this debilitude is due to infected "nuciform sacs," he is acutely uneasy until he has had the chance to remove the offending appendage. Only one logical difficulty faces him—some people he has not operated on are healthy; but he solves this problem by concluding that they are mere medical curiosities, born sacless. His operation has become the rage among fashionable women who are hypochondriac enough to want and wealthy enough to afford it. Thus, a personal monomania and lay credulity go hand in hand to create a surgical fad.

Walpole is temperamentally an alarmist. Sir Ralph Bloomfield Bonington, Shaw's royal physician, is, by contrast, pontifical, theoretical, and soothing. While the surgeon's mania is specific, Sir Ralph indulges in the widest speculations about "the fundamental truths" of science. Here, one imagines, is the genuine scientist as opposed to the mere empiric. But he, too, has his *idée fixe*: he imagines that all diseases can be fought by "stimulating the phagocytes" through inoculations.[7] His enthusiasm for this pet notion leads him to defend it with a series of hilarious *non sequiturs*, "post hoc ergo propter hocs," and circular arguments. Thus every recovery from illness is ascribed to inoculations, every death without them to their lack, the deaths of the inoculated and survival of the uninoculated being ignored. When two patients recover despite Sir Ralph's carelessly mixing up two different antitoxins, his conclusion is not that the human organism is remarkably capable of surviving all kinds of medical abuse, but that all antitoxins are interchangeable and can be used indiscriminately. The point is that, given his favorite hypothesis, all medical experience whatsoever falls into a pattern which fits the interpretation he wants to put on it.

Shaw's treatment of the medical profession is in the tradition of Molière's *Le Malade imaginaire*, *L'Amour médecin*, and *Le Médecin malgré lui*. The broad satire is balanced in turn by a serious dramatic plot: a beautiful and devoted wife, Jennifer Dubedat, pleads with the newly famous Colenso Ridgeon to treat her tubercular artist husband; and Ridgeon is forced to choose between curing the talented painter and the honest, but unglamorous, medical drudge, Blenkinsop. If the psychology of the play is that of William James, Shaw's handling of the Jennifer-Louis-Ridgeon triangle has something of the oblique subtlety of a novel by his famous brother. Even the theme involved—the relation of personal honor to professional and domestic obligations—is a Henry James theme, different though Shaw's approach is from what the novelist's would have been. This combination of indirectness and ironic reserve on Shaw's part has made it hard for critics to grasp his attitude toward the play's three central characters and his judgment on them. Indeed, it would probably be no exaggeration to say that their relations to one another have been the most misunderstood in all of Shaw's writing. One common view of the matter, for instance, is that Jennifer is an ideal wife, the artist a man whose amorality is a typical artistic trait, and the doctor a practitioner who fatally compromises his honor by plotting the artist's death in the hopes of marrying his widow. As we shall see, such a reading of the play represents the exact opposite of Shaw's intentions.

The idea of writing about such a woman as Jennifer Dubedat seems to have entered Shaw's mind at least a decade before he began work on *The Doctor's Dilemma*. Rather than regarding her as an ideal wife, however, Shaw began with the conviction that husband-idolizing women of Jennifer's sort were dangerously deluded. In the lectures on Ibsen which he delivered to the Fabian Society in 1890, he speaks of "the devoted woman who pictures a noble career for the man she loves" as suffering from "perhaps the most mischievous of the many crazes of feminine idealism," just because the desire to sacrifice herself for such a man has the "loftiest, purest, most seductively romantic aspect of all."[8] Four years later, reviewing a play in which a woman sacrificed herself to help a man of genius, Shaw declared, "In such an error of the feminine imagination, and in its fearfully real consequences, there is material for a tragedy."[9]

Shaw intended that Jennifer should make a very powerful appeal to our sensibilities; she is glamorous after the style of a movie star or fashion model, intensely idealistic, dignified, persuasive, and at first genuinely touching in her concern for her sick husband. Shaw gives her a name from Celtic legend and endows her with Celtic delicacy, sensitivity, impetuosity, and imaginativeness. On the surface she seems every man's dream of a woman, since she adds to her external attractions and grace of character the final winning trait of an over-whelming concern for a member of the male sex. Yet, for all this, she mistakes scoundrelism for its opposite just because she worships Louis as a god and assumes that he can do no wrong. Hence the strength of Shaw's revulsion against her. "I am sorry to have to tell you," he warned Lillah McCarthy, the actress who created the role, "that the artist's wife is the sort of woman I hate; and you will have your work cut out for you in making her fascinating."[10] There was perhaps even a touch of irony in the situation, since, though Shaw's relations with the actress were perfectly friendly, Lillah McCarthy shared at least one important trait with Jennifer.

> The first natural qualification of an actress who is not a mere puppet, impotent without a producer, is imagination. Lillah had a great deal too much of it: she was of imagination all compact. It was difficult to get her feet down to the ground, and almost impossible to keep them there. Her life was rich in wonderful experiences that had never happened, and in friendships with wonderful people (including myself) who never existed. All her geese were swans, flying about in an enchanted world. When, as inevitably occurred from time to time, real life and hard objectivity brought her down with a stunning collision, she could be tragically disappointed or murderously enraged; but she could not be disillusioned: the picture changed: but it remained a picture.[11]

In her girlhood Jennifer had nurtured the romantic dream of marrying a talented man she might help and protect from the harshness of the world. She is thus Louis's natural victim, who makes of her dishonest husband a revered idol free from every mortal taint. She does not object to his swindling, but invents excuses for it simply because she wants to believe in him. The worst she can find it in her heart to say about Louis's unscrupulousness in money matters is that it "gives people a wrong idea." That is, it will limit the circle of her fellow worshipers, for Jennifer has divided the world into just two classes—those who share her admiration of Louis, and those who, through blindness or envy, refuse to acknowledge his greatness. Her bias in his favor, based on her affection for him as a husband and her admiration for him as an artist, makes it impossible for her to see him as he really is.

Jennifer's strain of egotistical hero worship may remind some readers of the young Dorothea Brooke in *Middlemarch*. However, Shaw's moral is the exact opposite of George Eliot's. In the novel the principal women characters face crises in their relations with uncongenial, foolish, or scoundrelly husbands. George Eliot makes the test of each woman's mettle her ability to minister comfort to the bruised man. Shaw, taking exactly the opposite view, objects to the sentimental notion of marriage as involving unconditional loyalty from a wife. He is more concerned about the social danger of a woman who effectively encourages a rascally husband than about the

woman who fails to soothe a sympathetic one. Nor does the fact that
Jennifer has substituted emancipated bohemian standards for pious
Victorian ones save her in Shaw's eyes. Punctiliousness in money
was one side of middle-class morality Shaw could respect.

Shaw made no secret of the fact that he had based the character of
Louis Dubedat on Edward Aveling, the well-known socialist and
atheist lecturer. Aveling was notorious in radical circles for borrowing
money shamelessly and for embezzling funds in a peculiarly cold-
blooded fashion. Having entered into a common-law liaison with
Karl Marx's daughter Eleanor, Aveling abandoned her for another
woman when his legal wife's death made marriage possible. H. M.
Hyndman even suggests that Aveling inveigled Eleanor into a suicide
pact and then reneged after she had killed herself.[12] Whether or not
one believes this story, the fact that Hyndman obviously did gives
some notion of the reputation Aveling bore in radical circles, despite
his idealistic and selfless devotion to unpopular causes. In Shaw's
play Dubedat thus stands for the type of the plausible and attractive
scoundrel, clever, unconventional, fair-spoken, and even winning in
manner.

Jennifer's belief that the artist stands outside and above conventional standards of judgment allows her to brush aside the alarming
discoveries she makes about her husband. It was this dangerous
tendency of imaginative people to idealize artists that led Shaw to
turn Aveling into a painter. He was not, as some critics have maintained, raising "the eternal question as to how far genius is a morbid
symptom."[13] The whole of Shaw's essay The Sanity of Art is devoted
to the thesis that there is no more connection between artistic genius
and morbidity than between morbidity and, say, plumbing. Moreover, under the heading "Artist Idolatry" in the preface to Misalliance, Shaw declared emphatically that "nothing is more pitiably
ridiculous than the wild worship of artists by those who have never
been seasoned in youth to the enchantments of art."[14] In issuing his
warning, Shaw had in mind the influence of Oscar Wilde over the
young Robert Ross, though he was too chivalrous to mention Wilde
by name. Shaw believed the delusion that "the great poet and artist
can do no wrong" was mischievously erroneous; in The Doctor's
Dilemma, he explained, he had "recognized this by dramatizing a

rascally genius, with the disquieting result that several highly intelligent and sensitive persons have passionately defended him, on the
ground, apparently, that high artistic faculty and an ardent
artistic imagination entitle a man to be recklessly dishonest about
money and recklessly selfish about women." [15]

Louis's most remarkable faculty is his power of casting an imaginative spell over others. He has the cleverness to divine, and the
histrionic talent to live up to, Jennifer's conception of him. As a
painter, his talents are those of the artist-magician, not of the
artist-philosopher. In his hands the muddy Thames becomes trans-
formed into the "Silver Danube." On his deathbed, the prospect of
his ultimate cremation appeals to his artistic sense as a kind of
transfiguration. So potent is the aura of glamor he casts about him
that Jennifer is totally baffled as to how Ridgeon can be concerned
about the dull, elderly Blenkinsop after he has seen her darling. And,
despite all the humiliating exposures he undergoes before the doctors,
Louis never for a minute shows anything but total self-satisfaction,
his belief in his own artistic talents being enough to give him an
impenetrable cloak of self-respect. When the doctors berate him, he
easily puts them at a disadvantage by treating them as stuffy philistines. By a final stroke of choice irony, Shaw even has Dubedat
justify himself on the grounds that he is a "disciple of Bernard
Shaw," and, consequently, does not "believe in morality." In short,
Louis's intellectual agility and cool self-assurance allow him to
score off with the greatest of ease the "honest" men who challenge
him.

Because of the poetic ambiance that surrounds the artist and his
wife, most critics have looked upon them as the central characters of
the play, and have tended to ignore Sir Colenso. It is, indeed, rather
the exception than the rule to find a review of a production that even
mentions the doctor. Yet Ridgeon is the real center of Shaw's play,
and the real drama is the one that takes place in his mind. His
mental processes deserve all the more scrutiny because he is not only
the most complex character in the play, but also, from the point of
view of self-revelation, one of the most reticent of all Shaw's pro-
tagonists. With his mixture of passionate truth-seeking and cool
skepticism, he is, to begin with, Shaw's ideal scientist among the

doctors, as Almroth Wright was his ideal investigator in real life.
But a man may be a first-rate scientist and yet misjudge people
badly. Ridgeon's Achilles' heel is his susceptibility to feminine
charm. He is subject to spells of romantic unrest, and in the manuscript version of the play Shaw makes him complain to Schutzmacher
in the opening scene that he has been composing little waltz tunes in
his head and finding them beautiful.[16] His foible is well known to his
old servant, Emmy, who recommends Jennifer to him as the very
sort of woman to whom he is likely to respond. But just because Mrs.
Dubedat is a strikingly beautiful woman, Ridgeon, knowing himself,
sets out to resist her. His struggle, however, is comically ineffectual.
Her combination of elegance and sympathetic warmth are all but
irresistible to him, and he seizes with some relief on the drawings she
has brought to prove Louis's worth as tangible evidence that will
sanction his helping her. When she leaves, he realizes with a touch of
chagrin the extent to which his feelings have got the better of his
judgment and discretion.

Thus even before the dinner at Richmond, Ridgeon is more than
half disposed to accept Louis as a patient. By its conclusion, Louis's
boyish good looks, guileless blue eyes, and charmingly candid manners have completely won over the panel of doctors, whose mood of
sentimental indulgence has been further intensified by Jennifer's
attractive pathos, the beauty of the evening, and the plentiful wine.
Only one man, the old Irish doctor, Sir Patrick Cullen, reserves
judgment. Since, however, Sir Patrick's dry comments on each turn
of the drama unfailingly reflect Shaw's own views, his act is highly
significant. Sir Patrick is not wholly surprised when Louis turns out
in the after-dinner revelations to be a conscienceless scamp who
fleeces his male acquaintances through sponging or blackmail, and
his female ones by marrying them for their money. Now Ridgeon is
forced to face up squarely to his dilemma: Will he save the talented
but corrupt artist or the dull but honest Blenkinsop, who is also
afflicted with the disease his new discovery can cure?

Ridgeon's first impulse is to discount Louis's blackguardism out
of sympathy for his wife and admiration for his talents. He even
affects a moral skepticism which Sir Patrick challenges by asking
why he himself does not behave as Louis does and whether he would

really prefer a world of good pictures and bad men to one of good men and bad pictures? Nevertheless, when Ridgeon arrives at Louis's studio a few days later, he has decided to save him. His motive, from the point of view of a sentimentalist, is a pure and even noble one. He has confessed to Sir Patrick that he loves Jennifer and would marry her if she were free, but he does not succumb to the temptation to turn Louis down on that account. On the contrary, he wants to cure him for the simple reason that he believes it will make Jennifer happy.[17] Nor, when he reverses his decision shortly afterwards, is he acting inconsistently. Having in the meantime discovered that Louis is quite as willing to exploit his wife as anyone else, Ridgeon is still concerned primarily to protect the woman he adores. Later, Jennifer's hysterical threat to commit suicide if Louis fails her has the unintended effect of placing the final nail in the artist's coffin. It is his chivalrous desire to protect Jennifer that makes Ridgeon tell her that only if Louis is treated by Sir Ralph can her ideal hero be "preserved." Thus Ridgeon does the right deed for the wrong reason, acting not on public grounds as Sir Patrick counsels, but on private, sentimental ones. Louis is condemned, not because he is a social menace, but solely because his crookedness specifically threatens his wife's happiness.

As Ridgeon anticipates, Louis does indeed die as a result of Sir Ralph's benevolent but inefficient care. Shaw puts the scene before us on the stage and seizes the opportunity to write a brilliantly sardonic commentary on theatrical deathbeds. At least four different considerations prompted Shaw to use all the histrionic trappings usually considered appropriate to stage deaths, but to present them in such a way that—whatever the response of the conventionally minded—perceptive members of his audience would remain coolly critical. There was, to begin with, the impetus of his newspaper controversy with William Archer over the artistic validity of Ibsen's deaths. There was also his knowledge of the ironic circumstances surrounding the death of Louis's prototype, Aveling. In addition, Shaw wanted to criticize and parody the high-flown rhetoric and false emotionalism of some of Shakespeare's more famous stage deaths. But above all he wanted to attack the orthodox religious view of the significance of deathbeds, and to show how the lugubriousness

men reserve for such occasions can seriously obscure moral
issues.

The controversy with Archer sprang out of the obituary Shaw
wrote for Ibsen in the *Clarion* in 1906. There Shaw praised Ibsen for
showing Europe that "our fashionable dramatic material was worn
out as far as cultivated modern people are concerned," and that
"what really interests such people on the stage is not what we call
action ... but stories of lives, discussions of conduct, conflict of
characters in talk, laying bare of souls, discovery of pitfalls—in
short, illumination of life for us." At the same time he objected to
Ibsen's use of suicides and accidental deaths as artistically dishonorable blows below the belt, on the grounds that they depended
for their effects "on a morbid horror of death and a morbid enjoyment of horror."[18] In rebuttal, Archer took issue with Shaw in a
column headed "Bernard Shaw and Death" in the *Tribune*, arguing
that instead of being a relic of barbarism, the ability to write death
scenes was a real test of dramatic genius, since death was the ultimate
human adventure—"the touchstone of character, the supreme test
of fortitude, the refuge of despair, the consecrator of greatness, the
desecrator of loveliness, the crass intruder and the deliverer yearned
for in vain, the matchless stimulant, the infallible anodyne, the
signature of the stave of life, the mystery and the solution, the
problem and the key."[19] In reply, Shaw dryly saluted Archer for his
"remarkable dithyramb to Death," but conceded nothing more than
that his next play would be "all about death" and that it would be
"the most amusing play" he had ever written.[20]

Shaw noted that death made most men solemn and platitudinous,
paralyzing their minds into the acceptance of mawkish banalities
they would not countenance without protest at other times. In *The
Doctor's Dilemma* he sets this uncritical mood against the audience's
full knowledge of the enormity of Louis's deeds. The fact that the
unspeakable Aveling had died in an atmosphere of secular sanctity,
with great rhetorical effect, "like an atheist saint, spouting Shelley
in the glory of the setting sun,"[21] had appealed to Shaw's sense of
humor and no doubt gave an extra incentive to his satire of funeral-
parlor attitudes. Aveling, who was nothing if not self-dramatizing,
had even written a deathbed poem, "*In Articulo Mortis*," in which a

dying atheist, true to his creed to the end, declaims, "Oh, yes, my life's been a failure, and fortune has not been kind," [22] hitting a note close to Louis's own mixture of self-pity and self-congratulation. Louis's valedictory speeches on his devotion to the cause of art are presented by Shaw with deliberate irony. They are full of amusing clichés ("Ive played the game," "Ive fought the good fight," etc.) and exalted sentiments carefully selected by the artist for their effect on his audience. Shaw had looked forward to writing the episode with considerable relish. He promised Granville Barker, who created the role, that "you will have a deathbed scene (to please Archer) which will, both in sublimity and blasphemy, surpass anything that ever gave Redford a nightmare. The spectacle of a hopeless blackguard dying a beautiful and imposing death, with his wife adoring him, and everyone else in the room knowing the truth about him, will satisfy my soul completely." [23] The speech in Wagner's tale "An End in Paris," which gave Shaw his idea for Louis's credo, goes as follows:

> "Now,"—the dying man continued, after a pause occasioned by his growing weakness,—"now one last word on my belief.—I believe in God, Mozart and Beethoven, and likewise their disciples and apostles;—I believe in the Holy Spirit and the truth of the one, indivisible Art;—I believe that this Art proceeds from God, and lives within the hearts of all illumined men;—I believe that he who once has bathed in the sublime delights of this high Art, is consecrate to Her for ever, and never can deny Her;—I believe that through this Art all men are saved, and therefore each may die for Her of hunger;—I believe that death will give me highest happiness;—I believe that on earth I was a jarring discord, which will at once be perfectly resolved by death . . . ." [24]

In Wagner's story, this speech moves us because the dying musician is an earnest, if comic, down-and-outer who is pathetically asserting his dignity *in extremis*. Shaw, on the other hand, is warning us, in Louis's case, of the power of fine words and sonorous phrases spoken impressively to enchant people out of their moral senses. With wonderful self-assurance his dying swindler reviews the part he has played in life, presents himself as a put-upon victim, and utters his belief in "the redemption of all things by Beauty everlasting." In a letter to Trebitsch, Shaw underlines the fact that Dubedat is highly conscious of the effect of his speeches on the assembled audience, and especially on the newspaper reporter.[25]

Shaw also repeatedly objected to Shakespeare's propensity to let worthless characters die in a glow of sentiment and histrionic glamor. Cleopatra was Shaw's prime example, but he might have chosen Richard II as an even more outrageous case, since there is at least nothing in Cleopatra's dying that quite touches Richard's comparison of himself to Christ. Sir Ralph's comic mishmash of Shakespearean quotations is meant to demonstrate the distance of Shaw's point of view from that of a writer who loved to exploit popular emotions connected with death and apparently had a natural feeling for the undertaker's trade. For Shaw, death in its racial aspect was a clearing of the ground for new generations, in its individual aspect, merely the consignment of a man to the scrap heap as a used-up organism. The evolutionary and metaphysical meanings of death Shaw later made the subject of *Back to Methuselah*; in *The Doctor's Dilemma* he is concerned with death as a personal drama. Popular Christianity has traditionally given a special moral significance to the state of a man's soul at the time of death, making this moment the most important one in his whole life, since his eternal destiny in the afterworld is conceived as bound up with it. When Louis dies, Sir Ralph pronounces the usual encomium, "He died extremely well," showing that he is still unconsciously thinking in those terms. But it is Sir Patrick who delivers Shaw's judgment when he declares that it is not how a man dies but how he lives that matters. Shaw even has him quote the Seventy-third Psalm on the death of the wicked, as a corrective to the popular view that bad men die in remorseful agony:

> For there are no bands [i.e., pains] in their death;
> But their strength is firm:
> They are not in trouble as other men.

Louis's performance succeeds completely as far as his wife is concerned. In accordance with his desire that she should wear beautiful dresses and jewels to create a "great atmosphere of wonder and romance" around the dead man's name, Jennifer appears in a radiant mourning costume. (Lillah McCarthy has recorded the sensational

effect her reappearance in flame-colored silk instead of the traditional black had on the first-night audience.) Ecstatically enraptured
by the drama of the moment, she tells the departing doctors that they
have shared a "wonderful experience," and that henceforth, "life
will always be beautiful to us." Even Thackeray's irony in showing
the duped Amelia worshiping the dead George Osborne in *Vanity
Fair* or Conrad's in depicting the fiancée idolizing the unspeakable
Kurtz in *The Heart of Darkness* hardly touches Shaw's portrait of
misplaced, doting devotion.[26]

The last act of *The Doctor's Dilemma*, which takes place a year
later, has most often been regarded as either unintelligible or super-
fluous. Walkley objected to it as a "brief, quaint, not entirely com-
prehensible, epilogue."[27] Siegfried Trebitsch seriously proposed
publishing, and Max Reinhardt actually produced, a German version
with the fifth act omitted. Yet if we look at the scene carefully, we
will see how the accidental encounter of Ridgeon and Jennifer at a
showing of Louis's pictures a year after his death completes Shaw's
dramatic intention. During the interval Ridgeon has been living in a
state of acute self-consciousness with regard to Jennifer, at once despairing of healing the breach between them which Louis's death has
caused, yet at the same time, with a lover's optimism, hoping against
hope that he might win her over. Jennifer, for her part, shows the
resentment she feels towards Ridgeon for his refusal to treat Louis by
attacking all doctors as monsters who practice vivisection. It may at
first strike us as surprising that Shaw makes a woman to whom he is
so antipathetic an antivivisectionist, since he himself attacks vivisection so emphatically in his preface. But we soon discover that
Jennifer's antivivisectionism is not, as in Shaw's case, the recognition
of a bond of honor between all living things, but merely an extension
of her sentimental, maternal instinct. Indeed, Louis's appeal to
Jennifer's sense of beauty and affectionateness was largely that of a
pet animal whom she refused to judge by mundane human standards
of honor and decency.

At last, to break the impasse, Ridgeon, desperate with the des-
peration of a man who feels he has nothing to lose, frankly admits
that he let Louis die. But this is too great a revelation for Jennifer
to take in all at once. Mistaking his meaning, she thinks he is only

confessing that he made a mistake in turning Louis over to Sir Ralph, and in response she is all forgiveness. The result is to present Ridgeon with a serious temptation. He can, if he wishes, regain Jennifer's friendship by leaving her in error, but his male pride revolts at such a deception. Instead, he makes a clean breast of it by telling her he let Louis die on purpose, because he was, and is, in love with her. But in delivering this blow he receives one himself. From their first meeting, Ridgeon had fondly nursed the illusion that Jennifer might love him, misconceiving her warmth for the doctor she hoped would save her hero for sentimental feeling for the middle-aged man, despite the fact that the snub she had earlier given Blenkinsop should have warned him that older men made no appeal to her protective side at all. Now Ridgeon undergoes the shock of hearing Jennifer ask how he could conceivably have imagined she had any feeling for him.

Jennifer is so surprised by Ridgeon's avowal of his love that it takes her a minute to grasp the fact that he actually intended Louis should die. When she finally comprehends it, she threatens to kill him. Ridgeon in turn embraces the idea enthusiastically: to be the victim of violence at her hands would be delightful. Still not guessing the chivalrous nature of his motives, Jennifer accuses him of acting out of jealous envy. He tells her gently that she owes her present happiness to him, that Louis dead is more of a blessing to her than Louis alive could ever have been. But Ridgeon's reference to the difficult side of their marriage only leads her to declare in an insane fit of self-recrimination that she was unworthy of the dead man. This, however, is in turn more than Ridgeon can bear; exasperated at her tormenting herself in such a foolish fashion, he blurts out the truth about Louis, hotly and bluntly. His loss of balance allows Jennifer to resume her former air of superiority. If Ridgeon has failed to appreciate Louis's true worth, others—including her new husband—have been more perceptive. Thunderstruck at the totally unexpected news of Jennifer's remarriage, which shatters once and for all his dream of a romantic relation between them, Ridgeon can only stammer incoherently and then admit, with mocking self-irony, that he seems, after all, to have "commited a purely disinterested murder."

Readers should here be cautioned against taking Ridgeon's final statement, with its ambiguous wording, as an expression of guilt, which it is not. In motive, his decision to let Louis die was disinterested in that he would have taken it to protect Jennifer even if he had not also nursed the hope of marrying her. Now he has discovered it is also disinterested in its effect. It is Ridgeon's judgment which Shaw impugns, not his honor as a doctor.[28] His folly lay in his failure to gauge the depth of Jennifer's demented passion and in his wanting to make her his wife. At the opening of the play Sir Patrick had warned him that he might be about to make a fool of himself. In the end that is exactly what he has done. Shaw subtitled his play "A Tragedy," and this description fits it well enough if we think of Louis, whose life exemplifies Ridgeon's contention that "the most tragic thing in the world is a man of genius who is not also a man of honor." But if we look, not at Louis, but at Ridgeon, whose emotional entanglement is the real heart of the play, we see that Shaw in fact wrote, not a tragedy, but a tragicomedy about a well-intentioned sentimentalist.

Throughout his long career, Almroth Wright showed an unflagging interest in what he called the psychology of "the feminine mind." In the chapter in his *Alethetropic Logic* which he devoted to the subject, he took a gleeful delight in exposing women's incapacity for rational thought. There he prints no fewer than five dozen epigrams against women, from Dr. Johnson's "There is always something a woman prefers to the truth" to Nietzsche's "Woman belongs to the logical underworld." He takes particular issue with Shaw's counter-contention that "there is not any specific psycho-physiological difference between men and women."[29] Though men may on occasion place public concerns above personal and domestic ones, when woman acts altruistically, Wright tells us, "that altruism is exercised towards those who are linked up to her by a bond of sexual affection, or a community of blood, or failing this, by a relation of personal friendship."[30] *The Doctor's Dilemma* is an ironic commentary on these views of Wright's, with their presumption that men are more rational than women. By the end of the play we have come to realize that Ridgeon has, in fact, idealized and indulged Jennifer in just the same way that she has idealized and indulged Louis. The man of science has been just as purely emotional in his amatory infatuation as the hysterical wife. From the point of view of logic and social morality, there is nothing to choose between them. Having set out to show the aberrations to which the human imagination is prone under the powerful emotional stimuli of love, death, art, and the (wholly honorable) desire to cure human illness, Shaw was not willing to recognize any distinctions between masculine and feminine folly in such matters.

CHAPTER NINE

Pygmalion

Pygmalion, as all the world knows, is the story of a flower girl who passes as a duchess after taking phonetics lessons. Shaw himself did not rank this adaptation of the Cinderella story very high among his plays, calling it deprecatingly the last of his "pot-boilers." It has, of course, fully achieved the popularity he aimed at. Its sensational triumphs as a drama, as a film, and as a musical comedy, however, have not been without their ironies. The paperback edition of the musical, for instance, claims to recapture "one of the most beautiful love stories the world has ever taken to its heart."[1] The reader who knows Shaw and the ways of Broadway may be amused at this, reflecting that what the world takes to its heart the world is likely to remold after its heart's fancy.

It is perhaps to be expected that producers, actors, and the general public should have delighted in the fairy-tale aspect of Shaw's play, and have steadfastly repudiated the antiromantic side of *Pygmalion* as so much perverse nonsense from a man who always insisted on teasing as well as pleasing. But the joke deepens when we look at scholarly journals and discover that professors of literature are just as prone as advertisers to assume that Shaw should have let Higgins marry Eliza.[2] In reaction one is inclined to recall gently but firmly such amiable sentimentalists to their senses by reminding them that *Pygmalion* is, after all, not a comedy by James M. Barrie, but a serious study of human relationships by the author of *Caesar and Cleopatra* and *Back to Methuselah*. It is, in fact, just this refusal to sentimentalize that gives the play its distinction.

It must be admitted at the start, however, that Shaw's preface is a somewhat misleading guide to the meaning of the play. There Shaw enthusiastically applauds the new scientific approach to language by

141

phoneticians, if only because it raised pronunciation above the intense self-consciousness and class snobbery which had always bedeviled the subject in England. Then he goes on to imply that the main theme of his comedy will be phonetics. But it takes only a little reflection to realize that dialects, in and of themselves, have no intrinsic dramatic or social significance. Our response to them as pure sounds is largely arbitrary: a Brooklynite's pronunciation of "girl" may strike one ear as exquisitely refined (it did Shaw's) and another as comically vulgar. The real basis for our reaction to anyone's dialect is our association of particular kinds of speech with particular classes and particular manners. Here we are much closer to the real stuff of drama, and especially of comedy. Manners have been a central concern of the comic stage from Roman times through Shakespeare and Molière down to our own day. And, for all the shop talk about phonology, it is possible with a little analysis to see that it is really manners and not speech patterns that provide the clue to the character contrasts in *Pygmalion*, accents being, so to speak, merely their outer clothing.

Shaw's opening scene is admirably suited to bring out these contrasts. It is a brilliant little genre-piece that sets a group of proletarians—some timidly deferential, some sarcastically impolite—over against an impoverished middle-class family with genteel pretensions, a wealthy Anglo-Indian, and the haughtily self-sufficient Professor Higgins,[3] all jostling beneath a church portico. The moment is chosen to show class antagonisms and personal idiosyncrasies at their sharpest. Brute necessity prompts a flower girl to wheedle a few last coins from the opera-goers while they in turn face that acid test of middle-class manners, the scramble for taxis in a sudden squall. The scene highlights two kinds of vulgarity. The first is the comico-pathetic, specifically lower-class vulgarity of the flower girl. Eliza is vulgarly familiar when she tries to coax money out of prospective customers, and vulgarly hysterical when she thinks she is suspected of soliciting as a prostitute, on the theory that, as she belongs to a class that cannot afford lawyers, she had best be loud and vigorous in her protestations of virtue. Later, she is vulgarly keen on lording it—or ladying it—over her neighbors with her windfall of coins. What is interesting, however, is that Shaw by no means regards vulgarity as specifically a class trait. All the time he is treating us to Eliza's plangent diphthongs he is also dissecting the manners of the girl in the middle-class family, Clara Eynsford Hill. Compared to Eliza, Clara comes off the worse. For Clara is also pushing, and, in her dealings with strangers, as vulgarly suspicious and as quick to take offense as the flower girl, her rebuke to Higgins—"Dont dare speak to me"—being less comically naïve than Eliza's "I'm a good girl, I am"—but just as silly. And Eliza's pushiness at least has the excuse of springing from her wholly understandable desire to escape from the squalor of the slums into a bourgeois world which can offer her some kind of independence and self-respect.

The next day in Higgins' laboratory Eliza is first vulgarly determined not to be cheated, and then suspicious of being drugged and seduced, as the impetuous professor bullies and tempts her. Later, *Pygmalion* reaches its climax as a comedy of manners at Mrs. Higgins' at-home, where Eliza, now master of enunciation as a parrot might be master of it, delivers pompous recitations and spicy Lisson Grove gossip with the same impeccable air. The joke lies in the way the old vulgarian peeps out from behind the new façade, as in her theories about her aunt's death. At the same time, Eliza, for all her absurdity, still manages to think and feel naturally behind the veneer. By contrast, Clara is mere bright affectation, a much less vital person. She even outdoes Eliza's parroting when she repeats her slum expletive as the latest thing. Shaw, who disliked hearing the word "bloody" used "by smart or would-be smart ladies as a piece of smartness," was trying to kill its vogue by ridiculing Clara's callowness.[4]

Shaw's attitude toward manners was not a simple one. Obviously, he preferred social poise and considerateness to mere crudity. He seems even to have harbored some limited admiration for the dignified code of manners of the Victorian period, though he found its artificialities cramping. He gives Mrs. Hill, Mrs. Higgins, and the Colonel exquisite manners to contrast with the girls' lack of them. Yet Shaw is clearly no latter-day Castiglione here or elsewhere. His hero is, after all, the creative rebel, not the courtier. He preferred Beethoven to Liszt, and the rough-tongued Joan of Arc to Ninon de Lenclos. He would have been the first to remind us that on the score

of mere gentlemanliness, Charles I would carry the day over Cromwell, and Czar Nicholas II over Lenin. And in *Back to Methuselah*,
Shaw's Superrace cannot even imagine what the word "manners"
could have meant.

Professor Higgins, Shaw's Prometheus of phonetics, is equally
without manners. Consider the Olympian tirade he visits on Eliza's
head while she sits snivelling in Covent Garden:

> A woman who utters such depressing and disgusting sounds has
> no right to be anywhere—no right to live. Remember that you are
> a human being with a soul and the divine gift of articulate speech:
> that your native language is the language of Shakespear and
> Milton and The Bible; and dont sit there crooning like a bilious
> pigeon.[5]

Clearly, the man who can vent such splendid wrath upon a street
vendor is neither a snob nor a vulgarian, but neither is he a gentleman, and he just as certainly has no more manners than the petulant
daughter or the disgruntled flower girl. At home he takes his boots
off and wipes his hands on his dressing gown. In creating Higgins,
Shaw was assuredly driving at something more than a definition of
true gentility.

Before we consider what it is, however, we may pause for a moment
to look at the part Eliza's father, Alfred Doolittle, plays in the
comedy. Here Shaw turns from the question of social manners to the
deeper question of social morality. The farce of the dustman turned
moral preacher has always delighted Shaw's audiences. But just as
they have rested content with the Cinderella aspect of the main
story, so the ironic intention in this second transformation has been
missed. One critic has even held that since Doolittle is less happy
after coming into his fortune than he was before, Shaw's aim was to
demonstrate the "vanities of philanthropy."[6] This is not so much to
miss Shaw's point as to turn it completely upside down. What Shaw
is saying is that Doolittle after his escape from Lisson Grove is a
much better social being, albeit a less comfortable one, than he was
before. Critics have simply overlooked the ironic amusement with
which Shaw views the dustman's discomfiture, which he regards as
pure gain from the point of view of society.

Shaw seems to have been inspired to create the fable of Doolittle's sudden wealth by Dickens' use of a similar story in one of his novels. In *Our Mutual Friend*, Dickens contrasts two poor men, one a Thames-side water rat named "Rogue" Riderhood, and the other an honest garbage collector, Mr. Boffin, who unexpectedly comes into a large inheritance. Each is treated as an all-black or all-white figure in a popular melodrama. Riderhood, whom Dickens describes bluntly as a piece of "moral sewage," remains unrelievedly villainous throughout, while Boffin, a kind of illiterate Pickwick, is a paragon of benevolence both before he becomes wealthy and after. Shaw's approach is to roll Dickens' pair of poor men into one, and then to show how the man's behavior is a consequence not of his character, but of his situation.

Alfred Doolittle first appears in Wimpole Street in the hypocritical role of virtuous father, rather after the fashion of Engstrand in Ibsen's *Ghosts*, his intention being to blackmail the two men who have taken up Eliza. When Higgins bullies him out of this scheme, he changes his tack and becomes the ingratiating pimp: "Well, the truth is, Ive taken a sort of fancy to you, Governor; and if you want the girl, I'm not so set on having her back home again but that I might be open to an arrangement." This approach fails too. But Doolittle is nothing if not a resourceful rhetorician. He forthwith throws morality to the winds and argues for consideration, in an eloquent flight of philosophical oratory, as an undeserving poor man done out of his natural right to happiness by the narrow-minded prejudices of middle-class morality.[7] Higgins and Pickering, enchanted, now offer him five pounds, which he accepts after rejecting ten as too likely to entail sobering responsibilities. But alas, the man who shrinks from ten pounds comes into several thousand a year before the play is over and finds his free and easy life at an end. What, then, is the meaning of this fable?

First of all, Doolittle's moral and social attitudes contrast strongly with Eliza's. Eliza yearns above all things to join the respectable lower middle class. Doolittle, finding that his job as garbage collector is too low on the social scale to have any moral standards attached to it, realizes that he already has, in a sense, the prerogatives of a duke, and is loath to rise. He protests that he likes a little "ginger" in his life, "ginger" to his mind being the privilege of beating his female paramours, changing them at will, indulging in periodic drinking bouts, and pursuing life, liberty, and happiness on his own terms. But Shaw, like Carlyle, did not consider personal happiness the end of human existence. Hollow as three-quarters of middle-class morality may be, and damaging to the race on its higher levels, the imposition of minimum standards of decency on Doolittle is clear gain, any standards being better than the impunity he enjoys as a result of his poverty. If we leave his engaging impudence aside, it is a difficult thing to admire a man who wants to sell his daughter, and it is impossible to like a blackmailer. Shaw's aim as a socialist was to abolish the poor as a class on the grounds that such people were dangerous and contemptible. Shaw held it against poverty that it made Doolittle's kind of happiness all too easy. In a Shavian Utopia the Industrial Police would no doubt have bundled Doolittle off to a labor camp with as little compunction as they would a rent-collecting millionaire who took a similar view as to the world's owing him a living. Doolittle's character does not change, but he is as effectively moralized by coming into money as any hooligan athlete who has ever won a world's championship or any hillbilly moonshiner whose land has brought him a fortune in oil royalties. When Higgins, on the occasion of his marriage, asks if he is an honest man or a rogue, his answer is "A little of both, Henry, like the rest of us." Doolittle is, in short, whatever society wants to make of him.

Conventional farce would have ended with Eliza's fiasco at Mrs. Higgins' at-home, conventional romance[8] with her triumph at the ambassador's reception and a love match between her and Higgins. But Shaw contended that most ordinary plays became interesting just when the curtain fell. What, he wants to know, will be Galatea's relation to her creator after the transformation has taken place? It was one of his favorite theories that people of high culture appear to savages or even to the average man as cold, selfish, and unfeeling simply because of their inaccessibility to the common emotions and their freedom from ordinary affectionateness or jealousy. The development of Eliza's relation to the professor in the last two acts is meant to illustrate this perception.

Higgins is in many ways a paradoxical being. He is at once a tyrannical bully and a charmer, an impish schoolboy and a flamboyant wooer of souls, a scientist with a wildly extravagant imagination and a man so blind to the nature of his own personality that he thinks of himself as timid, modest, and diffident. Like Caesar in *Caesar and Cleopatra*, he is part god and part brute; but unlike Caesar, he cannot boast that he has "nothing of man" in him. It is this manliness,[9] which takes the form of obtuseness to the feelings of others, that leads to his first comeuppance. He and Pickering alike have both failed to grasp the fact that Eliza's heroic efforts to improve herself have not been based merely on a desire to rise in the world, and still less on any desire for perfection for its own sake, but are first of all the result of a doglike devotion to two masters who have taken trouble over her. When the men fail to pet and admire her after her triumph, her thwarted feelings turn to rage, and, desperate to provoke an emotional response from Higgins, she needles him so she may enjoy the spectacle of a god in a vulgar human fury.

Yet however much her spitfire vehemence may put us in mind of the street girl, the Eliza of this scene is far from the original Eliza of Covent Garden. There is a new dignity and even calculation in her emotional outburst. She has now mastered more than the pronunciation of the educated classes. When she meets Higgins at his mother's the next morning she is a model of poised reserve, even cuttingly cold in manner. Obviously her old commonness has forsaken her at the very moment that the experiment has ended and she must find her way independently in life. Nevertheless, Eliza's development, marked though it is, is limited in one important respect. She never gets past the stage of judging the world wholly in relation to herself. In this respect she remains a typical petite bourgeoise, who, as Higgins puts it, sees life and personal relations in commercial terms. She has nothing of the impersonality of the world-betterer, nothing of Higgins's scientific passion for reform.[10] Once again, as with Caesar and Cleopatra, it is a case of the superhuman face to face with the all-too-human. Higgins tells Eliza he cares "for life, for humanity," and her objection is that he does not care personally for *her*. On hearing that she is going to marry Freddy, Clara's amiable but brainless brother, Higgins objects—"Can he make anything of you?" He is chagrined at seeing his duchess, so to

speak, thrown away. Eliza in her turn finds such a question unintelligible: "I never thought of us making anything of one another;
and you never think of anything else. I only want to be natural."

To all but the most inveterate sentimentalist the relation between
Eliza and her mentor does not appear to have the makings of a
marriage. Higgins lacks not only the personal tenderness Eliza craves
but even the tact necessary to avoid hurting her repeatedly. Not that
he wants cunning in his treatment of women. He knows, Eliza tells
him, "how to twist the heart in a girl." But in the end, Higgins, who
has devoted his life "to the regeneration of the human race through
the most difficult science in the world," does not need a wife any
more than Plato, or Swift, or Nietzsche, or Tolstoy did. Indeed,
Tolstoy's marriage, a real-life instance of the world-betterer married
to a flesh-and-blood woman, had a good deal of the same tragicomic
conflict in it. Higgins explains to Eliza that he has grown accustomed
to her face and voice and that he likes them as he likes his furniture,
but he makes it brutally clear that he can also get on without them
and that he does not really need her. Knowledge of these facts does
not endear him to Eliza, who infinitely prefers Freddy's simple-
hearted homage. As Shaw tells us in his prose sequel to the play,
"Galatea never does quite like Pygmalion: his relation to her is too
godlike to be altogether agreeable." Eliza is not yearning after godhead; she likes Freddy Eynsford Hill.

The central theme of *Pygmalion* is the contrast between the
Promethean passion for improving the race and the ordinary human
desire for the comforts and consolations of the domestic hearth. The
history of Shaw's struggle to keep this dramatic conception from
being travestied in productions is in itself a long-drawn-out comedy.
The first published text of the play ended with Higgins giving Eliza
a string of items to shop for, including a ham and some ties; when
she retorts, "Buy them yourself," he merely jingles his change in his
pocket, "highly self-satisfied" at the new independent spirit she is
showing. Beerbohm Tree, the original English Higgins, neatly subverted this Miller-of-Dee ending in the 1914 production:

> I had particularly coached him at the last rehearsal in the
> concluding lines, making him occupy himself affectionately with
> his mother, & throw Eliza the commission to buy the ham &c,

over his shoulder. The last thing I saw as I left the house was Higgins shoving his mother rudely out of his way and wooing Eliza with appeals to buy a ham for his lonely home like a bereaved Romeo.[11]

When Gabriel Pascal undertook to make a movie of the play in 1938, Shaw once more found he had a problem on his hands. To begin with, Pascal, in casting the part of Higgins, chose not the kind of crusty character actor Shaw wanted, but the dashingly handsome and debonair matinee idol, Leslie Howard, which led Shaw to protest, "It is amazing how hopelessly wrong Leslie is," and to add that the audience would all want him to marry Eliza, "which is just what I don't want."[12] Shaw's own personal suggestion for the movie ending was a shot of Freddy and Eliza in their new flower and fruit shop, selling grapes.[13] This is not, of course, the way the film actually ends. In the movie, Eliza creeps back to the laboratory after her spat with Higgins, finds him alone, and hears him ask for his slippers.

Critics who argue for a romantic reading of the play, and who dismiss Eliza's marriage to Freddy in the prose sequel as a mere piece of perversity on Shaw's part, have used what they have considered to be Shaw's condoning of this conclusion to bolster their interpretations. Donald Costello, in his meticulous comparison of the play and the film, wonders what kind of "hypnotic powers" Pascal and Howard used over Shaw to get him to accept it in lieu of his own proposal. But it is clear from Mrs. Pascal's account of the matter that Pascal did not get Shaw's approval at all:

Pascal's answer to the additional scene in the flower shop with Freddy as Eliza's husband was silence.
But at the sneak preview of *Pygmalion* a very nervous Pascal was tightly holding Mrs. Charlotte Shaw's hand. Mrs. Shaw and Pascal were great friends. Beside them, the white beard of Bernard Shaw seemed to be fluorescent in the darkness. Pascal was sure enough that the white beard would soon be ruffled with anger. Eliza was *not* going to marry Freddy, and there was not going to be a flower shop. Instead the rebellious Galatea-Eliza would return to her maker, Pygmalion, with the soft and humble words:
"I washed my face and hands before I came, I did."
And the love-stricken Higgins, finding his old upper hand fast, instead of running to her would turn his chair with his back toward

Eliza and, leaning back, he would push his hat up as if it were the crown of a newly anointed king, and say:

"Confound it, Eliza—where the devil are my slippers?"

When the lights went on, Shaw didn't say a word. But there was a faint smile above the white beard.[14]

Evidently Pascal presented Shaw with a *fait accompli* he was powerless to undo. What did he think of Pascal's intimation that Eliza would devote herself happily to a lifetime of slipper fetching? The best answer to this question is the speech on the subject (omitted in the movie) which Shaw gives Higgins in the play:

> I dont and wont trade in affection. You can call me a brute because you couldnt buy a claim on me by fetching my slippers and finding my spectacles. You were a fool: I think a woman fetching a man's slippers is a disgusting sight: did I ever fetch your slippers? I think a good deal more of you for throwing them in my face. No use slaving for me and then saying you want to be cared for: who cares for a slave? . . . If you dare to set up your little dog's tricks of fetching and carrying slippers against my creation of a Duchess Eliza, I'll slam the door in your silly face.[15]

With these sentiments ringing in his ear, anyone contemplating Pascal's ending is bound to find it amusingly bathetic.

In the screen version of the play published in 1941, Shaw added a number of scenes he had written for the movie, including the scene at the ambassador's party, but, far from following Pascal, he took pains to reword the final speeches of the play to make it clear that Eliza would marry Freddy.[16] The well-established tradition of improving on Shaw, however, still continues. Tree and Pascal have now been succeeded by Alan Jay Lerner. In adapting *Pygmalion* to the musical stage, Mr. Lerner has retained the dialogue and business of the movie ending. In the published libretto of *My Fair Lady* he has gone a step further and added some stage directions of his own to Pascal's ending. When Higgins hears Eliza returning to the laboratory, Mr. Lerner comments, "*If he could but let himself, his face would radiate unmistakable relief and joy. If he could but let himself, he would run to her.*" When Eliza reappears, he tells us that there are tears in her eyes: "*She understands.*"[17] How Shaw's ghost would chuckle over this, if he could read it.

Of course such a sentimental curtain ignores the whole meaning of the encounter between the professor and the former flower girl in the final act. When Eliza, piqued at Higgins's brusque treatment, proclaims defiantly, "I can do without you," Higgins, far from being hurt or disappointed, congratulates her quite sincerely and tells her, "I know you can. I told you you could." Her emotional independence he takes as a sign of growing self-respect. He is equally candid in his counterboast about himself, "I can do without anybody. I have my own soul: my own spark of divine fire." For Eliza, the very essence of human relations is mutual caring, for Higgins it is mutual improvement. True enough, the rage the professor rouses in her is the rage of thwarted affection, but her affection is that of an emotionally sensitive pupil, not of an amorous woman. Freddy appeals to her because he is "weak and poor" and considerate, but also because he is young and handsome and sexually to her taste. But above all, she knows Freddy wants and needs her, while Higgins doesn't. Eliza's life is the warm, passionate life of embraces, mutual recriminations, even violence, and her temperament is the volcanic temperament that makes scenes when her feelings are wounded. Higgins can be equally volcanic, but only when professional matters are concerned. His is the cold, superhuman passion for changing the world. Eliza's code is "I'll be nice to you if you'll be nice to me," Higgins's that of the artist-creator to whom human material is raw material only. The insistence that they end as lovebirds shows how popular sentiment will ignore any degree of incompatibility between a man and a woman once it has entertained the pleasant fancy of mating them.

CHAPTER TEN

Heartbreak House

Heartbreak House is a curious paradox among Shaw's dramas: it is at one and the same time a novel experiment and a very reactionary play. The experimentalism lies in Shaw's use of Chekhov as a model, a choice he signalized by his subtitle, "A Fantasia in the Russian Manner on English Themes." There is no question of Shaw's enthusiasm for his mentor; he once declared that watching *The Cherry Orchard* made him want to tear up his own plays and begin afresh. He had unbounded admiration for the quiet realism with which Chekhov dissects his characters' contradictions and futilities, and for his rigorous avoidance of stereotypes and the clichés of conventional comedy and melodrama. Even the secondary characteristics of Chekhov—the naïve self-absorption of his people, the absurd *non sequiturs*, the tragicomic impasses, and the sense of boredom and frustration that infect his country-house gatherings—attracted Shaw to the extent of leading him to pay the Russian master the compliment of imitation.

Yet the spirit of *Heartbreak House* is at the same time so diverse from Chekhov's that some writers have objected that its Chekhovism is wholly superficial.[1] This is not my view: the whole spirit of the Chekhovian vintage is, I believe, here; what happened is that Shaw has added to it a pungent ingredient to make a much headier brew. Never one to take a simple view of a matter, or to be satisfied with another man's formula, no matter how sophisticated, Shaw has added to Chekhov a strong dash of the nineteenth-century writer who of all writers would appear to most critics to be Chekhov's exact opposite—Thomas Carlyle.

There is more of Carlyle—and, indeed, of the Old Testament—in *Heartbreak House* than in any other of Shaw's plays. This is what I

153

have had in mind in calling *Heartbreak House* a markedly reactionary drama as well as a technically advanced one. To understand the reason for the sudden upsurgence of the stern Victorian prophet in Shaw we need only to consider the change in manners and social outlook that had taken place in the decade since the writing of *Man and Superman*. As the author of that comedy's satiric irreverences, Shaw had looked like the very midwife of the twentieth century, the man best fitted to lay the ghost of the Victorian proprieties. Now, a decade later, Shaw renders his judgment on the era that followed the old Queen's death. The new prospect did not reassure him. The smug philistinism that Arnold and Dickens had pilloried a generation earlier was now in full retreat, but the new age, having thrown off the shackles of Victorian moralism, had also thrown off with them the Victorian sense of purpose. Instead of trying to realize Utopia, it had followed the more seductive course of wandering where its sentimental and romantic impulses led it. A narrow world had given way to one that was sophisticated, skeptical, and pleasure-seeking: Bohemia, the devil's kingdom, had superseded Mrs. Grundy's Philistia. But whatever the gain in charm and intelligence, Shaw thought it more than outweighed by the loss of will, social energy, and public conscience. Far from inspiriting him, the spectacle of a country in which Edward the *bon vivant* had replaced Victoria the good as the national exemplar aroused his deepest apprehension.

The result was to fire Shaw with a neo-Victorian prophetic ire. In *Heartbreak House*, Shaw visits upon the age of Bloomsbury with its cult of sentimental personal relations the same scorn Carlyle visited upon the age of Brummel with its Byronism and its pococurantism. Hence the paradox already referred to, for *Heartbreak House* is an *avant-garde* drama, designed to titillate the subtle and refined palates of the hedonists and dilettantes at the same time that it is meant to scourge them. Like Carlyle's *French Revolution* and Dickens' *Bleak House*, it is an adaptation to the author's own purposes of the Calvinist–Old Testament theory of history as a series of divine judgments upon human behavior. Shaw is telling us in his tragicomedy that we must be prepared, if not as "sinners in the hands of an angry God," at least as mortals in a world of men, to abide the consequences of our social actions—or negligences—as they issue in war, plague, famine, and revolution. Nowhere else in Shaw's writings does he express such sardonic joy in human misfortune as in the passage in the preface to *Heartbreak House* which begins, "Apostolic Hapsburg has collapsed; All Highest Hohenzollern languishes in Holland," where, in rhythms as mockingly derisive as the choruses in Handel's *Israel in Egypt*, he celebrates the downfall of the Central Empires in the course of World War I.

But if the spirit behind *Heartbreak House* is that of Micah, Jeremiah, and the Book of Exodus, Shaw's avowed literary strategy, as we have seen, was to appeal to the most highly developed taste of the intelligentsia he was attacking. Shaw knew that Captain Shotover, his spokesman in the play, must first of all, like Coleridge's Ancient Mariner, hold his audience spellbound if he was to strike home with his message. As Shaw himself put it, "The funny old captain, having lured them into his ship by his sallies, ties them up to the gangway and gives them a moral dozen."[2] The result is Chekhov reorchestrated, so to speak, with tubas and drums added, to allow for the playing of a *Dies Irae* at the end.

Heartbreak House is thus a redistillation of Chekhov and at the same time a passing beyond him, for Chekhov's world is static and directionless. Though his characters often talk grandly and eloquently about the future of humanity, it is obvious that they are not going to act on their convictions, and Chekhov records their orations with a sympathy that is undercut with humorous skepticism. His aim is to present men and women to us dramatically, not to point the way. As a result some critics have exalted his detachment into an end in itself and attacked Shaw as the perverter of the master. But this is to ignore the fact that Chekhov himself found the lack of commitment in contemporary writing its greatest failure and contemporary nihilism the age's bane. In a letter to the critic Alexei Suvorin, written in the first flush of his fame, he put the case sharply enough:

> Science and technology are passing through a great period now, but for our writing fraternity it is a flabby, sour, dull time. . . . Remember that the writers whom we call eternal or simply good and who intoxicate us have one very important characteristic in common: they move in a certain direction and they summon you there too, and you feel not with your mind alone, but your whole

being that they have a goal . . . . The best of them are realistic and paint life as it is, but because every line is permeated as with sap, by the consciousness of a purpose, you are aware not only of life as it is but of life as it ought to be, and that captivates you. And we? We! We paint life as it is, and beyond that neither whoa! nor giddap! Whip us and we cannot go a step farther. We have neither immediate nor distant aims and our souls are a yawning void, we have no politics, we don't believe in revolution, we have no God . . . .[3]

Like the clear-eyed medical man he was, Chekhov diagnosed the disease of will-lessness from which cultivated Europe suffered before the war, but he felt powerless to cure it. Shaw agreed with the diagnosis, but desired to rouse the sleepwalkers of *The Cherry Orchard* and *The Three Sisters* to a recognition of their plight.

Shaw started writing his play in 1913 in a moment that to the casual observer looked peaceful enough. Europe had not known a continent-wide convulsion since the time of Napoleon. But Shaw saw clearly that behind the calm, the intensification of international hatred, fear, and envy, coupled with the paralysis of the foreign offices, was causing a slow but dangerous drift toward war. Sensing that time was running out, he took up the public advocacy of a triple alliance between Britain, France, and Germany as a way of staving off the disaster. Consequently, though Shaw did not know what the end of his drama would be when he began to write it—he even declared that he did not see one speech ahead but let the play write itself—his premonitions were of the direst, and there is an ominous undercurrent in the Captain's electrically charged warnings from the first scene on.

For all his preoccupation with foreign affairs, Shaw does not set his play in Whitehall or the Quai d'Orsay. Instead he comments on the situation obliquely by taking us to a country house in Sussex on a fine September evening when five visitors arrive. Four of them—Ellie, Ariadne, Mangan, and Randall—suffer some sort of heartbreak in the course of the evening. Ostensibly, it is these disappointments that give the play its name. Yet in point of fact, as Shaw made clear to Trebitsch, it is not this kind of heartbreak he is really alluding to in his title. The word "heartbreak," he explained, meant a "chronic complaint, not a sudden shock." Its real meaning is the despair felt by the social philosopher who has come to realize that these charming, "advanced, unprejudiced, frank, humane, unconventional, democratic, free-thinking" men and women are totally feckless in social matters and quite incapable of realizing the danger in which they stand. Shaw added that he was using the word in the way Carlyle had used it when he referred to the blind faith of nineteenth-century liberalism in the beneficent effects of laissez faire as "heartbreaking nonsense."

To the Chekhovism of the play Shaw has added his own poetic symbolism. The shiplike room in which the action takes place is meant to put us in mind both of England's maritime history and of the allegory of the ship of state in *The Republic*.[4] Captain Shotover, who designed it, is a very old man who was born in the 1820's. He was thus a contemporary of the great explorers like John Hanning Speke and Sir John Franklin (whose Arctic adventures seem to be echoed in his tales), and of those other Victorian navigators such as Ruskin, Mill, Marx, and Tolstoy, who attempted to chart the course of man's social and spiritual destiny. During his adventures as a commercial trader he was forced to pretend to sell his soul to the devil as the only way of striking awe into his crew of desperadoes. This pretense led to his real damnation, from which he was only redeemed by an informal marriage to a West Indian negress, who presumably forced him for the first time to see natives as fellow humans. The main characteristic of his life, however, has been his heroic sense of purpose, which has led him to brave every new hardship and danger undaunted. Throughout all his hairsbreadth adventures his code has been, like that of Tennyson's Ulysses, "to strive, to seek, to find, and not to yield." Above all, he has lived in fear of happiness, contentment, acquiescence, and purposelessness.

But the warnings of the prophets have gone unheeded. What Carlyle called the "hog philosophy" of free enterprise has triumphed in a world that has avowed a faith in the survival of the fittest, the fittest in this case being the greediest and least public-spirited. Worse still has ensued, for the Captain eventually made the mistake of abandoning the humanizing, mundane negress to marry a captivating and seductive Eastern enchantress—a kind of oriental houri who is

referred to in the play as a "black witch" of Zanzibar—and from
this union has sprung a daughter who combines his vitality and
intellectual brilliance with her mother's exotic beauty.[5] Hesione
Shotover is of the race of Kundry, Circe, and Astarte. Her appearance
and manner are those of Mrs. Patrick Campbell, whose potent spell
had fascinated Shaw first over the footlights, and then from much
closer range while he rehearsed her for her part in *Pygmalion*. Mrs.
Campbell combined a sensitive poetic culture with a feckless charm,
an impish sense of humor, and a statuesque Italianate beauty at once
classical and Pre-Raphaelite. Edward Burne-Jones, whose style she
adopted as her own, was sufficiently struck by her *femme fatale*
attractiveness to paint her as a "Vampire," and this painting no
doubt provided the epithet which Shaw has Hector hurl at his wife
in the play.[6]

Hesione represents a post-Victorian world in which the cultivation
of private feeling has superseded an interest in public affairs. Her
function is not to create heroes, but to enchant them and minister to
their pleasures by realizing in real life their favorite poems and stage
romances. But she is no sensual monster; she is a refined, cultivated
society hostess whose bohemianism is part of her fashionable smartness. Her aim is to make existence a thing of poetry and sentiment
which will find its culmination in happy love affairs. Her faith in this
ideal has been bolstered by her own lifelong passion for her dashing
and romantically handsome husband, Hector. Their love match has
seemed so satisfying to her that she is preoccupied in arranging
similar matches or liaisons for others. One result of her highly
gratifying marriage has been to remove her far above mere jealousy
or possessiveness; indeed, she is willing to connive at latter-day
amorous escapades on her husband's part, and even to promote
them, since she is sincerely puzzled by the restlessness and discontent
that possess him, and sure enough of her own power to risk such
experiments.

Shaw complained that the first audiences of the play could not
make head or tail of Hesione's husband. He sought to enlighten them
by explaining that Hector was to be interpreted as a "liar, boaster,
hero, stylist, Athos and D'Artagnan rolled into a single passionately
sincere humbug."[7] Once more, as in *Arms and the Man*, Shaw is

analyzing that strange anomaly, uncommon in literature but not unknown in life, the hero-poseur. To those naïve souls who imagine that men are either strong, silent heroes or simple frauds, Shaw points out that there are in fact brave men (of whom at a later date he might have chosen T. E. Lawrence as an example) with courage, imagination, and dramatic flair, who, though they have had a whole series of amazing real adventures, deprecate these and satisfy their modesty and literary inventiveness at once by making up a series of false ones. Hector is, of course, none other than our old friend Sergius Saranoff, the comedic Hamlet of *Arms and the Man*, making his appearance again after the career of writing and adventuring Bluntschli had recommended to him—and twenty years of marriage. That Shaw once more had the Scottish aristocratic revolutionary author Robert Cunninghame Graham in mind in creating his swash-buckling disillusioned romancer seems clear enough from the pseudonym, Darnley, that he gives him (with its hint of royal Scots blood), his sheik's costume (Cunninghame Graham had traveled through Morocco disguised in native dress), and Ellie's description of him as a Socialist who "despises rank, and has been in three revolutions fighting on the barricades."

Hesione appreciates and respects her husband's courage even though she recognizes that it is part schoolboy bravado and part fear of being thought a coward. She also understands and forgives him his lies. What she does not understand is his political side, for Hector is a born reformer who has been diverted from his mission by Hesione, to whom revolutionary politics are merely another excuse for risking his life needlessly. She has beguiled him into a life of erotic and social pleasures and encouraged him to play the picturesque traveler in oriental robes while the burden of supporting the household falls on her aged but still resourceful father. Yet all this cannot hide from Hector that it is Hesione who is the haremkeeper and he who is the sexual ornament or male sultana. Like Shakespeare's Cassio, he is a man "damn'd in a fair wife," and his sense of damnation expresses itself in the scraps of wild poetry and Hamlet-like imprecations he utters—not against his beautiful captress, but against himself. In his analysis of Hector's relation with Hesione, Shaw is following the idea developed by Ibsen in *Little Eyolf* and by

Tolstoy in *The Kreutzer Sonata* that marriage may on occasion be the most dangerous and soul-destroying of all sexual relationships.

What Shaw is trying to say is that happiness, particularly in its most refined, cultivated form, is damnation. By contrast, heartbreak of the sudden-shock type may be a step toward salvation. Unless one grasps this idea he will go hopelessly wrong in trying to understand *Heartbreak House*, and in particular he will be merely baffled by the development of Hesione's young protégée, Ellie Dunn, which forms the chief dramatic action of the play. Desmond MacCarthy, for instance, has denounced Ellie's sudden transformation from a "green girl" into an "acute, collected woman" as a "thundering impossibility."[8] Ellie first arrives at the Sussex country house in a contentedly happy daze, which we soon discover is the consequence of her clandestine but thrilling meetings with a mysteriously romantic gentleman who calls himself Marcus Darnley. It is Ellie's escape from this state first into a condition of hardheaded cynicism and then into discipleship to the Captain that has puzzled critics.

Ellie's two remarkable changes of heart can be fathomed only if we first of all consider her father and her relation to him. Shaw seems to have based the character of Mazzini Dunn on an idealistic entrepreneur of his acquaintance, Ebenezer (later Sir Ebenezer) Howard. Howard was perhaps the exact temperamental opposite of the flamboyant Cunninghame Graham. He was nevertheless an equally unusual personality. As a young man he had come under the influence of Emerson and Whitman in the 1870's during a sojourn in Nebraska and Chicago. He then returned to England to live the life of a high-minded, self-effacing dreamer, all the while cheerfully enduring the dreariest poverty. Yet for all his lack of personal success, he was destined to have a profound influence on the twentieth century as founder of the international city-planning movement. Beginning with Welwyn City near Shaw's home at Ayot, the movement he inspired led to the founding of some score of model towns in England and America. One of his biographers wrote of him:

> Howard's personality was a continual surprise to strangers knowing nothing of his astonishing achievements. He was the mildest and most unassuming of men, unconcerned with personal appearance, rarely giving evidence of the force within him. Of

medium height and sturdy build, he was the sort of man who could easily pass unnoticed in a crowd; Mr. Bernard Shaw, who much admired what he did, only overstates a truth when he says that this "amazing man" seemed an "elderly nobody," "whom the Stock Exchange would have dismissed as a negligible crank."[9]

Ellie worships her father and has even become engaged to his fifty-year-old colleague, "Boss" Mangan, who has helped him through a financial crisis. The idea of a marriage of gratitude between Ellie and the dull and unattractive financier naturally shocks Hesione, whose favorite pastime, as we have seen, is arranging for other people's sentimental gratification. She is delighted to hear of Ellie's interest in Darnley, and not offended but only sorry on Ellie's behalf when the romantic dream hero turns out to be none other than her own philandering Hector incognito. But Ellie, though she is momentarily shaken, does not in the long run react at all as Hesione expects her to. Among Chekhovians who sigh, agonize, fascinate each other, and laugh and weep at their own follies without changing their ways, Ellie discovers that she is in their world but not of it.[10] Ellie is shocked but she also is brought suddenly to the realization that "heartbreak is not like what I thought it must be." She means that she is not a stage Ariadne who bemoans her lost lover and enjoys heartbreak (after the style of Octavius Robinson in *Man and Superman*) for the theatrical and poetic possibilities of that much dramatized condition. Her hurt and chagrin are in fact overborne by her self-scorn, and she becomes hard and clear-eyed, not tearful.

Ellie survives heartbreak. The Captain's second daughter—who actually does bear the name of Ariadne—wants to think of herself as heartbroken but in reality has no heart to break. Ariadne had left home at nineteen and married a hidebound colonial governor named Hastings Utterword in order to escape a family whose easygoing bohemianism irked her. Now, twenty-three years later, she returns to what she imagines will be a sentimental reunion with her father and sister. Shotover, however, receives her woodenly, and Hesione, amazed as she is at Ariadne's reappearance, shows none of the warm interest in her she takes in Ellie. Ariadne is intensely annoyed with this cool reception, but she cannot hide, even from herself, that her chagrin is not really sentimental disappointment, but simply her old exasperation with her family's lack of conventionality. It is her sense of decorum, not her heart, that is bruised. In her frustration she turns to Hector, and he, in his own despite, reacts as spontaneously to his wife's sister's sexual vitality as he does to his wife's. The ironic result is that he finds himself playing Don Juan against his will without the least illusion that he loves or even likes Ariadne. For though she lures Hector on, Ariadne has none of her sister's frank candor, and plays the game of sex after the fashion of one of Blake's "angels," that is, clandestinely, behind a façade of propriety. The situation is rendered one degree more absurd when Ariadne's brother-in-law, Randall Utterword, appears and turns out to be an aging *cicisbeo* with the nerves of a lovesick adolescent and a more than husbandly sense of jealousy.

Behind this cat's cradle of amorous intrigues stands the Captain, half dotard and half seer. While the Chekhovians nurse their broken hearts, he keeps the family in money by selling new lethal inventions to the militarists, and ponders the problem of social power. The problem presents itself to him this way: If blindly selfish men like Mangan and Hastings are willing to fight for their private wealth and class privileges, what are the public-spirited to do in the face of such determination? The Captain hopes to create a death ray which will act at the mere will of the benevolent, exactly as the psychological power of awe operates to control tyranny and violence in Shaw's utopian society in *Back to Methuselah*. The Captain is thus a pre-figuration of the Ancients of the succeeding play cycle; his quest for the seventh stage of concentration is none other than their quest for godhead through the union of omnipotence and good will and for the inauguration of the rule of the philosopher-king that is the culmina-tion of Shaw's social and political hopes. There is reason in Shotover's madness, even as there is in Lear's. It was this visionary side of the drama that made Shaw commend *Heartbreak House* as his own favorite among his plays on the grounds that "it has more of the miracle, more of the mystic belief in it than any of my others." [11]

The critics' obtuseness to the play's political implications made Shaw complain to St. John Ervine on the occasion of its first pro-duction:

> The criticisms are all stupid (except Hope in the New Age) because every situation in my plays has a public interest; and

critics, leading a Savage Club life, are incapable of public interests. They grin at the burglar as the latest Gilbertism, and never reflect on the fact that every day malefactors exploit the cruelty of our criminal law to blackmail humane people. They are not interested in Mangan because they are not interested in Lord Devonport. What use are such political imbeciles to me?[12]

The Lord Devonport whom Shaw used as a model for Mangan was Hudson Kearley, the founder of a national chain of grocery stores who became a Liberal member of parliament and in 1907 was appointed first chairman of the Port of London Authority, a post that brought him into acrimonious opposition with the dockers' union. To Shaw he must have appeared as a prime example of a businessman unfitted for public service through his economic and social philosophy, the exact antithesis of the selfless Howard.[13]

Mangan proves no match for a clever seductress like Hesione when she employs her wiles to lure him away from Ellie. Unfortunately, however, Hesione's plot backfires, for Ellie makes another surprising discovery about herself. When Mangan tries, under Hesione's influence, to break off the engagement, she comes to realize that his wealth was more than an incidental attraction—she had in fact counted on it to escape from her family's poverty. With this realization she now fights to keep him to his pledge, and he is startled to find what power of will the frail girl has when her mind is made up to a course of action. He squirms and writhes, and even reveals to her that, far from being her father's friend in need, he had made him his own cat's-paw and dupe, but to no avail; she holds him in a grip of steel, meeting each revelation with a counterrevelation and each threat with a counterthreat.

It is the Captain who loosens her grip by warning her that she must not sell her soul. She fences with him by paraphrasing Ruskin and Morris—and Shaw—to the effect that only well-fed bodies are capable of spiritual life, but he relentlessly brushes this sophistry aside: the material happiness she is now pursuing in her mood of cynicism is a far hollower ideal than the sentimental happiness she yearned for before. She must renounce both kinds of happiness as an end of existence if she is to escape damnation and despair. His own philosophy has been one of struggle and self-discipline, not a dream of bliss. The horror of old age is just the fact that it may inevitably bring happiness in its wake—"the happiness that comes as life goes, the happiness of yielding and dreaming instead of resisting and doing, the sweetness of the fruit that is going rotten." To save herself, Ellie must live as a free soul, unenamored and unbought.

Shortly after this, the calm is shattered by the arrival of a pseudo-burglar who purposely lets himself get caught in the act of stealing. The scene of the burglar's intrusion has been repeatedly decried as farcical and irrelevant, but it is really neither. Far from being stock comic relief, the burglar is a thoroughly unpleasant fellow, and the predicament he puts the others in is a genuinely uncomfortable one. In his preface on prisons Shaw explained his intention: "In most cases it costs nothing to let a thief off, and a good deal to prosecute him. The burglar in Heartbreak House, who makes his living by robbing people, and then threatening to put them to the expense and discomfort of attending his trial and enduring all the worry of the police enquiries is not a joke: he is a comic dramatization of a process that is going on every day." [14] The point is that the enlightened and sensitive part of our community has not only abdicated its responsibility for guiding the nation's economic and political affairs; it has also failed to evolve a humane and sensible penal code, so that it is faced with the choice between punitive retaliation based on a superstitious ideal of expiation it no longer believes in, and an irresponsible granting of impunity to offenders.

The final act takes place on the terrace later that evening. Earlier in the play the *crise de cœur* of the various characters have been interspersed with a good deal of comic bustle and fantastical farce. Now as the house party relaxes to hymn the beauty of the moonless night, the mood becomes musical and operatic. Shaw gives an indication of the tone he was aiming at in a note to his French translator correcting the overly prosaic style in which he had at first translated Ellie's speeches—"Après la reveille de Mangan, jusqu'à la fin de la pièce, Ellie est une figure de poésie, rêveuse, lyrique, jamais terre à terre, quoique toujours forte." [15] Musical feeling pervades the scene, and Hesione even detects the sound of a "splendid drumming in the sky." However, as we soon see, this background music has an ominous ambiguity. Shaw first evokes the night of Tristan with its voluptuous languor, but gradually the echoes of Isolde's invocation fade into the drumbeats of *Götterdämmerung*, and the ecstasies of love-pain pass into ecstasies of danger and destruction as *Heartbreak House* comes to judgment.

The idea that it is Tristan's story and not Siegfried's that is the natural prelude to the "Twilight of the Gods" is the central idea of Shaw's play. Victorians like Morris had proclaimed that "love is enough," and moderns like Auden tell us that we "must love one another or die" and then on second thought change it to "love one another *and* die," which is worse. Shaw simply announces the futility of love as a serious value: Ellie nurses love's young dream and sees the bubble burst; Randall represents the tragedy of a man who never achieves his heart's desire, Hector the tragedy of the man who does, Ariadne the comedy of a vigorous woman duped by convention into believing in sentiments she does not feel or even really want to feel. Hesione, the self-appointed patroness of lovers in the play, finally wonders "just how much longer I can go on living in this cruel, damnable world." Much modern pessimism—Jean Anouilh's might be taken as a typical instance—has exactly the same basis. What Shaw does is tell us that such feelings are wasted. He wants us to digest our sentimental disappointments and brace ourselves for nobler and more urgent business. His advice to us is comparable to Carlyle's advice to his age to close its Byron and open its Goethe.

The scene on the terrace now becomes a moment of truth for the whole group. Ellie, who has at last won through to salvation, hails the Captain as her soul's natural master and her spiritual husband. Mangan admits his political talent is largely obstructive and reveals that he has no inkling whatsoever of how to steer the ship of state. Lady Utterword counsels abandoning England's sham democracy and putting Hastings at the helm to rule by a colonial governor's methods of brute coercion, but the Captain scoffs at this as "not God's way." The natural leader of the country is the idealistic Hector, but his self-disgust at his enthrallment to women makes him the most Byronic of all. He interprets the sounds in the sky as "Heaven's threatening growl of disgust at us useless futile creatures," and looks forward to the holocaust he expects with the suicidal fervor of the baffled idealist. Hesione, puzzled by the men's discontent and sublimely ignorant of its cause, turns to them and asks

despairingly, "Arent you happy . . . ? Open your eyes: Addy and
Ellie look beautiful enough to please the most fastidious man: we live
and love and have not a care in the world. We women have managed
all that for you. Why in the name of common sense do you go on as
if you were two miserable wretches?"

What is remarkable about this scene is that for all its intellectual
intentions—here analyzed somewhat nakedly—the dialectical structure remains largely implicit. The characters, as in Chekhov, assert
their own convictions and express their feelings very much as if the
others were not present. They inhabit separate, self-sufficient
worlds and are not here debaters in a Platonic dialogue, as they are
in the last act of *Major Barbara*, for instance. The plangent expression of conflicting feeling, musically composed, dominates over
abstractions, as the voices interweave symphonically. At last, however, one voice rises above the rest, as Mazzini joins Hesione in
rebuking the others. The bohemian informality and casual ease of
this country-house week end, he tells them flatteringly, represents all
that is most pleasant and charming in English life. At one time,
fearing disaster, he had joined socialist societies to fight poverty and
avert revolution, and pacifist societies to combat militarism and avert
war, but now he is convinced that he took too melodramatic a view
of matters. Obviously, there is a Providence that looks out for men
and prevents catastrophes.

His willingness to bask in the apparent halcyon calm and savor the
sweet life accurately reflects the mood of Asquith in Downing
Street and Grey in the Foreign Office on the very eve of World War
I. The mood was endemic in Paris and Vienna and St. Petersburg
among all but the one per cent of European society that had resolved
to pin its hopes on blood and steel. Nothing ever happens, Mazzini
assures the company. The Captain, from the depths of his Victorian
conscience, demurs, with the grimmest Carlylean realism: "Nothing
but the smash of the drunken skipper's ship on the rocks, the
splintering of her rotten timbers, the tearing of her rusty plates, the
drowning of the crew like rats in a trap."

A moment later the first bombs fall and we realize that the moonless night has been an invitation to enemy airplanes. The play which
Shaw had begun in 1913 was finished in 1916, the year of Verdun.

The first zeppelin raids had been greeted with the same amazed delight as a relief from boredom and routine with which Hesione and Ellie greet the bombs at the final curtain. Bombs had fallen near Ayot, and a workman who had wantonly lit a flare in a field to attract aircraft (as Hector lights up the house) had been killed. Shaw declared that his plays were

> interludes, as it were, between two greater realities. And the meaning of them lies in what has preceded them and in what follows them. The beginning of one of my plays takes place exactly where an unwritten play ended. And the ending of my written play concludes where another play begins. It is the two unwritten plays [the critics] should consider in order to get light upon the one that lies between.[16]

It is not too difficult to accept Shaw's challenge and sketch a sequel to *Heartbreak House*. The play ends just as the war begins. Presumably Hesione will organize entertainment for the troops, and Ariadne war drives, while Hector will go to his death as a dashing cavalry officer, and Hastings as a general will blunder into massacres and be quietly relieved of his post. Ellie, in whom the spirit of an Edith Cavell lies latent, will be a nurse in France; Mazzini will work silently and efficiently without acclaim organizing industry and then be swept out of his post when peace with its cry for normalcy returns, while Mangan's surviving counterparts will be put in charge of wartime industries until their incompetence and the necessities of the situation force their replacement. Mangan's own death by bombing at the end of the play parallels the "spontaneous combustion" of the mock Lord Chancellor in Dickens' *Bleak House*, the two deaths symbolizing the final explosion of the false values, commercial and legal, the men are associated with. So the inhabitants of Heartbreak House will enter history and find their fulfillment or doom, not through any will of their own, but through the brute compulsion of political forces they refused to try to control.

Shaw repeatedly called *Heartbreak House* his greatest play. Some critics have agreed with this estimate and placed it high among his achievements; others have dismissed it as mere fantastication. One common reaction has been an initial delight with its surface attractions, followed by a later revulsion.[17] In such cases one is tempted to suspect that the critic did not at first get past the brilliant exterior, and that the response that found the work unpalatable was, if hostile, nevertheless the more profound, since he had at least become aware of what Shaw was opposing and of the weight of social responsibility being laid on his shoulders. I would myself place it among Shaw's best works. If it has not the intellectual brilliance of *Man and Superman* and *Major Barbara* or the heroic *élan* of *Saint Joan*, it is unsurpassed in the Shavian canon for the subtlety of its art, its depth of poetic feeling, and the fascination of its symbolism. On these merits it may be ranked next after his three greatest master-pieces. And, on the realistic side, as a fable of the way civilizations can drift into catastrophes, it is still all too chillingly to the point.

CHAPTER ELEVEN

Back to Methuselah

Two leading ideas obsessed Shaw throughout his long career. One was the possibility of achieving social equality through socialism; the other was the need to conquer man's propensity for violence through evolutionary progress. Obviously, the latter theme offers special difficulties when it comes to the stage, not the least being that significant evolutionary development is patently not a matter of days or even years, but of millennia. Don Juan gives us an intellectual account of the process in *Man and Superman*, but only in the five full-length plays that make up *Back to Methuselah* does Shaw tackle the all-but-impossible task of presenting his vision of mankind's racial future dramatically.

In so doing he has left some critics seriously confused on a vital point. Since socialism is not an issue in Shaw's "Pentateuch" after the third play, Edmund Wilson, for instance, thinks that Shaw here abandoned his socialist aspirations—that socialism in *Back to Methuselah* is shown to have "misfired."[1] But this is to misread Shaw's intention. Socialism is the one thing Shaw is optimistic about. By Part III, socialism has triumphed and done its necessary work. That crucial social difficulties remain after the economic problem has been solved is not, for Shaw, a criticism of socialism, but of the human race as it exists at present. *Back to Methuselah*, then, does not repudiate socialism; it merely goes beyond it to ask, After socialism, what? The answer reveals Shaw's pessimistic side, for he does not, in the last analysis, think the human race good or clever enough to live up to the Christian-anarchist standards he sets for it. The fourth play shows humanity as we know it dying out, and by the fifth it has vanished and been wholly replaced by a new species. Here, however, we may logically raise the question whether "pessimistic"

169

is the appropriate word. Shaw repeatedly insisted that he held no
special brief for the human race as such; his faith was in life rather
than in man, and on this account even the possibility of the destruction of mankind by atomic warfare did not especially daunt him.
Why, he once asked, should we look forward to a Superman and not
a Supersnake? For him, as for Nietzsche, mankind was only a bridge
to the future, and if this bridge failed, others might be found.

When Shaw called *Back to Methuselah* his "world classic" he
meant that he was consciously entering into competition with other
literary philosophers who had set forth their conceptions of life's
highest capabilities.[2] The questions the cycle asks are of the broadest
possible scope: What lies at the root of social suffering? What
institutions and what human traits have to be changed to alleviate it?
What form should an ideal commonwealth take? These are not
ordinarily matters the dramatic stage has considered at all; they are
rather the concerns of utopian fictionists from Plato, More, and
Campanella, down to Samuel Butler, Bulwer Lytton, and William
Morris. In his five plays Shaw sets out to explore the origin of evil
(like Milton in *Paradise Lost*), to excoriate modern European civilization (after the fashion of Swift in the first three books of *Gulliver's
Travels*), and finally to give us his vision of the City of God (as Plato
does in the *Republic*). The poles of the cycle are represented by the
Lilliputians and Yahoos of Parts I through IV and the philosopher-
kings of Part V. In the final play Shaw shows us a Platonic society
which is not, however, authoritarian, but anarchist in its organization, or lack of it. This ultimate achievement comes about not from
rational planning, but as the result of a biological leap forward. Thus
Shaw, beginning with the problem of man's unfitness for a decent
political life, and holding a view of the pettiness, cruelty, and blood-
thirstiness of man not far different from Swift's, looks for salvation
in the same direction as Bergson, Julian Huxley, and Teilhard de
Chardin. As he put it in his 1944 postscript to the play:

> The history of modern thought now teaches us that when we are
> forced to give up the creeds by their childishness and their conflicts
> with science we must either embrace Creative Evolution or fall into
> the bottomless pit of an utterly discouraging pessimism. . . . Had
> Swift seen men as creatures evolving towards godhead he would

not have been discouraged into the absurdity of describing them as irredeemable Yahoos enslaved by a government of horses ruling them by sheer moral superiority.[3]

I have said that Shaw's decision to write evolutionary utopian drama put him outside the tradition of the stage. This is nearly but not quite wholly true. Wagner's *Ring* also depicts, in allegorical form the moral development of the human race, and even deals with two typical Shavian themes—the corruption of man's social instincts by economic greed, and the struggle of the human spirit to disembarrass itself of the crutches of Church and State. It is not, then, surprising to find Shaw, the "perfect Wagnerite," comparing his cycle (which was also at first conceived as a tetralogy) to Wagner's in a letter to Trebitsch.[4] As in Wagner's case, what binds Shaw's plays together is not a common cast of characters or a single dramatic situation, but a set of leitmotifs. One such motif which occurs repeatedly throughout *Back to Methuselah* is the war theme, which accompanies Cain in Part I, enters into the background of Part II (set in 1920), reappears with the figure of Napoleon in Part IV, and then sounds for one brief final moment in the boasts of Ozymandias in the last play. Another subtler example would be the discouragement theme which Shaw first introduces when Adam contemplates the possibility of immortal life, then again in the excogitations of the brothers Barnabas, but develops fully only in "The Tragedy of an Elderly Gentleman." Still another is the theme of the triumph of life over death and matter. As an artist Shaw is writing philosophical opera à la Wagner without music. But instructive as a theme-by-theme analysis of the five parts of the cycle might be, to proceed with it here would obscure the coherence of the separate plays and the connection of the themes with each other. With a warning, then, that Shaw's symphonic method means that variations on his main subjects will appear in nearly all the dramas, we will leave the reader to identify them himself, and look at the plays in chronological order.

Part I, "In the Beginning," is a kind of allegorical theodicy in which Shaw tries to trace the origin of evil and its social consequences. In it Adam and Eve discover death and face the threat posed by Cain's acts of violence. These are two themes Milton deals with in *Paradise Lost*, but Shaw differs profoundly from Milton both in his artistic style and in the interpretation he gives to the Genesis story. To begin with, his Adam and Eve are not ideally beautiful demigods in an Arcadian landscape. Instead, Shaw the Pre-Raphaelite goes back beyond the Renaissance to the tradition of medieval drama and makes Adam a rough farmer and Eve a discontented housewife. Shaw even has Cain quote the rhyme with which the medieval priest John Ball launched the Peasants' Revolt—

> When Adam delved and Eve span,
> Where was then the gentle man?—

in order to establish clearly Adam's rank as a mere humble tiller of the soil. But Shaw's Gothic-Marxist Adam is anything but a social revolutionary: having invented the spade to help him dig, he has stopped there. The typical conservative countryman, dull, suspicious, and hostile to innovation, he characteristically invents marriage to ensure comfort and certainty in his domestic life, while the serpent laughs such vows to scorn. In the quartet of voices which contrast with each other in Part I, Shaw clearly intended him to be the gruff peasant bass whose earthiness is set against Eve's soaring soprano, the serpent's seductive contralto, and Cain's brilliant *heldentenor*.

Philosophically, Shaw's treatment of the Adam and Eve story presents another contrast with Milton. Shaw asks Milton's question —What "brought death into the world and all our woe"?—but gives an entirely un-Miltonic answer. Where Milton makes death man's punishment for sinning against divine law, Shaw, looking at the phenomenon from the perspective of modern evolutionary theory and Schopenhauerian metaphysics, restates Milton's question so that it becomes, Is death an inescapable biological fact? His answer, startling as it may seem to the average reader, is no. Shaw was led to this conclusion by none other than August Weismann, the neo-Darwinian biologist he berates so roundly in his preface. In the chapters on "Life and Death" and "The Duration of Life" in his *Essays upon Heredity*, Weismann noted that various species have had radically different life spans at different periods of evolutionary history and that certain primitive forms, such as the amoeba, which reproduce by fission, can even claim to be immortal.[5] Thus death, for Weismann, is an event occurring only among the organisms of higher sort which appear later in the evolutionary process. It is not a necessity but a convenience introduced by nature to prevent over-crowding by feeble and worn-out organisms.

Throughout his essay, Weismann, always a rigorous determinist, explains death as the result of natural selection, without, however, realizing the logical paradox this so-called explanation lands him in, for it is manifestly impossible to argue that death has survival value for the individual, and to say that it has survival value for the species would follow only if death were the consequence of intense reproductive activity, a possibility Weismann considers and rejects. Shaw recognizes the paradox and solves it with a much bolder speculation. Where others have thought of death as an affliction, Shaw, taking the opposite view, regards it as a boon wrested from nature by living things which would otherwise be faced with the intolerable burden of eternal life:

> If some devil were to convince us that our dream of personal immortality is no dream but a hard fact, such a shriek of despair would go up from the human race as no other conceivable horror could provoke. With all our perverse nonsense as to John Smith living for a thousand million eons and for ever after, we die voluntarily, knowing that it is time for us to be scrapped, to be remanufactured, to come back, as Wordsworth divined, trailing ever brightening clouds of glory. We must all be born again, and yet again and again.[6]

Thus Shaw posits a basic will to die, as fundamental in higher organisms as the will to survive. Of course, by making death a matter of volition, Shaw will appear to the unreflecting reader merely to be talking fantastically; but, in reality, Weismann's scientific effort to explain death in terms of orthodox mechanistic biology also contains a hidden teleological and voluntaristic premise, since he is also saying in effect that organisms die because nature (that is, they themselves) finds it expedient that they should do so.

Shaw's Adam wills natural death for himself as a way of escaping immortality. But his invention of death frees him from one anxiety only to bring him face to face with another—that of the possible extinction of the race. In this crisis, Eve appeals to the serpent for aid,

and the subtle snake responds by recounting two myths. The first is
the myth of the single-sexed Lilith, Adam and Eve's progenitor, who
by a supreme act of will divided herself in two. This is Shaw's
allegorization of the gynecocentric theory we have already en-
countered in the Don Juan dialogue, according to which primitive
organisms are to be regarded as feminine and bisexual reproduction
seen as a later stage in evolution. The second myth is the story of the
serpent's conception of young within her body, an achievement she
urges Eve to emulate by coupling with Adam. At this point Shaw
makes Eve's reaction on hearing the facts of human sexuality one of
repulsion. But this is not to say that he regarded the sex act as intrinsically unpleasant. Shaw explained to St. John Ervine that,
though Eve was initially repelled at learning the physiological details
of sex (especially the fact of the union of the sexual and excretory
organs), it would not preclude her enjoying pleasurable relations with
Adam later, once the shock wore off.[7]

Eve imitates the serpent by desiring, imagining, and willing, thus
completing the cycle of creation Shaw exalts throughout his five
plays. Unfortunately, the first result of this creativity is Cain. When
the second scene opens some centuries later, Cain has invented the
political and economic order peculiar to tribal or feudal society, and,
with it, most of the social inequities that are still with us. Cain, the
first military aristocrat, is the Superman of this society: he is a
romantically dashing figure, full of high spirits and vaunting bravado,
who has been goaded by his mother's discontent with his stick-in-the-
mud father to surpass his parents. In doing so he has introduced first
murder, then organized warfare, and finally exploitation and slavery
into the social system. In the name of progress he has instituted class
privileges, ostentatious wealth, passionate love, luxurious idleness
for spoiled wives, and a penchant for blood sports, and in the process developed a contempt for his father's manual labor as beneath
the dignity of a landowning fighter. Shaw's Cain corresponds to
what Plato in his analysis of inadequate forms of government in the
Republic calls a "timarch," or leader in an aristocratic oligarchy
which bases its rule on a code of military honor. Plato's vignette of a
warrior-chieftain, which is remarkably like Shaw's, was influenced
by the ancient Spartans, while Shaw, in creating Cain, presumably

had in mind feudal Europe as it existed in its prime from Charle-
magne to Richard III.

But Shaw did not see Cain simply as a social anachronism. What
Shaw elsewhere calls the Junker spirit was not totally dead in 1914—it
lingered on in the minds of men like the Kaiser and Winston
Churchill. Shaw counseled the actor who first played the part to
underline this by stressing Cain's contemporariness. "Cain," he
wrote, "should open this scene in quite a modern vein, with the high-
pitch and haw-haw of a stage cavalry officer, and with conceited
superiority and self-satisfaction. He is not a savage. By contrast
with Adam he is highly civilized and a gentleman. He does not scowl:
his swagger is a gay swagger."[8] Shaw even gives him a certain
attractive panache, which suggests that he agreed with Plato that the
military aristocrat is not a bad fellow at heart. Nevertheless, when
they speak as political scientists, both men finally reject the fighting
aristocrat because his insane pride of rank makes him equate the
good of society with the welfare of his special class. Shaw even adds
a telling indictment of his own: such men, whose very ideals of honor
are bound up with duels and battles, are at bottom in love with death.
Eve's divine discontent is not assuaged by Cain; she strongly prefers
her artist, scientist, and prophet sons to the heroic warrior, whom in
the end she denounces as anti-man for his love of killing.

In Part II, "The Gospel of the Brothers Barnabas," Shaw invites
us to contemplate the works of the sons of Cain as they appeared in
the wake of the Great War, when half of Europe lay in ruins with
millions dead and millions more starving. Like Shaw's pamphlets on
the war, this dramatic tragicofarce is a protest against "the poisoning
of the human soul by hatred, the darkening of the human mind by
lies, and the hardening of the human heart by slaughter and destruction and starvation"[9] that made the conflict so abhorrent to him.
Shaw's disgust parallels the *saeva indignatio* the War of the Spanish
Succession aroused in Swift, and these pages of Part II, which show
Britain's wartime Prime Ministers indulging in mutual recriminations
over its horrors even as they jockey for positions in the next election,
are perhaps the bitterest Shaw ever wrote. "To me," one character
says, "the awful thing about their political incompetence was that
they had to kill their own sons." Thus *Back to Methuselah* is, among

other things, Shaw's commentary on the catastrophe the feckless denizens of Heartbreak House failed to prevent.

As political leaders, the Cainites, in the persons of the Hohen-zollerns, Hapsburgs, and Romanoffs, have at last been totally dis-credited. Liberal democracies are now the order of the day. How successful are they, Shaw asks, in providing the statesmanship neces-sary for solving the momentous tasks before them? Shaw's judgment on the two democratic politicians in his play, Lubin and Burge, is withering. Lubin is a portrait of Herbert Asquith, the Liberal Prime Minister who took England into the war. Shaw saw Asquith as an easygoing, talented man of the world, capable of dealing with day-to-day problems, but destitute of any real statesmanship, conscious policy, or capacity for vital action. Shaw thought it sufficiently revealing that in moments of serious difficulty he should have taken refuge from unpleasant political realities in the minor social pleasures of golf and bridge. But it was not only his bland tendency to let things drift in the hope that crises would wear themselves out that struck Shaw about Asquith's Horatian temperament. He was also convinced that the best and most prestigious education England had then to offer, the *Literae Humaniores*, or "Greats" program in classical literature at Oxford, had in fact seriously crippled Asquith and other leaders of similar background by cutting them off from modern sociology and economic thought, and leaving them, in those areas, to fall back on an uncritical acceptance of early nineteenth-century laissez faire social doctrine, which in the long run merely justified their natural indolence and penchant for *la dolce vita*.[10]

Burge is Lubin's opposite in Shaw's theater as David Lloyd George, who supplanted Asquith after a munitions crisis during the war, was the latter's opposite in real life. Full of push and bustle, a man who took up popular grievances with zest and indignation, Lloyd George had inveighed against Tory landlords and bishops with the partisan zeal of a Harry Truman flailing Republicans. Beatrice Webb acknowledged his executive ability but found him brainless on all subjects except the consolidation of political power, in the pursuit of which his deviousness in wooing left-wingers like herself revolted her. Decrying the low moral and intellectual stature of "the little Welsh conjurer," she confided to her diary that she felt physically sick when she read of "the frenzied appeals of the Coalition leaders—the Prime Minister, Winston Churchill and Geddes—to hang the Kaiser, ruin and humiliate the German people—even to deprive Germany of her art treasures and libraries. These preliminaries of peace have become almost as disgusting as the war itself." [11] It was above all else the meanness and brutality of the appeals to popular anti-German rancor in the so-called Khaki Election of 1919 that gave the edge to Shaw's contempt and led him to represent his politicians as befuddled and conscienceless pygmies.

When *The Times* reviewer scolded Shaw for the sharpness of the personal satire in Part II, he defended himself by arguing that he had simply intended to show "our Parliamentary politics in contrast with politics *sub specie aeternitatis*" in order to demonstrate the disastrous inadequacy of the former.[12] But where, then, does salvation lie? Conrad Barnabas, Shaw's biologist spokesman, thinks the only solution is the breeding of a race whose lengthened life span will allow them to grow up sufficiently to deal with the quandaries that now beset mankind:

> It is now absolutely certain that the political and social problems raised by our civilization cannot be settled by mere human mushrooms who decay and die when they are just beginning to have a glimmer of the wisdom and knowledge needed for their own government.[13]

Today men perish just as they make the first tentative steps past childish immaturity. But if nature, against all probability, has created *Homo sapiens* with his talent for such things as music and mathematics, may she not, out of her very despair, create a race with political capacity? Can the life force, Shaw wonders, produce a *Homo* or *Serpens* or *Equus politicus*?

Contemporary biologists have balked at the idea. Julian Huxley, writing as a post-Weismannian neo-Darwinist, has rejected the conception of creative evolution as a "pseudo-explanation" and dismissed Shaw's speculations as wishful thinking.[14] But Shaw would reply that wishful thinking is in the last resort the only kind of thinking that really matters, since even a mathematician must want to solve a problem before he can work out its logic. Huxley and other

experimental scientists, scorning metaphysics, have explained evolution solely in terms of the operation of a blind, automatic natural
selection—that is, up until the moment of the appearance of man,
whom Huxley admits is free to alter and direct the course of his own
biological destiny. But can Mr. Huxley demonstrate in the laboratory
the free will which he posits as suddenly appearing with man? The
fact is that, as soon as one defines knowledge as only what can be
demonstrated by controlled experiments, he is by the very nature of
things committed in advance to determinism, mechanism, and anti-
voluntarism. Under such conditions free will becomes as much an
extraneous hypothesis as the life force, which is only free will in its
racial and historical form.

Frankly regarding metaphysics as inescapable, Shaw treats the
idea of the will not merely as a scientific but also as a philosophic and
even a moral concept. In this sense, his neo-Lamarckism is as different from the Lysenkoism of Russian science as it is from the neo-
Darwinism of the West. Lysenkoism is deterministic, resting on the
assumption that changes induced in the organism by the environment
are inheritable. But Shaw's idea is a much more mystical one:
organisms, Shaw believes, first feel a need and then develop the will
to change. Thus we would not, in his view, have eyes or ears if
primordial creatures had not willed to see and hear. Shaw first links
this vitalist metabiology with the mutation principle enunciated by
Hugo de Vries in 1910, according to which the most significant
advances in evolutionary progress are represented as coming, not
from minute variations accumulated over the ages, but from startling
new spores that plant and animal life throw off from time to time.[15]
Then, combining these two ideas with Weismann's speculations on
the potential variability of the life spans of species, Shaw has Conrad
Barnabas conjecture that the next significant biological development
in the human species will be an increase in human longevity to several
centuries.

Part III, "The Thing Happens," takes place two hundred and fifty
years later. Two people are shown actually to have survived—a silly
parson and an empty-headed parlor maid. The experiences of their
long lives have matured this unlikely couple into fully responsible
adults. The society in which they survive has also changed. Socialism

has succeeded in redistributing wealth and labor on a rational plan, and its citizens no longer face the constant threat of economic destitution. But in *Back to Methuselah*, as we have pointed out, Shaw is interested principally in looking beyond the triumph of socialism to the problems of human government that remain. Here his premonitions are by no means reassuring. As his name suggests, Burge-Lubin, the Prime Minister of England in 2170, is little more than a composite of his twentieth-century predecessors, and no more impressive as a national leader. Indeed, this cheerful, good-natured barbarian is hardly different from the typical democratic ruler whose picture Plato drew in the *Republic* five hundred years before the Christian era:

> Yes, [Socrates] said, he lives from day to day indulging the appetite of the hour; and sometimes he is lapped in drink and strains of the flute; then he becomes a water-drinker, and tries to get thin; then he takes a turn at gymnastics; sometimes idling and neglecting everything, then once more living the life of a philosopher; often he is busy with politics, and starts to his feet and says and does whatever comes into his head. . . . His life has neither law nor order; and this distracted existence he terms joy and bliss and freedom; and so he goes on.[16]

If Shaw has no abiding faith in democratic politicians, he has no more in democratic institutions. So lazy have the British become politically in the twenty-second century, and so convinced that the real life of the country is the life of its pleasurable week ends, that they have imported Chinese and Negroes to do the governing for them. To the British boast that, as foreigners, they governed India better than the less impartial Indians could, Shaw in effect replies that sauce for the goose is sauce for the gander, and Britain is shown as better run under its colored bureaucracy than it would be under white men. The British salve their self-esteem in this situation by clinging tenaciously to their myth of inherent racial superiority, and to their pride in being pioneers of liberty, though Confucius, the Prime Minister's Chinese secretary, tells him that the British have earned that reputation only by their "steadfast refusal to be governed at all."

The essential drama of Part III, however, lies in the discovery by the shortlived humans that there are two beings of a new, longlived race in their midst. The parson and the maid, with centuries of administrative experience behind them, have no more difficulty in overawing their ministerial colleagues than the average adult has in impressing a small child, but the shortlivers neither like the pair nor feel comfortable in their presence. Burge-Lubin finds their taste for serious political work simply unintelligible; Confucius, more long-sighted, is shocked to foresee the inevitable breakdown of family ties and incest taboos; while the stupid and irascible Accountant General simply recoils in hatred and terror, his instinctive reaction to the inexplicable superiority and unanswerable self-possession of these people being a desire to kill them forthwith. Shaw is reminding optimists who think ability and merit breed affection that the world has in fact been a dangerous place for its Lincolns and Gandhis. Part III ends with the two longlivers going off to breed a new race, while Burge-Lubin, suddenly aware of a sobering possibility, calls off a prankish assignation with his beautiful negress Minister of Health. The dip in the sea this amorous rendezvous was to involve may lead to rheumatism, and though, as a frivolous shortliver, the Prime Minister might chance it, as a man who may live for three hundred years, he is unwilling to risk two centuries of discomfort. With this farcical joke Shaw drives home philosophically his antideterminist point that it is not men's past that dictates their actions, but their anticipations of their futures.

By Part IV, "The Tragedy of an Elderly Gentleman," the new race has proliferated and established its own culture. Each Super-being spends a century of his lengthened life educating himself, a century as a practical administrator, and a final hundred years as a senatorial oracle. What is most striking about this utopian existence in the year 3000, however, is the disappearance of all conventional political and judicial machinery. Like Karl Marx, Shaw appears to have believed that once mankind has been re-educated along socialist lines into a sense of communal responsibility, the state can be allowed to wither away, so that the final condition of Shavian society is the anarchist ideal envisaged by such antistate philosophers as Godwin, Wagner, Bakunin, and Morris. The difference is that Shaw does not regard the achievement of such a peaceful and equitable society as an inevitable development of the present institutions of human society. Quite the contrary: desirable as such a consummation of man's troubled political and social history would be, Shaw thinks it beyond the capacity of mankind as it exists at present. When the Elderly Gentleman, the representative of shortlived humanity in Part IV, boasts of the whole "galaxy of Christs" that arose in the twentieth century, his longlived mentor merely points to the fate of pacifists and conscientious objectors in a world of war-mad ordinary mortals:

> But did any of their disciples ever succeed in governing you for a single day on their Christlike principles? It is not enough to know what is good: you must be able to do it. They couldnt do it because they did not live long enough to find out how to do it, or to outlive the childish passions that prevented them from really wanting to do it. You know very well that they could only keep order—such as it was—by the very coercion and militarism they were denouncing and deploring. They had actually to kill one another for preaching their own gospel, or be killed themselves.[17]

Like Swift's Superhorses, Shaw's Superrace has no organized system of power, government, war, law, or punishment. Again, like the Houyhnhnms, and like Plato's Guardians, they are passionless, stern, ascetic, kindly, responsible, and unbending. Shaw departs from Plato, however, in that his communist philosopher-kings are not a ruling caste at the top of a hierarchy: no man in his Utopia stands in a hero-follower, master-servant, prophet-disciple, or teacher-pupil relation to any other. The only advantage that any man has over his fellow is that which comes naturally from age and experience. Moreover, the emotional child-parent nexus of our society has also vanished. After the manner of most philosophical utopians, Shaw desires to limit the influence of the family as a social unit, first because he thinks the sentimentalism it fosters is intrinsically unhealthy, and second, because it narrows its members' vision of the common good. Once again he follows Swift and Plato in making the breeding of children a political and eugenic and not a personal matter, so that mothers treat all children in the same fashion and lose track of their own offspring after ten years. And, under the system of group marriage which obtains here, as in Plato, fatherhood is presumably a relation that is not ascertainable at all.

The adventures of the Elderly Gentleman are too rambling to engross us as drama, but Shaw's treatment of the psycho-evolutionary situation in Part IV is full of interest. Now the relations of Part III are reversed, and it is Shaw's Superrace who in thirtieth-century Ireland outnumber the shortlived visitors and set the norms for society. The instinctive estrangement between common humanity and superior men is a notion which had engrossed Shaw for at least three decades. In an unpublished lecture on fiction delivered in 1887, he demonstrated that he had already at that date worked out the psychology of moral evolution he was to dramatize in *Back to Methuselah* and had even anticipated by a quarter of a century the verdict of those who were to denounce his Supermen as bleak, cold, and inhuman:

> We are all familiar with the popular verdict on Goethe, the most highly educated of the great fictionists. He was cold; he was selfish; he was callous; he was unsympathetic and exclusive. Just so we hear complaints of George Eliot having talent but no genius, lacking feeling, being a soulless pedant, and the like. This is an inevitable result of evolution. I have no doubt that if the tigers and monkeys were to express their opinion of mankind they would vote us cold, passionless, calculating, and mysteriously dreadful. The Celtic peasant, who, when a member of his family dies, weeps, hires men to howl with him, and finally exhausts his grief in a drunken orgie, would be scouted as a callous monster if he acted like the self-controlled, sober, tearless ladies and gentlemen of our acquaintance. . . . In Lord Lytton's "Coming Race," he represents an ordinary man—a mining engineer—of our own time straying by accident into a subterranean country, inhabited by a race several centuries ahead of us in evolution. He meets a man of that race, and though there is nothing grotesque or frightful about him, the mere facial expression of superhumanly passionless and serene wisdom scares the unfortunate engineer almost out of his wits. And though he stays in that country for some time, and is kindly used there, he never gets used to these comparatively godlike people, nor ever overcomes his instinctive dread of them. The mistrust and aversion excited by Goethe and George Eliot are part of the same conflict between the highly evolved men and those who are still comparatively savage.[18]

Back to Methuselah, then, does not mark any sudden dropping by Shaw of his Fabianism in favor of salvation through evolution, but the final working out of the conviction he had held since the age of thirty that the most vexing difficulties facing mankind could be solved only through a radical biological advance.

The "Tragedy of an Elderly Gentleman" makes the same point as the lecture of 1887. The Elderly Gentleman has made a pilgrimage to the Irish home of his ancestors—now the domain of the longlivers— aglow with patriotic sentiment, nostalgic feelings for historical associations, and a desire to interview the oracular race, who he innocently imagines will resemble the older ecclesiastics, academics, and statesmen of his own experience. As a "Baghdad Briton," he looks to the British Isles as a citizen of the new Roman Empire based in Constantinople might have looked to ancient Rome. To his consternation, he discovers that not only is his patriotism incomprehensible to the longlivers, but they have remorselessly razed the very monuments he hoped to visit. In addition, their code of manners is profoundly shocking to him, for they know nothing of good taste, propriety, embarrassment, insults, or sexual or social distinctions. In short, he is as much adrift as a tribal chief would be in the halls of a scientific congress. So discomfited is he by the disappearance of the moral landmarks he has been accustomed to that he is soon thrown into an acute state of psychological shock.

Shaw calls this condition of psychological disorientation "discouragement." In his postscript he conjectures that pessimists like Swift and George Eliot suffered from it in the eighteenth and nineteenth centuries and that Shakespeare was dramatizing the effects of such a frame of mind in the death of Timon of Athens. The conception, and the term for it, Shaw seems to have borrowed from the anthropological speculations of Francis Galton. In his *Inquiries into Human Faculty* (1883), Galton postulated such an influence at work in native tribes on their first contact with white civilization.[19] Apparently Galton had in mind such phenomena as the collapse of morale of the American Indian and the actual extinction of some races, such as the Caribs and Tasmanians. But perhaps we can grasp Shaw's idea most clearly if we think of the cultural plight of the Elderly Gentleman and his friends as parallel to that of a group of primitive Neanderthal men who had strayed into a colony of the more highly developed *Homines sapientes* who were destined eventually to supplant them.[20]

Shaw derived his theory of discouragement not only from Galton but also from a novel he had read. Bulwer Lytton's utopian fantasy, *The Coming Race*, which Shaw mentions above, is a work which exercised a remarkable influence over his imagination. As we have seen, the book defined for Shaw the distance between the Goethean or Olympian temperament and the temperament of the average citizen. Both politically and morally, Bulwer Lytton's tale is in the Platonic-Swiftian tradition. What makes it a direct forerunner of *Back to Methuselah*, however, is the fact that the underground Superrace in the story has achieved its moral and social advantages over the human race through biological evolution. In particular, they have solved the problem of power by developing a kind of personal magnetic force called "vril" to the point where they can apply it with deadly effect. It is this force with which Shaw endows his long-livers in Part IV and their successors, the Ancients, in Part V. An episode in his own life had persuaded him that such an influence might well become a potent factor in human relations. As a young man in his twenties, the ordinarily unfazable Shaw had met a venerable Jewish rabbi whose impassively placid personality so overwhelmed him that he found himself struck dumb:

> . . . by some power in him, magnetic or mesmeric or hypnotic or whatever you like to call it, which reduced me to a subjection I had never experienced before and have never experienced since. I was simply discouraged by him. Since then my observation, and the stories I have read about the dying-out of primitive tribes at the impact of civilized invaders, have convinced me that every living person has a magnetic force of greater or less intensity which enables those in whom it is strong to dominate those in whom it is relatively weak, or whose susceptibility to its influence, called shyness, is excessive.[21]

This force comes most dramatically into play when the longlivers have to deal with the formidable Emperor of Turania. The Emperor, like Cain, is a warrior, but he is not simply Eve's son revivified. Politically he is an entirely different phenomenon, the dictator whose power rests, not on birth or rank, but on his popularity with the masses. The great archetype of this kind of adventurer is, of course, the historical Napoleon, and Shaw makes clear the sort of politico-military leader he has in mind by giving his character the Corsican's name. Plato, in the *Republic*, represents the kind of society such men preside over as the least stable of all the imperfect societies, and the one in which the situation of the leader himself is least happy, since the tyrant's regime is more likely than not to end in a bloody revolt. This is exactly the new Napoleon's difficulty. Too clear-sighted and strong-willed to put up with misgovernment by others, he has been able to consolidate his power only by making his people drunk with dreams of military glory, and he fears their reaction once disillusionment with his costly adventures sets in. But he finds no sympathy among the longlivers. The oracle whom he has come to consult about his dilemma deliberately shoots him with his own pistol as one might shoot a dangerous animal. When her shot goes wild, Shaw ironically makes Napoleon curse her for having no sense of the sacredness of human life.

Besides possessing natural awe of lethal intensity, the longlivers are also skilled manipulators of the kind of artificial awe produced in our society by papacies and imperial courts, or by military, judicial, and legislative tribunals desiring to impress onlookers with their authority. Though they themselves despise such mummery, they find it necessary to resort to it because the shortlivers refuse to accept their dry, hard wisdom when it is communicated directly and undramatically. In the final scene of Part IV, the longlived Oracle, suitably accoutered to impress the human visitors, speaks to the Envoy, who, as British Prime Minister of the day, is the last of the line of Lilliputian politicians whom Shaw scourges throughout *Back to Methuselah*. The Envoy has no desire to learn statesmanship from the Superrace; his sole aim is to gain prestige through his trip abroad. Hoping for the same encouragement a predecessor had reportedly received, he asks the oracle to repeat her former message. When, amid thunder and lightning, the contemptuous oracle orders him to "Go home, poor fool," he realizes his former chief had lied to the electorate; after a moment's chagrin he decides that it is politically expedient that he do the same. But the Elderly Gentleman, who at first, like Gulliver, had boasted to his interlocutors of the glories of his own civilization, has had too many shocks in one day. He cannot stomach this last piece of chicanery. Rather than go home and connive at a lie, he begs for the privilege of staying behind, as Gulliver begged the

Houyhnhnms to be spared the ignominy of a return to England. In reply to his anguished cry, the Oracle, knowing he will perish slowly in the new rarified moral environment, gives him the only help she can by lifting him in her arms and compassionately killing him.

At this point it may be well to take our bearing and ask where we stand at the end of the first four plays of Shaw's new Bible. Is *Back to Methuselah*, the reader may be tempted to ask, a plunge into nihilism which negates the general tenor of Shaw's whole life work? Edmund Wilson thought it was, and that Shaw had here given up politics in despair. Certainly the parallel between the Elderly Gentleman's final state of mind and Gulliver's at the conclusion of Swift's satire is striking. Both are overwhelmed with acute depression when they contemplate man's distance from a more perfect species, and the decision of the Houyhnhnm council to let the race of Yahoos die out is matched by the decision of the Elderly Gentleman's mentor to join the growing faction of longlivers who favor exterminating ordinary humanity. As far as man is concerned, Shaw is a Swiftian pessimist. As we have noted, it is on the post-human that Shaw pins his faith, though his hope will strike those who are committed to mankind as nature's last word as no hope at all.

Be this as it may, Part V, "As Far as Thought Can Reach," shows us Eve's dreams bearing fruit in a Utopia of longlivers thirty thousand years from now. Along with mankind, the spirit of Cain, the spirit of Napoleon, and the spirit of Torquemada have all vanished, taking with them all fraud, needless bloodshed, coercion, and punishment. From the pessimistic ending of Part IV we move to a dawn beyond the darkness. Indeed, the last play of the cycle, radically different in mood and form from what has gone before, is a kind of final "Ode to Joy," which shows us Superhumanity progressing on its road to godhead.

Since life's social problems have all been solved, no government at all exists, and we find ourselves in a kind of anarchist paradise of free, self-determining individuals. Nevertheless, Shaw's City of God is not without its dramatic struggles, though these are no longer with economic necessity or human bellicosity. The necessity Shaw's free race now strives against is not bound up with the social order, but with the laws of physics and chemistry as they touch on biology.

Like most vitalists, Shaw is a dualist with respect to body and soul, mind and matter. The last great contest he sees life engaged in is the contest with matter itself. The *élan vital* has involved itself with matter in a desperate effort to make the body an instrument of the will, but in so doing it has in fact become, as Shaw laments, the "slave of a slave." In *Creative Evolution*, Bergson expresses his sense of the dilemma of the mind-body relation in a way that closely parallels Shaw:

> The whole history of life until man has been that of the effort of consciousness to raise matter, and of the more or less complete overwhelming of consciousness by the matter which has fallen back on it. The enterprise was paradoxical, if, indeed, we may speak here otherwise than by metaphor of enterprise and of effort. It was to create with matter, which is necessity itself, an instrument of freedom, to make a machine which should triumph over mechanism, and to use the determinism of nature to pass through the net which this very determinism has spread. But, everywhere except in man, consciousness has let itself be caught in the net whose meshes it tried to pass through: it has remained the captive of the mechanism it has set up.[22]

Shaw would add that in the case of man the entrammelment is still overwhelmingly in evidence.

Life is first of all subject to matter through the power the material world has to enchant our senses. "As Far as Thought Can Reach" consists of a series of charmingly ingenious scenes dramatizing the effects of this power on the Superrace in babyhood, childhood, youth, and maturity, until it frees itself from them in old age. The Newly Born emerges from her egg as ecstatically enraptured by her flesh-and-blood playmates and toys as Miranda in her "brave new world." The young Strephon suffers the joys and frustrations of adolescent love when Chloe, who has passed beyond the age of sentimental amorism, drifts away from him. The older Acis sings the delights of nature and the pleasures of sex and of male comradeship. The more sophisticated Ecrasia finds life's all-in-all in the beauty and grace of ideal works of art. Beyond her stage of development is the sculptor Arjillax, who has ceased to worship bodily beauty and who makes busts of Ancients—the philosopher-kings of Part V—which reflect

the power of mind. Shaw weaves this exquisite polyphony of conflicting obsessions together with naturalness, humor, and clarity, so
that we are vividly aware of how each growing member of the Superrace is at odds with those younger or older than he is.

The result is a restatement of the themes of Plato's *Symposium* in
a kind of dramatic fantasy. But the setting, though Greek in style, is
not the compliment to Plato one commentator has thought it to be.[23]
Rather, the children's "Festival of the Artists" represents exactly that
side of Greek culture Plato was reacting against. The occasion is
intended to parody the sort of romantic Hellenism we find in Keats's
Endymion, Ingres's Arcadian idylls, or Pater's essays on Greek art.[24]
Its delights are meant to be viewed ironically, since the overriding
idea of Part V is the turning of the mind from visible and sensible
things to the world of philosophical ideas. In the *Republic* Plato
mocks the pretenses to wisdom of the dilettantes who "run round
the city and country Dionysia as if they were under contract to listen
to every performance." In "As Far as Thought Can Reach" Shaw
takes Plato's side against hedonistic aestheticians like Pater who
prefer the immediacies of sound and color and the intense emotions
of romantic love to abstract thought, as well as against more austere
modern theorists like Croce who regard man's image-making as a
self-justifying activity. In the speech of the older sculptor, Martellus,
to the younger Arjillax, Shaw translates Plato's objections to art into
his own vitalist terms:

> Your disillusion with your works of beauty is only the beginning
> of your disillusion with images of all sorts. As your hand became
> more skilful and your chisel cut deeper, you strove to get nearer
> and nearer to truth and reality, discarding the fleeting fleshly lure,
> and making images of the mind that fascinate to the end. But how
> can so noble an aspiration be satisfied with any image, even an
> image of the truth? In the end the intellectual conscience that tore
> you away from the fleeting in art to the eternal must tear you away
> from art altogether, because art is false and life alone is true.[25]

One consuming passion of the Superchildren is creating inanimate
art-dolls; another is playing with animated mechanical ones. Martellus, having abandoned art, has now entered into collaboration
with the inventor-biologist Pygmalion to produce pseudo-human

automata with the powers of speech and locomotion. Shaw introduces Pygmalion with the aim of complementing Martellus' critique
of image-making with a critique of modern science. Pygmalion commits the error of reducing life to a purposeless series of accidents and
reflexes, and mental processes to a thoughtless association of ideas.
Though he speaks of a "Life Force" in describing his animation of
Martellus' models, it is clear that Shaw does not consider Pygmalion
as a bona fide vitalist in the metaphysical tradition of Bergson or
John Scott Haldane. In his preface to the play Shaw calls these men
the New Vitalists and distinguishes them from such nineteenth-
century empiricists as Claude Bernard, or even Lamarck, who think
of the life force as just another mechanical force added to matter,
and not as a radical element involving free will.[26] It is to the latter
school of Old Vitalists that Pygmalion belongs; for him, there is no
crucial distinction between a live body and a dead one, and automatism is indistinguishable from life itself.

Shaw's objection to laboratory science was that it began with
hypotheses and then manufactured evidence through controlled
experiments to prove them, ignoring unexpected or disappointing
results:

> A laboratory may be a fool's paradise or a pessimist's inferno:
> made to order either way. Its door may be shut against metaphys-
> ics, including consciousness, purpose, mind, evolution, creation,
> choice (free will), staring us in the face all over the real world. It
> may assume that because there is no discoverable difference
> between a living body and a dead one there is no difference. It may
> rule out as metaphysical delusion every fact that is incompatible
> with the determinist creed, practically official in professional
> science, that everything that has yet happened or ever can happen
> is inevitable and unalterable no matter how human will and con-
> science may desire and strive to alter it.[27]

Pygmalion's automata dance, answer questions, bicker jealously, and
grandiloquently assert their majesty. Ozymandias and Cleopatra-
Semiramis proclaim their natures to be "logical and predetermined
and inevitable" in vaunting speeches whose sonorous rhythms,
relentless repetitions, and loud anathemas satirically recall the
Athanasian Creed. Though Pygmalion refuses to distinguish their
reflex reactions from human life, Martellus, for whom automatism,

no matter how intricate, is mere automatism still, denies their vitality. Even their death speeches are mere mechanical rhetoric, parodies of Shakespeare's stock dying adieux.

Above the children in Part V stand the Ancients, who embody Shaw's ultimate vision of wisdom and power. These elders—who are passionless, sexless, and, when the welfare or safety of the community demands it, deadly—have evoked no more general enthusiasm among Shaw's readers than they do from the Superchildren of the play. But Swift's Houyhnhnms have never been popular either, nor Plato's Guardians: the average man has never found the ideal creations of utopian philosophers much to his taste. The children cannot imagine that beings who have given up dancing, love, friendship, and art- and nature-worship can possibly find any pleasure in life. When the Ancients tell them that the ecstasy that accompanies their intellectual activity is more intense than any ecstasy of the senses, they laugh incredulously. Yet, though Shaw obviously has a quarrel with the body comparable to Plato's or Paul's, the asceticism of the Ancients does not rest on any puritanical sense of sin. The Ancients neither repress, scold, admonish, nor sermonize the young. The only advice they give is "Do what you please," which is not the lesson we usually inculcate in our Sunday schools.

The children are absolutely free to roam through the Venusberg and the Palace of Art until they outgrow such pleasures. This peculiar attitude toward sex and matter is, to say the least, unusual in Western thought. Writers in what may be called the Manichean tradition within Christianity, like Paul and Augustine, have decried both at once; most sexual libertines, on the other hand, have been materialists to whom matter is good. In making his young people promiscuous sexual communists benignly patronized by a group of absolute idealists who treat matter with contempt, Shaw adopts a position which is all but unique, though an obscure second-century Alexandrian heretic named Carpocrates seems to have hit on the same unusual attitude, despising matter but regarding sex as a morally indifferent activity. Obviously, such views are bound, on the one hand, to shock moral legalists by implying that people should be free to have the sexual relations they want, and on the other, to repel those Lawrentians who find it impossible to imagine that sex is something mature beings outgrow. But Shaw's objection to the body is only that it is not perfectly at the service of the will and the intellect. After we are freed from the lures of sense, the enfeeblement of the body eventually debilitates us so that "when a man dies of old age, he kills a lot of mental babies with which he is pregnant."[28] If our bodies lasted longer, our mental development, Shaw thinks, might proceed indefinitely. The Ancients in the first power of their maturity experiment by turning themselves into many-limbed Hindu gods; then they give up such efforts and try instead to escape from the "body of this death" into dematerialized astral essences. Like Bergson, Shaw images life as finally becoming disengaged from the matter to which it has subjected itself.

At the end of his cycle Shaw takes us back to its beginning. As the children retire to a rest sweetened by the caresses of real lovers or the dreams of imaginary ones, three familiar figures appear in the twilight. Adam, the eternal conservative, can make nothing of a world in which men do not grow crops or raise animals and are not bound to the wheel of economic necessity. Cain the warrior, though still jaunty, is forced to admit that there is now no place for his seed. But the serpent and Eve stand vindicated, the snake by the results of her willingness to tempt and dare, the woman in the triumph of her favorites among her children, the thinkers and creators, over the plodders and killers. Finally a new apparition, Lilith,[29] the "mother" of Adam and Eve, a personification of the "Eternal Feminine," or life force itself, speaks her doubts and aspirations in a great concluding aria. Despite its moments of surpassing horror, life, she tells us, at last stands redeemed from the vileness of slaughter and man's baser passions. But best yet, the creative urge is still unsatisfied. The World Will must push on, as Shaw puts it in his essay on "Modern Religion," until it attains "on its infinite way the production of some being, some person if you like, who will be strong and wise, with a mind capable of comprehending the whole universe and with powers capable of executing its entire will—in other words, an omnipotent and benevolent God."[30]

Thus Shaw takes us through the valley of the shadow to a Pisgah view beyond. *Back to Methuselah* ends gloriously for all its becloudedness. Yet, despite its triumphal close, it still remains by far the least popular of Shaw's major works. In part, as we have seen, this is due to the austerity of its final vision, with its utopian contempt for mundane social and domestic pleasures. But more than anything else, it is the result of the artistic failure of the second, third, and fourth plays. What Shaw himself clearly recognized as the "dull and irritating" qualities [31] of the people in these plays was an intentional effect he aimed at in order to rouse in us a conviction of the pettiness and absurdity of human life as it now exists. Shaw was determined not to flatter humanity by making his characters more eloquent, or touching, or witty, than they would be in real life, or to beguile us with any diverting vivacity of comic invention. But the unfortunate result of this self-denying ordinance was that he failed to keep the "unsatisfactoriness" (as he himself called it) of the people in the three intermediate plays from being ultimately tedious. Rather than being closely engaged by them, we are in the end bored by their actions and talk. The triviality which was meant to provoke our disgust finally wearies us. This is a pity, first, because the opening and concluding plays reveal Shaw exploiting a fascinating new vein at the top of his form, and second, because, for all its faults, the Methuselah cycle nevertheless contains Shaw's subtlest thoughts and his widest, deepest, and most steadfast look at human existence.

CHAPTER TWELVE

Saint Joan

Back to Methuselah is not only a dramatic essay on politics and biology. It also provides the iconography, as Shaw called it, for the religion Don Juan first preached in the hell scene of *Man and Superman*. Adam's fall, in Shaw's interpretation of the Eden story, is due to his original sin of negligence, that is, to his failure to exercise his will effectively once his limited life span gave him only a limited interest in the future. From his failure of will and from Cain's desire for self-aggrandisement spring the social evils of idleness, violence, and exploitation. After presenting the fall in this new perspective, Shaw first announces a new gospel, and then shows us a new elect who are biologically redeemed from the fallen state of man. Finally, the ministers of godhead triumph over matter, death, and evil. But Shaw did not, however, find virtue only in the future: man's present corrupt state did not preclude the appearance from time to time of exceptional individuals who constitute an order of sainthood. It is logical, then, that Shaw, having dramatized a new body of myth for his religion of creative evolution in one set of plays, should next have undertaken to write a chapter of its hagiography.

For his subject Shaw chose Joan of Arc. But why did he pick this particular medieval saint? Perhaps we may best see what Shaw is about if we look at his play in the light of the philosophy of history. John Stuart Mill, following the French critic Saint-Simon, has pointed out that ages of faith and of doubt have tended to succeed each other historically. Nowhere is this theory better borne out than in the historiography of Joan. No one has ever been more trenchantly debunked or more piously exalted. Rationalistic ages have deprecated her, while the alternating ages of faith have reaffirmed their belief in her greatness. To see the contrast clearly we need only set Voltaire's portrait of Joan side by side with Schiller's or Southey's: the eighteenth century, which laughed at saints and heroes, pooh-poohed her, while the nineteenth century put her back on a pedestal. On the one hand we have a hilarious spoofing of her story, on the other a spurious romantic idealization.

Shaw's relation to these various currents of faith and skepticism is by no means simple, since he was at the same time the spiritual heir of the Enlightenment and of the transcendental reaction against it. Among his intellectual forebears are both Voltaire, the mocker, and Carlyle, the arch-anti-*philosophe*. He shared with the utilitarians both their distrust of moral traditions based on mere custom or taboo, and their determination to take a hard look at the practical consequences of human actions quite apart from high motives and good intentions. But though he found the negative weapons of utilitarian criticism useful for demolishing dead ideals, he is not, in a positive sense, a utilitarian at all, since he rejects both their rationalistic logic and their hedonist ethics. When it comes to beliefs and values, he is, on the contrary, a Platonist, an apriorist, an antipragmatist, and a mystic.

Mill thought the best of all worlds would combine the free critical spirit of a skeptical age with the coherent convictions and fervor of an age of "organic" faith. Shaw's *Saint Joan* is an attempt to achieve a Millite synthesis through the evaluation of one remarkable historical figure. If we want to understand the play we must be aware of how these two opposing currents mingle in it and find their resolution. To take two points on each side of the balance: in its rejection of supernaturalism and its indictment of orthodoxy (as embodied in the Inquisition), *Saint Joan* is an infidel drama; in its view of Joan's visions as superratiocinative and its celebration of her mystic sainthood, it belongs to the tradition of faith.

Shaw read scores of writers on Joan. He mentions at least a dozen by name—Shakespeare, Voltaire, Schiller, Michelet, Henri Martin, Henri Wallon, Marcel Poullin, Mark Twain, Tom Taylor, Percy MacKaye, Anatole France, and Andrew Lang.[1] Their writings include, respectively, a political melodrama, a mock-heroic poem, a tragedy, four historical studies, a novel, two more plays, and two critical biographies. Most of these works fit clearly into one or the other of the infidel and the fideist traditions. The one exception is the play by Shakespeare—or whoever was responsible for the disputed authorship of *Henry VI, Part I*. Here the playwright violates the general rule that the fideist plays are favorable to Joan and the infidel ones critical of her and her admirers. The author clearly believes in Joan, but he believes in her as the agent of diabolical, not of heavenly, powers. Reflecting the scurrilous popular Anglo-Burgundian estimate of Joan current in England until the seventeenth century and most accessible to Elizabethan readers in the pages of Holinshed's *Chronicles*, the play treats Joan as a harlot-witch who owes her victories to the devil. Yet even this melodrama cannot be said to be without influence on Shaw, for he takes the anti-Joan bias that runs throughout and ascribes it to his English chaplain, De Stogumber.

The most influential debunking works on Joan have been Voltaire's *La Pucelle* (*c.* 1730) and Anatole France's *Vie de Jeanne d'Arc* (1908). Voltaire's poem is less an attempt to write history than an exuberant exercise in anticlericalism. Voltaire is above all else interested in poking fun at miracle-mongering, saint-worship, and belief in the magical powers of virginity as they persisted into the Age of Reason. While anti-Joan sentiment lingered in England, a pro-Joan cult had grown up in France, carefully fostered by the clergy as a prop to popular religion. To counter this, Voltaire impishly turns Joan into a bouncing chambermaid whose seduction is the chief aim of English strategy. Ribald, satirical, and wildly extravagant at every turn, Voltaire has no compunction about departing from history by marrying Joan off to Dunois and ending his poem with their wedding. Anatole France's biography, by contrast, is a model of scholarly sobriety, completely free from Voltaire's comic and erotic license. Yet for all its difference in tone and method, it is still the work of a man who is patently grinding the same axes. France is reacting against Joan's nineteenth-century rehabilitation as Voltaire reacted against her seventeenth- and eighteenth-century cult. Nor, though France (like Voltaire) is sympathetic to Joan as a person, does he believe in her greatness. From his skeptical point of view her visions are simply hysterical hallucinations, her mission a priestly stratagem to increase the prestige of the Church in the national struggle, and her military prowess a mere legend grown up around a simple young girl who was no more than the army's mascot.

Shaw's play is not without its Voltairism, particularly in its treatment of popular credulity. Moreover, though he gives us dignified churchmen who are models of personal integrity rather than absurd figures of fun, Shaw is not, in the last analysis, one whit less anti-ecclesiastical. Shaw's basic approach, however, is distinctly closer to the line of mid-nineteenth-century French liberal historians, of whom Jules Michelet was the most important.[2] These writers, though outside the Church, were much more sympathetic to the Middle Ages and to Joan's messianic side than the *philosophes* had been. Yet Shaw is as critical of several aspects of nineteenth-century Johannamania as he was of Voltaire and France. He especially decried the tendency to make Joan a romantic heroine or a melodramatic victim. Here Schiller and Mark Twain struck him as the prime offenders. Schiller wrote *Die Jungfrau von Orleans* (1801) as a corrective to Voltaire's farcical irreverence. In it, Joan is a lyrically eloquent warrior-prophetess, torn between patriotism and love for an enemy soldier. Her amorous dilemma, and the fact that Schiller's Maid dies, not at the stake, but on the battlefield, removes her story as far from history in the direction of high romance as Voltaire's mock-epic does in the direction of freewheeling satire. Shaw praised *Die Jungfrau* as a "tender and beautiful picture" but complained that Schiller had idealized Joan out of all recognition. Nor did Mark Twain's serious fictionalized biography, purportedly the memoirs of Joan's page, please him better. Twain's book is sympathetic melodrama, or *Henry VI* turned upside down. His *Personal Recollections of Joan of Arc* (1896) transforms Joan into a sweetly pathetic child saint, surrounded by ugly monsters. Cauchon is an obese butcher, so that Joan's relation to him is not unlike Little Nell's to Quilp. And though Twain is not antipathetic to Catholicism, he is intensely hostile to the fifteenth century, which he denounces as the "brutallest" and "rottenest" era since the Dark Ages.

Depictions of Joan on the English stage were no novelty before Shaw. Two versions he was personally familiar with were those of Tom Taylor, the Victorian dramatist, and Percy MacKaye, a contemporary American littérateur. Taylor's *Joan of Arc* (1871) was a popular melodrama not far removed from Twain in spirit, with a suborned spy in place of Cauchon as the stage villain. Then in 1902 an event occurred which put English-language treatments of Joan's story on a new footing. In that year T. Douglas Murray published a full translation of Quicherat's transcriptions of the trial of 1431 and the rehabilitation proceedings of 1456 under the title *Jeanne d'Arc, Maid of Orleans, Deliverer of France: Being the Story of Her Life, Her Achievements and Her Death, as Attested on Oath and Set Forth in the Original Documents*. Later, this translation was to become the immediate source for Shaw's own play, but in the meantime Mrs. Patrick Campbell drew MacKaye's attention to it as possible material for the stage. The resulting drama, *Jeanne d'Arc* (1906), belongs, like Shaw's, to the literary tradition of English Pre-Raphaelitism. But MacKaye's Pre-Raphaelitism is not of the vigorous Shavian sort; rather it is Yeatsian—that is, poetically romantic and picturesque. MacKaye's Joan is no robust farm girl, but a recognizable cousin of Yeats's wistful Countess Cathleen, and like the latter, a great breaker of hearts. The play's highly self-conscious neomedievalism, though very pretty, is far from the rough realism of the popular medieval stage. After watching Julia Marlowe perform the title role, Shaw remarked that MacKaye's heroine was "pitiable, sentimental, and in the technical melodramatic sense, 'sympathetic'" and about as much like Joan "as Joan's kitten was like Joan's charger."[3]

After all this abuse, adulation, bawdry, debunking, melodrama, and romance, the reader may be tempted to exclaim skeptically, "Tot homines, tot Johannae," and to decide that men have simply recreated Joan from age to age after their own image. Obviously, to write about Joan is, like writing about Christ, to reveal not only one's religious beliefs, but also one's conception of the possibilities and limits of human life itself. It is also to reveal one's views on sainthood and heroism, on the capacities of women, and on the political and historical forces that shape society. Shaw, in writing *Saint Joan*, had all these matters in mind.

We may begin with Joan's sainthood, since from among the multitude of epithets bestowed on her by friend and foe, Shaw has chosen "Saint" for his title. His choice was not simply a way of pointing up the irony of the Church's turnabout at her canonization in 1920.

Traditionally, saints, in the orthodox ecclesiastical sense of the word, have been distinguished from other men by their miracle-working, by their self-mortification, and by their expiatory martyr-doms, which have been regarded as contributing to a vicarious treasury of merit for mankind. All of these notions of sainthood Shaw emphatically rejects.[4] Far from countenancing supernaturalism, Shaw treats miracles as satirically as Voltaire and France do. He is even more adamant on the subject of self-mortification. While Schopenhauer had praised Christian above Greek tragedy on the ground that the Christian saint negates his will, "joyfully forsaking the world," Shaw, who does not share Schopenhauer's belief in human depravity, thinks man is saved by affirming his will, not by negating it. Joan's triumph lies just in this—her assertion of her will —and the pride which the Archbishop, looking at her from the Greco-Christian point of view, denounces as *hubris* is for Shaw the source of her salvation, pride and its concomitant, self-respect, being exactly what the Dauphin, the court, and the French ecclesiastics have been lacking.

As to the horrific side of martyrdom—the side which has always made the greatest appeal to the popular imagination—Shaw considers it on exactly the same level with the attraction of grisly tragedies reported in sensational newspapers. When he gave a radio speech in 1931 on the five hundredth anniversary of her death, he begged his audience to forget Joan had ever been burned.[5] Furthermore, he strongly condemned the moral theory that regarded such deaths as expiatory sacrifices. Strangely enough, even liberal historians have been tinged with such notions: Michelet, though strongly in reaction against clericalism, nevertheless imagined Joan as longing for a "purifying death." This stupid attitude, which finds something morally efficacious in torture, so tried Shaw's patience that on one occasion he was moved to cry out in exasperation that he hated the cross as he hated all gibbets.

Yet sainthood is for Shaw something more than the mere absurdity it was for Voltaire and Anatole France. For all his unorthodoxy, Shaw is a man who looks at the world primarily in theological terms, and the epithet of his title makes a serious claim for Joan's eligibility in a Shavian "Communion of Saints" whose canon, including as it does non-Christians like Socrates and Mahomet, and even professed atheists like Shelley, is more catholic than the canon of Catholicism. Carlyle also speaks of a "Communion of Saints" in this broader sense, and Shaw follows the Carlylean tradition further in calling the power which moves Joan miraculous and mystical, since, though it is not supernatural, it is nevertheless superpersonal and outside the realm of logic or reason. In so doing, he equates the life force, or evolutionary appetite, with what a theologian would call the will of God. Joan's suffering is holy, not as an expiation, but because it is the consequence of her struggle to advance the race, and as such is "the food of godhead." Obviously, such a view of Joan was calculated to provoke dissent from rationalists and orthodox Christians in equal measure. It is not, then, at all paradoxical that a churchgoer like T. S. Eliot should have applauded what he called the "steam-rollering" of Shaw by J. M. Robertson, the arch-rationalist, in the latter's *Mr. Shaw and "The Maid."* [6] Indeed, Shaw must have considered Eliot's attack on his play from the orthodox position a high compliment, since it implied that he had recognized that, in *Saint Joan*, a live religion was at work competing for men's souls with his own Anglo-Catholicism. In this light, Eliot's own *Murder in the Cathedral* can be regarded as an attempt to reaffirm the ecclesiastical ideal of sainthood in reply to Shaw's challenge.

Skeptical historians have not only denied the religious nature of Joan's inspiration; they have also cast doubt on her prowess as a warrior. Shaw's preface and play take direct issue here with Anatole France, who simply refused to credit the possibility that an uneducated girl in her teens could have acted as an effective military leader. Robertson in his turn accused Shaw of falling back on mere "historic polemic" in making his claims for Joan.[7] But whether or not this is the case may be seen by turning to the record of sworn testimony at the rehabilitation trial. Here the French general, Alençon, though he stresses Joan's naïveté in other matters, speaks of the amazement he felt on discovering that "for warlike things— bearing the lance, assembling an army, ordering military operations, directing artillery—she was most skilful." Dunois, too, states quite as unequivocally that Joan "executed many marvelous manoeuvres which had not been thought of by two or three accomplished generals

working together." [8] Since the aim of the rehabilitation proceedings
was specifically to establish Joan's sanctity and piety in order to clear
her of the charge of witchcraft, and since any evidence as to her
military ability was, so to speak, gratuitous, and even detrimental to
the view that her victories were chiefly the result of divine favor, we
may safely trust the record at this point and assume that for all his
trenchancy Robertson is here simply indulging in skepticism for
skepticism's sake.

Having shorn Joan's legend of its supernaturalism and her death
of its mystery as a ritual atonement, Shaw was also determined to
remove the accretions of popular romance. This meant de-eroticizing
Joan and desentimentalizing her. Before Shaw, nearly every literary
man who had dealt with her story added some sexual element for
dramatic interest: Shakespeare gives her the baleful attractiveness of
a villainess in a spy novel, Voltaire a luscious nubility, Schiller a
broken heart, and Mark Twain a winsomeness capable of engaging
male sympathies at a glance. Shaw, by denying that Joan had any
"touching and charming love affairs," and by citing her comrades'
testimony on her lack of sex appeal, broke radically with the traditions of literary history. His Joan is not a soft woman who melts
men's hearts, but a bossy one who stirs them. His models were not the
heroines of romance, but the militant leaders of the woman's suffrage
movement in the first decades of the twentieth century. [9] To this force
of will he adds a peasant directness of expression which is surely
closer to the mark than the chivalry Andrew Lang [10] and the Renaissance romance writers ascribe to her. Indeed, if one reads her letters,
there is more of the style of Khrushchev in them than of Chaucer's
"parfit gentil knight." There she reveals herself, as in Shaw's play, as
a woman lacking both aristocratic suavity and middle-class caution,
but amply endowed with courage, blunt vigor, and common sense.

Shaw's endorsement of Joan's nationalism is perhaps more surprising. In this matter he was anticipated by Schiller, who, moved by
embryonic pan-Germanism, made Joan not merely a French patriot,
but a champion of nationalism per se. But Shaw, after all, deprecated
national self-determination as an ultimate good in itself; on the
contrary, he held that it was a positive advantage for small, barbaric
countries to be conquered by larger, more civilized ones. Yet though

Shaw was an internationalist rather than a romantic nationalist in politics, he also believed that it was a law of history that countries should pass through a nationalist phase as part of their organic development:

> Here, then, we have to face an inevitable order of social growth. First, the individual will have his personal liberty, in pursuit of which he will at last weary out and destroy feudal systems, mighty churches, medieval orders, slave-holding oligarchies, and what else may stand in his way. Then he will enlarge his social consciousness from his individual self to the nation of which he is a unit; and he will have his national liberty as he had his personal liberty, nor will all the excellent reasons in the world avail finally against him .... The third step is the federation of nationalities; but you cannot induce him to forgo the achievement of national independence on the ground that international federation is a step higher.[11]

When Shaw wrote these words, he was thinking, not of medieval France, but of contemporary Ireland. Obviously, he considered the Hundred Years War an object lesson in the futility of England's trying to impose its rule on another country against its will. In a defense of the play he sent to the Theatre Guild, Shaw argued that he would not have written *Saint Joan* if he had not thought it had immediate relevance in "a world situation in which we see whole peoples perishing and dragging us towards the abyss which has swallowed them, all for want of any grasp of the political forces that move civilization."[12] Today, forty years later, America's frequent blindness to the meaning of nationalist and social revolutions throughout the world might have struck him as another cogent example of the consequences of an inadequate philosophy of history.

Shaw's ascription to Joan of crypto-Protestant leanings has aroused even more controversy than his making her a nationalist. Once again, Shaw was not the first person to set forth such a theory, though we may safely speculate that he was not familiar with the obscure German theological study in which it was originally formulated in 1841.[13] J. M. Robertson, who considered this idea of Joan's Protestantism a typical Shavian *jeu d'esprit*, rejected it as fantastically absurd. But since he also admits that the Church has had its Protestant dissenters from the first century on, there seems to be little reason why he should object to the adjective being applied to Joan. The real point of course is the meaning to be given to the word "Protestant." If it is restricted to someone who founds or joins a new church in opposition to the Church of Rome, then obviously Joan does not qualify. But Shaw freely admits Joan's devoutness and piety and her failure to challenge the Church on doctrinal grounds, and is careful to point out that he is using the term only to designate someone who reserves the right to place his private judgment above the authoritative decision of an ecclesiastical court.

Only at one point does it seem to me that Shaw seriously mis-interprets Joan's career, and this mistake has to do not with her character, but with her situation. Shaw sees Joan's trial as pre-eminently a confrontation between a new prophet and the representa-tives of the status quo. In this respect he endows it with the same significance for the Middle Ages that the trial of Socrates had for the history of Athens. But this is to miss a salient fact in fifteenth-century French politics—that the Hundred Years War was a French civil war as well as an Anglo-French conflict. Joan's party was opposed by a group of Frenchmen who were pro-English and pro-Burgundian because of their indignation at the Dauphin's complicity in the murder of Duke John the Fearless. To the extent that he belonged to this party, it is impossible to regard Cauchon as an unbiased spokes-man for medieval Catholicism. True, there is, on the other hand, no reason to stereotype Cauchon as a villain as Mark Twain does. But his sincerity at the trial was the sincerity of a man who had com-mitted himself to one side in a bitter political quarrel. Though he was punctilious about points of law even to the extent of exasperating Joan's more violent adversaries, his intimidation of witnesses and scribes at her trial reveals his real commitment. In brief, the court at Rouen was not the impartial tribunal the contemporary Council of Basel might conceivably have been.[14]

But if Shaw inadvertently distorts history, the lesson he is trying to teach—that the saint will encounter his strongest, most dangerous opposition from the most high-minded and best-intentioned members of society—is a true and significant one. Even as a misreading of history, it is more nobly generous than the view of Robertson, who simply affirms in his book that justice was denied Joan because the

Christian dogma of belief "excludes the conception of justice, once for all." In addition, it is more cogent than the Church's official argument exculpating itself from responsibility for Joan's death—that Cauchon was simply acting illegally in denying Joan's appeal to the Pope. Can the Church be honestly certain as to what the outcome of that appeal would have been? Joan's spirit, as Shaw noted, was as adamant as Hus's or Luther's. Surely his contention that Joan, if asked to deny her visions at Basel, would have stood her ground there just as firmly in the face of any command to recant, ought to give conscientious Catholics pause for thought. If Shaw, in creating his portrait of a fair and disinterested Cauchon, sought to make amends for the "abominable bigotry"[15] of his Irish Protestant boyhood, he nevertheless, by putting the question candidly and without animus, puts it all the more tellingly. As a result, any disinterested observer with a sense of irony will unavoidably feel there is a little too much that is comically self-congratulatory in the Church's decree of canonization.

Saint Joan, which was the occasion for awarding Shaw the Nobel Prize, did more than any other play to increase his prestige with the general public. Perhaps in reaction to this, some of his most sympathetic admirers have expressed large reservations about it. It is interesting to note the direction this criticism has taken. Where Victorian audiences would have been shocked by the lively irreverence of the play's opening scene, it has been what we may call the fideistic elements of the drama—its edification, its poetry, and its religious purpose—that have called forth the most significant twentieth-century attacks. In addition, formalist critics have objected to the explicit philosophizing and to the epilogue, which they have regarded as gratuitous to a dramatic tragedy. But, before we consider the play in relation to these matters, we may find it illuminating to look briefly at its individual episodes to see what they tell us about Shaw's intentions.

The first scene immediately makes clear Shaw's voluntarist, anti-rational view of Joan's temperament. Her encounter with the peppery squire, Baudricourt, is a piece of classical farce. As a feudal leader and a physically vigorous male, Baudricourt tries at first to impress his cringing steward with his own strong-mindedness. But when Joan enters, her soft-spoken determination turns aside the blustering soldier's fulminations as easily as the wind might turn the flame at a volcano's mouth. Baudricourt reveals himself as a fundamentally will-less person, Joan as a woman with a will of iron. Her triumph in the contest between them shows the power of will over circumstances and of belief over doubt. Yet Shaw treats these transcendental themes with positive breeziness, deliberately using his flair for humor to shake any conventionally pious or vapidly romantic preconception of the Maid the audience may be entertaining, even to the point of ending with the absurd pseudo-miracle of the eggs.[16]

Baudricourt has spirit but lacks direction. The courtiers at Chinon, by contrast, know what needs to be done, but are paralyzed, despairing, and unable to look beyond their own self-interest. They are all, in this sense, rational utilitarians. The Dauphin has so little force of conviction that he arouses only laughter, when, like the squire, he attempts to put his foot down. On the intellectual side, however, by far the most interesting member of the court is the Archbishop. He is the very spirit of skepticism in its most sophisticated and self-conscious form. Shaw is careful to place him historically by pointing out that he belongs not to Joan's world of medieval faith, but to the coming age of the Renaissance. He is a humanist scholar with so much of the doubter and cynic about him that Anatole France might either have satirized him as a worldly prelate or hailed him as kindred soul. A hollow fraud as a man of religion, he is nevertheless an astute statesman. He knows, for instance, that the faith of the multitude can very easily be sustained by clever stage effects and that the will to believe creates its own evidence. Still, he realizes that the faith that can move mountains is a force to be reckoned with, however silly the signs the mob accepts as pledges of divine favor. We thus watch the recognition scene with double vision, at once caught up in its drama and at the same time endowed with the Archbishop's skeptical detachment, as Joan unscrupulously (even "craftily," as Shaw expresses it [17]) exploits the superstition of the court for her own ends. For all this, we still inevitably thrill when selfishness and cowardice vanish before Joan's convictions. Faith, which appears to the court to have performed a miracle in guiding Joan to the Dauphin, has in all truth performed a greater miracle still in transforming supine men into potential fighters.

When Joan and Dunois meet at the Loire, Shaw suggests that the force that bears Joan onward is, like Shelley's West Wind, the *Zeitgeist* itself. Up to now we have simply seen this power objectified as the human will in dramatic conflict with obstacles in its way. Joan remains largely unconscious of the broader meaning of her mission, or has only the most naïve glimpses of its significance. Finally, however, in the tent scene, we have Joan's antifeudal nationalism and her Protestantism explicitly analyzed for us in the colloquy between Warwick and Cauchon. Edmund Wilson has taken exception to this discussion on the grounds that Chekhov would never have written it.[18] But this is to limit unduly the possibilities of drama as a commentary on human existence. Shaw admits in the play's preface the anachronism of the debate; but the function of the intellectual dramatist, he tells us, is to make his figures "more intelligible to themselves than they would be in real life" by revealing the hidden causes and currents that move individuals and nations. In a sense broader than Aristotle's, Shaw insists that drama must be "more philosophical than history."

The philosophical meaning of *Saint Joan* can be grasped only when we look at the play in relation to the conventional idea of tragedy. Here some teasing critical questions inevitably arise. For instance, is Shaw's philosophy of the life force compatible with the idea of tragedy at all?[19] To the extent that tragic drama is a drama of despair, obviously it is not. Schopenhauer's praise of tragedy as the highest form of poetic art because it dramatizes "the surrender not merely of life, but of the very will-to-live,"[20] would hardly have recommended tragedy to Shaw. In this regard, then, Shaw is essentially an antitragic dramatist, and belongs to the line of writers who have tended to dethrone tragedy from its place of honor among dramatic forms. But it is by no means possible to write Shaw off as a mere maverick on this account. We tend to forget that the critical tradition which is hostile to "pure" tragedy has been quite as persistent and is historically even older than the tradition which has exalted it. Plato, after all, thought tragedy demoralizing because it

fostered the emotions of grief and fear instead of courage and a sense
of civic responsibility. In our own day Karl Jaspers has warned us in
his *Tragedy Is Not Enough* that the cultivation of a tragic sense can
lead to a self-exaltation which is really a dangerous form of self-
indulgence. And even Hegel, one feels, if he had strictly followed the
logic of his own theory, should have placed a drama of reconciliation
like the *Oresteia* above a tragedy like *Antigone*, just as he places a
tragedy of ideological conflict like *Antigone* above a play of personal
misfortune like *Oedipus*.

Shaw attacks what might be called the infidel side of tragedy; he
wants to substitute for the tragedy of despair a tragedy of faith with
a radically different aesthetic. To this end he makes his play Hegelian,
neo-Gothic (or Pre-Raphaelite), and Promethean, and by implication,
anti-Aristotelian, anticlassical and anti-Shakespearean. The extent
to which this is the case has not been clear to most readers, some of
whom have argued that *Saint Joan* rigorously fulfills the canons of
classical tragic art. To a degree they have been misled by Shaw's
boast in his preface that he is writing classical tragedy, whereas in
fact he only intends by the term "classical" to distinguish any
serious, critical approach to literature from popular melodrama. If
we look deeper we will even find that the play, far from fulfilling, or
even simply ignoring, classical canons, is a deliberate repudiation of
classicism as it existed in Greek times and was revived by the
Renaissance. Moreover, since Aristotle is par excellence the theorist
of classical tragedy, it is specifically a negation of the conception of
tragedy set forth in the *Poetics*. Shaw makes this clear at the end of
the preface when he declares that the theater in its "Aristotelian
moments" is purgatorial, by which, through his punning reference to
the doctrine of catharsis, he means to imply that audiences are
ultimately bored by attempts to achieve perfection of artistic form
and can be fully engrossed only by drama which touches their lives
and interests at some vital point.

It should not surprise us to find that, just as *Arms and the Man* is a
critique of conventional romance, and *The Devil's Disciple* of conventional melodrama, so *Saint Joan* is a critique of traditionally held
theories of tragedy. Aristotle, for example, contends that the death on
the stage of a "pre-eminently just or virtuous" person can only out-

rage the sensibilities of an audience, and that a tragic hero must not be a saint, but a man capable of committing a tragic error.[21] Shaw, by contrast, goes out of his way to show that it is Joan's virtues, and not her defects, which bring about her death. This is the whole point of the cathedral scene, which attacks the sentimental idea that "we needs must love the highest when we see it" by showing how Joan's gifts inevitably provoke hostility. Those critics who, looking for Joan's *hamartia*, have ascribed her downfall to her vanity or her lack of prudence have put a false emphasis on minor details Shaw has introduced merely to humanize his heroine. Others have been deceived by the fact that the Archbishop, foreseeing the end of Joan's career, remarks. "The old Greek tragedy is rising among us. It is the chastisement of hubris."[22] But as we have already noted, Shaw conceives of the Archbishop as a man who belongs to a world alien to Joan's, who recognizes as his kin, not the saints, but Aristotle and Pythagoras. His Greco-Renaissance culture makes him wholly antipathetic to Joan. Those commentators who have quoted his words to show that Shaw is writing classical tragedy have simply missed the irony with which Shaw invests his pronouncements. As we have seen, pride is for Shaw a virtue.

The hostility to Renaissance ethics and aesthetics that pervades *Saint Joan* had its origin in one of the deepest-running currents of Victorian culture. Carlyle and Ruskin both attacked the Renaissance as an age which substituted commercial for religious ideals, and economic individualism for a sense of communal welfare. Ruskin went further and denounced it also as an artistic and cultural debacle in which theatricality and rhetorical posturing had replaced realistic observation and sincere expression of feeling in painting and literature. It is from Ruskin that Shaw derived the idea that Shakespeare had drawn no heroes, that is, men with a positive social or religious philosophy. Hence the "void in the Elizabethan drama" he deplores in his preface as the consequence of the pervading infidelism of the Renaissance. As an antidote to rhetorical neoclassicism in art, Shaw favored a return to what he calls the Gothic style, which, instead of requiring a uniform elevation of sentiment and diction throughout (that is to say, neoclassical decorum), combined imaginative sublimity with homely realism.[23] Thus *Saint Joan*, with its

mixture of broad farce and exaltation, is Pre-Raphaelite in style as
well as in substance, and closer, in its juxtaposition of comedy and
saintliness, to the religious drama of the Middle Ages than to anything in Elizabethan or later theatrical literature. Its aesthetic is that
of *Modern Painters* and *The Stones of Venice*, purged of Ruskin's
conventional evangelical piety and his nature worship.

The theory of tragedy which comes closest to Shaw's is that set
forth by Hegel in his *Philosophy of Fine Art*. This is not to say that
Shaw in *Saint Joan* consciously attempted to write a Hegelian drama
or that he had even read this or any of Hegel's other voluminous
writings on tragedy. Rather, the affinity with Hegel springs from
what we may call the natural Hegelianism of Shaw's mind. Certainly
Saint Joan is Hegelian in its treatment of historical processes,
dramatizing as it does the evolving forces of nationalism and individualism and the feudal and authoritarian reactions those move-
ments provoke. Hegel and Shaw both agreed that conflicts of this
sort were the very substance of drama. Both ruled out personal
ambition and the "hazards of crime" as adequate subjects for high
tragedy, though many playwrights (including Shakespeare) have
sought to make tragedy out of these ingredients. "Abstract evil,"
Hegel held, anticipating Shaw, "neither possesses truth in itself, nor
does it arouse interest." [24] For each of them the only really significant
tragic subjects were those collisions between different moral imperatives, both apparently "good," which make mutually contradictory
demands. This is why Hegel thought of *Antigone*, with its conflict
between family and social duties, as the archetypal tragedy. But
Hegel's most succinct and illuminating remarks on tragedy occur,
significantly enough, not in a discussion of a stage play, but of a real
historical event, the trial of Socrates:

> In genuine tragedy, then, [there] must be powers both alike moral
> and justifiable, which from this side and from that, come into
> collision; and such was the fate of Socrates. His fate therefore is
> not merely personal, and as it were part of the romance of an
> individual: it is the general fate, in all its tragedy—the tragedy of
> Athens, of Greece, which is therein carried out. Two opposed
> Rights come forth: the one breaks itself to pieces against the other:
> in this way, both alike suffer loss; while both alike are justified the

one towards the other: not as if this were right, that other wrong. On the one side is the religious claim, the unconscious moral habit: the other principle, over against it, is the equally religious claim—the claim of the consciousness, of the reason, creating a world out of itself, the claim to eat of the tree of the knowledge of good and evil. The latter remains the common principle of philosophy for all time to come.[25]

It is a view of tragedy akin to Hegel's Shaw has in mind when he insists that Joan's trial must not be seen as popular melodrama but as the confrontation of antagonistic historical forces of broad significance. Shaw's effort to objectify and depersonalize the situation has led some commentators to argue that he does not in effect even take sides. Eric Bentley, usually a perspicacious judge of Shaw's intentions, has described him as writing neither an "individualist defense of Joan" nor a "collectivist defense of social order," but as merely "depicting the clash."[26] Obviously, if we have a fatal disagreement between two apparent "goods," the problem does arise as to how we should interpret the resulting catastrophe. We might, for instance, merely respond with the same supine awe we feel on contemplating the *Titanic*'s smashing into the iceberg. Or, looking at the situation from the vantage of history, one might adopt the "unripe moment" attitude. This is, in sum, what Hegel does in the case of Socrates. Hegel thinks the Athenians were right in condemning Socrates for encouraging disobedience to parents and for setting his own private daemon above the state religion. He also maintains that they were right in reversing their verdict and condemning Socrates' judges a few years later. The Athenians were simply not historically ready to accept Socrates on the first occasion; later they had caught up with him, but he had in the meantime to pay for his forwardness.

But is this really Shaw's attitude toward Joan? Hegel's defense of the Athenians rests on his general premise that the state is an absolute incapable of wrong, a position Shaw emphatically rejected.[27] Shaw pointedly declared that a historian who would defend Joan's burning would defend anything. We must remember that for Shaw, the archetypal tragedy is not *Antigone*, but *Prometheus*. His aim is not to defend social stupidities but to educate us out of them. The reason

he enters so sympathetically into the mentality of the Inquisition is
not to exonerate it, but merely to make his point that the most
nefarious institutions and their administrators always seem perfectly
justified in their own eyes and in the eyes of most onlookers. Then,
too, he wants to destroy any smug suppositions we may be nursing
in our minds about a bad past and a good present, and to counteract
the all but universal human tendency to decry historical bogeys like
the Inquisition and to accept their modern counterparts uncritically.
Shaw forces us to look at the trial with the eyes of the fifteenth
century, not because he thinks the Inquisition was, even in Hegel's
conditional sense of the term, "right," but because the fifteenth
century regarded its procedures as perfectly respectable and was just
as mistakenly comfortable about them as we are about our own law
courts.

Most people have failed to grasp Shaw's real outlook simply
because he makes the Inquisitor at the trial a mild, scholarly, saintly
old man.[28] But apart from the fact that Shaw seems to have modeled
his Inquisitor on the historical Torquemada, who had such a temperament, his intention is to warn us that it is just the sweet, saintly
old men who make the most dangerous apologists for judicial crimes.
Like Britannus in *Caesar and Cleopatra* and Judge Hallam in *Captain
Brassbound's Conversion*, the Inquisitor is sincerely convinced of the
horrors that would befall society if the office of judge and our system
of social punishments were to be abolished. Allowing the Inquisitor
to present his case as cogently as possible, Shaw provides him with a
consummately skillful rhetoric which is nevertheless shot through
and through with Shavian antijudicial irony:

> Mark what I say: the woman who quarrels with her clothes, and
> puts on the dress of a man, is like the man who throws off his fur
> gown and dresses like John the Baptist: they are followed, as
> surely as the night follows the day, by bands of wild women and
> men *who refuse to wear any clothes at all*. When maids will neither
> marry nor take regular vows, and men reject marriage and exalt
> their lusts into divine inspirations, then, as surely as the summer
> follows the spring, *they begin with polygamy, and end by incest.*
> Heresy at first seems innocent and even laudable; but it ends in
> *such a monstrous horror of unnatural wickedness* that the most
> tender-hearted among you, if you saw it at work as I have seen it,

would clamor against the mercy of the Church in dealing with it. [Italics added.][29]

The most striking thing about his speech is the way it plays upon the audience's fears, and particularly, in the passages I have italicized, upon their sexual fears, to intimidate them and justify inquisitorial practices. The Inquisitor is a melodramatist who thinks the human race would run wild if there were no courts to restrain it. Yet so completely has the impression created by the Inquisitor's gentleman-liness numbed men's ability to detect the hysterical premises of his argument that Shaw found it necessary to remind critics of the drama that the man was, in his eyes, "a most infernal old scoun-drel."[30]

The Church's official defense of the Inquisition is to be found in the *Catholic Encyclopedia*. There, a brilliantly written article praises the "truly admirable sanctity" of many of the Inquisitorial judges, and adds, "There is absolutely no reason to look on the medieval ecclesiastical judge as intellectually and morally inferior to the modern judge."[31] Shaw, who apparently studied this essay most carefully in preparing his play, would have agreed; the modern judge and the Inquisitor stand side by side in his vision, too, but not as the saviors of civilization. Both justify terrorism out of panic fear. The rhetoric of Shaw's Inquisitor condemning heresy is identical with that of the defenders of our present-day laws on, say, sexual offenses, obscenity, or drug-taking. The notion that such Inquisitorial atti-tudes are historically obsolete is soon belied by a little experience of modern criminal prosecutions in these areas. The final irony comes from the fact that the arguments Shaw gives the Inquisitor are exactly those used by the nineteenth-century American Quaker historian H. C. Lea in his monumental *History of the Inquisition* to justify the extermination of the Albigensians, whose ultra-asceticism and contempt for marriage could only, in Lea's view, "have prob-ably resulted in lawless concubinage and the destruction of the institution of the family."[32] With certificates of indemnity like this from Protestant writers, the *Catholic Encyclopedia*, which quotes Lea at length, has no difficulty at all in establishing that the Inquisition was a bulwark of popular social virtues.

The Inquisitor (following the *Encyclopedia*) also argues that only the Inquisition stands between the heretic and popular wrath. Shaw disposes of this line of reasoning in his essay on imprisonment: "It is said, and it is to a certain degree true, that if the Government does not lawfully organize and execute popular vengeance, the populace will rise and execute this vengeance lawlessly for itself. The standard defense of the Inquisition is that without it no heretic's life would have been safe."[33] But, Shaw replies crushingly, a government that cannot control a lynch mob cannot rule at all. It is because of the parallels with modern administration of justice that Shaw puts a forensic tour de force into the mouth of the Inquisitor. The latter is a scoundrel not because he is a medieval ecclesiastic, but because of what he shares in common with most modern Protestants and atheists—a conviction that only through censorship, expiatory punishments, and cruel deterrents can the human race be kept from running amok. In the epilogue that closes the play Shaw pointedly makes him transcend his moment in history and speak for *all* judges in "the blindness and bondage of the law."

Shaw not only despises "justice" as the vengeance principle self-righteously parading in a moral disguise; he is particularly opposed to "the crime of imprisonment." Imagining ourselves superior to the age of the stake and the rack, we tolerate the refined torture of incarceration, and indeed accept it unthinkingly as a matter-of-fact routine until with us, as with the Inquisitor, who has become used to seeing girls burned, "habit is everything." When Joan thinks she can escape death by signing a recantation she sensibly signs it. The anger she shows on discovering that her choice lies not between the fire and freedom, but the fire and prison, matches Shaw's own contempt for a society that cages men and women without thinking twice about it:

> Bread has no sorrow for me, and water no affliction. But to shut me from the light of the sky and the sight of the fields and flowers; to chain my feet so that I can never again ride with the soldiers nor climb the hills; to make me breathe foul damp darkness, and keep me from everything that brings me back to the love of God when your wickedness and foolishness tempt me to hate Him: all this is worse than the furnace in the Bible that was heated seven times . . . . without these things I cannot live, and by your

wanting to take them away from me, or from any human creature, I know that your counsel is of the devil, and that mine is of God.[34]

It is a sign of our times that though literary critics have commented on Joan's diction in this speech, none have pointed out that, as members of a civilization capable of locking men up for fifty or sixty years, we are as guilty as her judges, and companion objects of her— and Shaw's—scorn.

This same blindness to the realities of human suffering afflicts De Stogumber, the Joan-baiting English chaplain in Shaw's play. In him, Shaw provides us with a fifteenth-century analogue of the anti-Hun jingoism of World War I and the insane patriotism that prompted the Black and Tan terror in Ireland. What chiefly characterizes the priest's hatred is its abstract, unimaginative quality. When De Stogumber actually witnesses Joan's burning he reacts hysterically, and his dramatic breakdown provides Shaw's tragedy with its note of pity and terror.[35] But Shaw does not want to purge us of these emotions: his aim is not to produce a catharsis. Instead, he introduces them with the intention of warning us of our own insensitivity to cruelty and of the danger of giving rein to the feelings roused by war panic.

The defeats of Prometheus are the "staple of tragedy," Shaw wrote in a review in the nineties.[36] Joan's life was for him a historical tragedy in the Promethean mold, in which "all the forces that bring about the catastrophe are on the grandest scale; and the individual soul on which they press is of the most indomitable force and temper."[37] Like Prometheus, Joan challenges the gods, and though, like him, she fails, she also resembles the Greek hero in showing a steadfast courage that speaks to the ages. But of course the failure is not the whole story. The defeats of Prometheus, looked at from the perspective of history, have a way of losing their tragic quality and taking on some of the ironic aspects of tragicomedy. That is what Shaw means by declaring in his preface that when we kill saintly prophets, "the angels may weep at the murder, but the gods laugh at the murderers." Eventually the moment of horror gives way to the moment of philosophical bemusement as we observe mankind revering and worshiping what it first feared and loathed.

In the epilogue to *Saint Joan* we hear the laughter of the gods. Shaw's seriocomic postscript tells us of Joan's canonization, but denies us any sentimental glow of pleasure at seeing the golden aureole fitted into place, or sense of gratification at the knowledge of justice done. The actors of her drama all praise her, but they also flinch at the idea of her return to life. Warwick, the eternal politician, admits that he would once more have to face political necessities; Cauchon, the eternal priest, can find no way of distinguishing private judgment from diabolical possession; and the Inquisitor is unable to see how the scourge he calls justice could be dispensed with. Only that modest pragmatist Charles VI is able to understand that what ails the leaders of Church and State is simply that they are "not big enough" for Joan. The world will continue to kill its saints and heroes until it has grown to their stature and produced a society of saints and heroes. Nor until we conquer that fear which is ultimately a fear of ourselves will this be possible. In the meantime, any certificate of sanctification we may issue for Joan remains factitious if it does not imply a toleration for future heretics.

Saint Joan is the last of Shaw's major plays. What he wrote after it is by way of postscript to his career as a playwright, a resetting of the themes of his major works in new keys. Such satires as *The Apple Cart, Too True to Be Good,* and *Geneva* show him responding to a new world mood and to new world crises. But delightful and provocative as some of these sunset dramas are, they add nothing essential to our understanding of Shaw as a world dramatist and critic of civilization. *Saint Joan* stands alone as Shaw's last great tribute to human greatness. As such it is one of the supreme statements of religious faith in a post-Christian world, the final masterpiece of a man who was willing to hope and think and challenge his readers to the end.

Notes

CHAPTER ONE   Unpleasant Prelude

1. Preface to *Three Plays by Brieux, Prefaces by Bernard Shaw* (London: Odhams, 1938), p. 196.

2. *Essays in Fabian Socialism* (London: Constable, 1949), p. 4.

3. Compare Dickens' *Hard Times*, with the curmudgeonly Bounderby and the blameless workman, Stephen Blackpool. Cf. also "Daly Undaunted" (July 18, 1896), *Our Theatres in the Nineties* (London: Constable, 1948), II, 192–193: "We are coming fast to a melodramatic formula in which the villain shall be a bad employer and the hero a Socialist; but that formula is no truer to life than the old one in which the villain was a lawyer and the hero a Jack Tar. . . . Take *Widowers' Houses*; cut out the passages which convict the audience of being just as responsible for the slums as the landlord is; make the hero a ranting Socialist instead of a perfectly commonplace young gentleman; make the heroine an angel instead of her father's daughter only one generation removed from the wash-tub; and you have the successful melodrama of tomorrow." All of the reviews reprinted in *Our Theatres in the Nineties* originally appeared in the *Saturday Review*.

4. Papers by command C4402, Sessions October 1884–August 1885, Vol. XXX, 1884–1885.

5. The longhand manuscript of *Widowers' Houses* in the Berg Collection, New York Public Library, contains a note by Shaw to the effect that the first two acts were written in 1885, the first part of Act Three in 1890, and the second part in 1892. The last page is dated August 1, 1892. Three additional pages were added on November 20. This version differs in its details from the Independent Theatre edition of 1893. There are a great many changes in the dialogue between this edition and the revised version issued in *Unpleasant Plays* in 1898. See Charles H. Shattuck, "Bernard Shaw's 'Bad Quarto,'" *JEGP*, LIV (October 1955), 651–663. The separate preface to the 1893 version is reprinted in Shaw's collected *Prefaces* (see note 1, above). Shaw published an interview about the play in the *Star*, November 29, 1892, p. 2. There is a shorthand early draft of the play in the British Museum (Additional MS 50594).

6. In Act Two (pp. 78–79) of the Berg Collection manuscript, Sartorius defends himself as follows: "As to my business, it is simply to provide

homes for poor people driven into the streets by sentimental acts of parliament by which the houses of 2000 laborers are pulled down to make room for fancy dwellings for 1000 artisans and small tradesmen. Do you think that such houses can be had for nothing? I have not found it so, I assure you. My houses must be paid for, otherwise they could not be obtained nor kept up. I could not let them for nothing even if I thought such mistaken philanthropy admirable, in spite of the pauperization of the people and the sapping of their independence that would certainly be the first result of it. . . . My young friend, these poor people do not know how to live in handsome residences: they would wreck them in a week. If I were to carry out your benevolent plan, they would wrench off the water-taps and gas fittings and sell them for a twentieth part of their cost. They would burn the woodwork and smash the glass and earthenware."

7. In a letter of June 8, 1909, to Iden Payne, Shaw wrote: "In the first act, you have two things to remember, and everything else to forget. The two things are your mortal anxiety about your wife and children, and your dread of Sartorious [*sic*]. What the scene wants is pathos & sincerity, and not comic acting. The great effect [in the third act] is produced by the change in Lickcheese. . . . You must put on exquisitely clean make-up. Your hands must look dainty. . . . But the main thing is the change in character. Lickcheese of course remains as incapable as he ever was of being any better than the world around him; but he proves—when properly played—the truth of his statement in the first act that he could not have collected the rents from the parents of the starving children if he had not known that his own children would starve if he did not. With money he becomes good natured, genteel, kindly, pleased with himself, enormously conceited about his business ability, and indulgent to everybody else. There should be absolutely no unpleasantness at all about him; he should come into the middle of the cat-and-dog life led by the other people as a humanizing reconciling element. The audience should delight in him in a thoroughly friendly way; and he should wallow in their friendliness. If you cannot see all this, then I give you up forever: you will never make a Shavian actor" ("Some Unpublished Letters of George Bernard Shaw," *University of Buffalo Studies*, XVI [September 1939], 120–121).

8. For a revealing analysis of this side of the play, see Paul Hummert, "Marxist Elements in the Works of George Bernard Shaw" (Ph.D. dissertation, Northwestern University, 1953). For a comparison of Shaw's use of the "misalliance" theme in this play with its treatment in other Victorian dramas, see Martin Meisel, *Shaw and the Nineteenth-Century Theater* (Princeton: Princeton University Press, 1963), pp. 161–169.

9. Christ's animadversions appear in their fullest form in Mark 12: 38–40: "Beware of the scribes, which love to go in long clothing, and love salutations in the marketplaces, And the chief seats in the synagogues, and

the uppermost rooms at feasts: Which devour widows' houses, and for a pretence make long prayers: these shall receive greater damnation." Cf. also Luke 20:46–47, and Matthew 23:14. Ruskin uses the phrase "widows' houses" repeatedly in his social criticism. See also Stewart Headlam's use of it in *Christian Socialism* (Fabian Society Tract, No. 42).

10. British Museum Add. MS 50596A–G is of unusual interest in that this draft of *The Philanderer* contains a third act totally different from the published one. This act takes place four years after Julia's marriage to Paramore. Each has grown tired of the other, and they discuss the possibility of a trip to South Dakota, the one part of the world with reasonable divorce laws. Julia proposes to marry Charteris afterward, but Charteris protests that they are intellectually incompatible: "You and I are capital playmates, but we are not helpmates" (50596F, f. 40). The diaries in the London School of Economics show that Shaw began the play on March 29, 1893, discarded the first version of the third act on June 17, and began the revised version on June 22.

11. Stanley Winsten, *Jesting Apostle: The Life of Bernard Shaw* (London: Hutchinson, 1956), p. 85. For Shaw's relations with these two women, see St. John Ervine, *Bernard Shaw: His Life, Work and Friends* (New York: Morrow, 1956), pp. 164–165. In a note to Augustin Hamon in the typescript of the French translation of the play in the Hanley Collection, University of Texas, Shaw objects to his translating the English word "philanderer" as "Don Juan": "Don Juan will not do. Don Juan is rather a woman's hero; but a philanderer is never a hero to them. A philanderer is a man who likes women and is always playing with women and making love to them, but who never marries or seduces them." He suggested "flirteur" as a better word. The French version was published under the title *L'Homme aimé des femmes*.

12. For two trenchant essays on the conditions which form the background of Shaw's play, see H. Dendy, "The Position of Women in Industry," *National Review*, XXIII (August 1894), 806–814, and Lady Emilia Dilke, "The Industrial Position of Women," *Fortnightly Review*, LX (October 1893), 499–508.

13. The most famous of these was the series entitled "The Maiden Tribute of Modern Babylon," published by W. T. Stead in the *Pall Mall Gazette*, July–November 1885. See also the report of the Committee for the Suppression in the Traffic in English Girls (1886); A. S. Dyer, *European Slave Trade in English Girls* (1885); and *De l'organisation de la traite des blanches à Bruxelles* (1881).

14. Geoffrey Bullough, in "Literary Relations of Shaw's Mrs. Warren," *Philological Quarterly*, XLI (January 1962), 339–358, relates Shaw's play to Maupassant's story "Yvette" and to Janet Achurch's unpublished play, "Mrs. Daintry's Daughter." In a letter to the *Daily Chronicle* (April 30,

1898), Shaw explained that Janet Achurch had told him about a dramatiz-
able story in an "ultra-romantic" French novel, which he did not read.
This does not sound like Maupassant; Shaw denied any influence from
him or Ibsen. He had remarked to Janet, "I will work out the truth about
that mother some day."

15. Shaw follows Edward Westermarck in believing that incest taboos
spring from a natural and instinctive sexual antipathy between close
relatives, but did not see any objection to the marriage of brothers and
sisters who had grown up apart. See *Major Critical Essays* (London:
Constable, 1947), 13–14 n. The British Museum manuscript of the play
has the following speech by Vivie: "Frank was the most unbearable
thought of all, for I knew that he would press on me the sort of relation
that my mother's life had tainted for ever for me. I felt that I would rather
die than let him touch me with that in his mind" (Add. MS 50598C, f. 7).
A note in Shaw's hand in the proof copy of the play in the Hanley Collection identifies the two words Vivie writes out for Frank in Act Four to
describe her mother as "Prostitute and Procuress." These proofs are
dated July 21, 1897.

16. The characters in *Widowers' Houses* are naïvely unreflecting men
and women whose self-justifications are merely worn shibboleths they
seize on when attacked. In *Mrs. Warren's Profession*, by contrast, Shaw
explores the psychology of the "conventionally unconventional." Frank
acts according to the playboy-gambler's code of "good form," Praed
according to the code of sentimental bohemian anarchism; even the brainless Crofts prides himself on his freedom from "cant," though his "unconventional" defense of his blackguardism is banal in the extreme. In
Shaw's first half-dozen plays one can note the growing self-conscious
articulateness with which the characters define their moral positions. This
process reaches its culmination in the debate between the Devil and Don
Juan in *Man and Superman*.

CHAPTER TWO *Arms and the Man*

1. Wylie Sypher, "The Meanings of Comedy," in *Comedy: An Essay on
Comedy by George Meredith and Laughter by Henri Bergson* (Garden City,
N.Y.: Doubleday, 1956), p. 241.

2. "*Arms and the Man*," *Specimens of English Dramatic Criticism*, ed.
A. C. Ward (London: Oxford, 1945), p. 191. This review first appeared in
The World, April 25, 1894. William Irvine, in *The Universe of G. B. S.*
(New York: Whittlesey House, 1949), p. 170, also holds to the Gilbertist
view of the play. Shaw thought the one reviewer on the right track was
A. B. Walkley, who clearly distinguishes between Shaw's psychology and

Gilbert's ("*Arms and the Man*," *The Speaker*, IX [April 28, 1894], 471–472).

3. "An Old New Play and a New Old One" (February 23, 1895), *Our Theatres in the Nineties* (London: Constable, 1948), I, 42–43. This is not an *ad hoc* position on Shaw's part, since he consistently raises the same objections to merely galvanic farcical comedy throughout his reviews. See also II, 120–121 and 230–231, where he complains of the empty-heartedness of such comedy. Shaw wants to go beyond superficial Gilbertist inversions to a truly Blakean transvaluation of moral values.

4. *Plays Pleasant and Unpleasant*, II (London: Constable, 1949), xiii. In the 1898 edition, Shaw wrote "are in tears."

5. See Irvine, *The Universe of G. B. S.*, and also particularly Louis Kronenberger's introduction to *Arms and the Man* (New York: Bantam Books, 1960).

6. For instance, Shaw alleged in the play that Austrian and Russian officers acted as advisors to the two sides during the war. For diplomatic reasons both major powers "recalled" their advisors, but according to Shaw's inside information this seems to have been mere pretense. In answer to a questionnaire sent him by the editors of *To-Day*, he replied that "in the original MS, the names of the places were blank, and the characters were called simply The Father, The Daughter, The Stranger, The Heroic Lover, and so on. The incident of the machine-gun bound me to a recent war: that was all. My own historical information being rather confused, I asked Mr Sidney Webb to find out a good war for my purpose. He spent about two minutes in a rapid survey of every war that has ever been waged, and then told me that the Servo-Bulgarian was what I wanted. I then read the account of the war in the *Annual Register* with a modern railway map of the Balkan peninsula before me, and filled in my blanks, making all the action take place in Servia, in the house of a Servian family. I then read the play to Stepniak, and to the admiral who commanded the Bulgarian fleet during the war, who happens to reside in London just now. He made me change the scene from Servia to Bulgaria, and the characters from Servians to Bulgarians, and gave me descriptions of Bulgarian life and ideas which enabled me to fit my play exactly with local color and character. I followed the facts he gave me as closely as I could, because invented facts are the same stale stuff in all plays, one man's imagination being much the same as another's in such matters, whilst real facts are fresh and varied" (Vol. II, April 28, 1894, p. 373).

7. In the draft of *Arms and the Man* in the British Museum (Add. MS 50601 A–C), Act One is called the "prologue," and its opening page is dated November 26, 1893. The flyleaf of the MS contains the following notes on the Serbo-Bulgarian War: "General Leshyanin . . . Timok . . . General Jovanovitch, Danube/ Lom Palanka/ Nov. 14th 1885. Servia . . . Servian victories on the advance . . . / Frontier crossed at Vlassina/, Trn,

Tsaribrod, Klissura, & Bregova/ 15 Nov. Tsaribrod occupied, slight resistance/ 16 Nov. Kula captured, severe engagement/ Leshyanin advances on Widdin/ Jovanovitch turns Bul. position in the Dragoman pass./ Adlijeh and Izvor—advanced posts come within a days march of Sofia & main body of Servian army encamps, on 17th Nov. at Slivnitza/ Servian army driven back toward Dragm pass/ full retreat/ 26 Nov. P. Alex. enters Servian Territory with 50,000 men/ 27th Nov. occupies Pirot—stopped there by threat of Austrian intervention/ Leshyanin still before Widdin. Beats back Bul. attempts/ S & B appeal to the Powers Dec. 11/ Reply on 14th Dec. Com. of military attachés at Vienna of Ger, Fr, Russ, Eng, Ital, sits at Belgrade./ 21 Dec. Commission signs protocol that/ (by) 25 Dec. Servians shall evacuate Bul. ter./ 27 Dec. Bulgarians shall evacuate Pirot/ Armistice to continue to 1 Mar. Accepted by both & carried out/ 3 Mar. Treaty signed at Bucharest/ 4 Mar. Serbian army demobilized (date of decree)/ 5 Mar. Bulgarian army demobilized/ 22 Aug. Kidnapping of P. Alex./ 28 Aug. Congratulations from Milan on his restoration." These notes are mainly based on the account of the war in the *Annual Register* for 1885. In the unpublished diaries Shaw mentions reading this material on March 19, 1894, when he added the "local color" to his play.

Despite his careful research into the history of the war, Shaw made light of his knowledge very airily in an interview published in the *Pall Mall Budget*, April 19, 1894, p. 13. After pretending to be uncertain whether there was such a place as Bulgaria, Shaw continued, "Well, let me give you the history of an idea . . . . A month or two ago I thought that Miss Farr would be wanting a play for her enterprise at the Avenue. It struck me that some interest might be got from the clash of romantic ideals with cold, logical democracy. The play was nearly finished before I had settled on its locality. I wanted a war as a background. Now I am absolutely ignorant of history and geography; so I went about among my friends and asked if they knew of any wars. They told me of several, from the Trojan to the Franco-German. At last Sidney Webb told me of the Servo-Bulgarian war, which was the very thing. Put a Republican—say a Swiss—into the tyrant-ridden East and there you are. So I looked up Bulgaria and Servia in an atlas, made all the names of the characters end in 'off,' and the play was complete."

8. In a letter dated February 6, 1908, Shaw scolded Lillah McCarthy (*Myself and My Friends* [London: Butterworth, 1933], pp. 93–94) for underplaying Raina and advised her to play in the high style of an actress of the Comédie Française performing the part of the Queen of Spain in Victor Hugo's *Ruy Blas*. "Raina," of course, means "queen"; in the manuscript version Raina was originally called Juana.

9. Shaw to Alma Murray, May 11, 1894, *Bernard Shaw: Collected Letters 1874–1897*, ed. Dan H. Laurence (New York: Dodd, Mead, and Co., 1965), p. 435.

10. See the important letter to Archer on the occasion of the opening of the play, April 23, 1894, replying specifically to the charge of Gilbertism: "I must really clear that Gilbert notion out of your head . . . . Gilbert is simply a paradoxically humorous cynic. He accepts the conventional ideals implicitly, but observes that people do not really live up to them. This he regards as a failure on their part at which he mocks bitterly. This position is precisely that of Sergius in the play, who, when disilluded, declares that life is a farce. It is a perfectly barren position: nothing comes of it but cynicism, pessimism, & irony. I do not accept the conventional ideals. To them I oppose in the play the practical life & morals of the efficient, realistic man, unaffectedly ready to face what risks must be faced, considerate but not chivalrous, patient and practical. . . . My whole secret is that I have got clean through the old categories of good & evil, and no longer use them even for dramatic effect. Sergius is ridiculous through the breakdown of his ideals, not odius from his falling short of them. As Gilbert sees, they dont work; but what Gilbert does not see is that there is something else that does work, and that in that something else there is a completely satisfactory asylum for the affections. It is this positive element in my philosophy that makes Arms & The Man a perfectly genuine play about real people. . . . If you could only rid yourself of the intense unreality of your own preconceptions, and of your obsession by the ideals which you grow pessimistic over, you would not find that an effect due to the ridiculous obviousness and common sense of realism breaking through the mist & glamor of idealism, was a mere mechanical topsyturvyism" (*ibid.*, pp. 427–428).

11. *Shaw on Theatre*, ed. E. J. West (New York: Hill and Wang, 1958), p. 22. This essay, which runs to some nine thousand words, first appeared in the *New Review* in July, 1894. The prefaces aside, it is the most elaborate analysis Shaw ever wrote of one of his own plays. Apart from Archibald Henderson and E. J. West, critics have almost universally overlooked it, though it is of basic importance for understanding *Arms and the Man.*

12. In a cancelled passage in the British Museum manuscript, Sergius tells Raina that Bluntschli had given him "excellent advice. He told me I was too much of a gentleman to make a good officer, and suggested that I should seek adventures and write books about them. A brother-in-law of his, he said, had done very well in that way" (50601A, f. 63). Later, Sergius denounces war as "a hollow sham": "I believed that there were two refuges left for our heroic instincts in modern life—love and war. You have shown me that they are both illusions. The cynics and the pessimists are right." Bluntschli protests, "Oh, I shouldnt bother about it if I were you. You'll find plenty of ways of making yourself useful," to which Sergius replies, "Make myself useful! I, Sergius Saranoff, the last of a race of 500 boyards, make myself useful like a laborer or a servant" (50601B, f. 58–59).

13. *Plays Pleasant and Unpleasant*, II, 56. In the British Museum version, this speech reads "whole English nation" instead of "whole Russian nation."

14. Vol. I (January 1901), pp. 289–315.

15. A. F. Tschiffeley, *Don Roberto: The Life and Works of R. B. Cunninghame Graham* (London: William Heinemann, 1937), pp. 328, 322.

16. Beatrice Webb, *Our Partnership*, ed. B. Drake and M. Cole (London: Longmans, Green, 1948), p. 23.

17. Robert Elliot develops these analogies in "Shaw's Captain Bluntschli: A Latter-Day Falstaff," *Modern Language Notes*, LXVII (November 1952), 461–464. Elliot thinks that though Hal represents Shakespeare's ideals, there are no serious ideals in Shaw's play: "In *Arms and the Man*, no choice between the conflicting worlds is possible, for neither has the power to command serious allegiance. (Surely this is Shaw's ironic comment—a comment implicit in the mock-heroic title of the play—on his own time.) . . . The practicality of Bluntschli is so practical and so low that one cannot take it seriously. The only character in *Arms and the Man* who in any sense transcends these worlds (as Hal transcends his), and is thus the real 'man' of the play, is Louka, the servant girl with a soul above her station. Louka is eminently practical, certainly, but she despises Nicola's 'cold-blooded wisdom,' and finally, she has the spirit and pride to bring the swaggering Sergius to heel." But, as we shall see below, Shaw regarded Sergius' engagement to Louka as a kind of *folie à deux*.

18. Vol. L (August 1888), pp. 279–292.

19. *The Century*, XXXVI (June 1888), 246–254.

20. *Shaw on Theatre*, p. 21.

21. "*Arms and the Man*," *Around Theatres* (London: Rupert Hart-Davis, 1953). This essay from the *Saturday Review* is dated January 4, 1908.

22. In a note on page 85 of the typescript of the French translation of the play in the Hanley Collection, Shaw comments on Nicola's relation to Louka: "Nicola is giving her a cold dry lecture. He objects to her showing any affection for him before other people, because it spoils her chance of catching a rich husband and becoming his customer instead of his wife. You really do not appreciate Nicola's greatness."

23. In a cancelled scene in the British Museum manuscript, Catherine warns Petkoff to hurry on the marriage with Sergius, since "Juana is not a bit in earnest about it" and may find this out before long (50601A, f. 52). Shaw wrote Archer a second letter on April 23, after he had seen the advance proofs of the latter's review, objecting strongly to several points: "Your 'transfer of Raina's affections' is a master piece of obtuseness. I offer to submit the point to your wife as arbitrator. The reference is to be 'Did Raina love Sergius & then *transfer* that love to Bluntschli; or did she, after imaginatively living up to an ideal relation with Sergius, and con-

ceiving a sub-conscious dislike for him under the strain, fall in love for the first time with Bluntschli?' . . . the latter is the true solution . . . . Poor Sergius, struggling with your idiotic view of the seamy side, and heroically marrying Louka because he *will* not be a coward and a trifler (as per that idiotic view) is patent even to a man's understanding" (*Collected Letters 1874–1897*, p. 429). Shaw dismissed Gilbert's *Engaged* as "nothing but a sneer at people for not being what Sergius & Raina play at being before they find one another out" (p. 427).

24. Shaw to Alma Murray, December 27, 1904, *Letters from George Bernard Shaw to Miss Alma Murray* (privately printed, 1927).

25. *The Universe of G. B. S.*, p. 170. A more recent adverse criticism of the play to be found is Michael Quinn, "Form and Intention: A Negative View of *Arms and the Man*," *Critical Quarterly*, V (Summer 1963), 148–154. According to Quinn, Shaw set out to write a classical comedy but instead wrote an artificial one. It fails as an attack on idealism because "the characters in *Arms and the Man* are not spokesmen for contrasting ideas as in Shaw's later plays but all are fakes of much the same kind." Moreover he finds characters inadequately motivated, so that we have only the stripping off of masks. Mr. Quinn clearly has not pondered "A Dramatic Realist."

CHAPTER THREE *Candida*

1. The British Museum manuscript (Add. MS 50603A–C) bears the subtitle "A Domestic Play in Three Acts." The first page is dated October 2, 1894 (the day the play takes place). The conclusions of the three acts are dated, respectively, October 15, November 6, and December 7.

2. Shaw's unpublished diaries at the London School of Economics state that he heard Yeats read his play on February 8, 1894, at 123 Dalling Road.

3. "The Philosophy of Shelley's Poetry," William Butler Yeats, *Ideas of Good and Evil* (London: A. H. Bullen, 1903), p. 128.

4. *Plays Pleasant and Unpleasant*, II (London: Constable, 1949), vii–viii.

5. There is a note to this effect on the typescript of the French translation of *Candida* in the University of Texas collection. Cf. the preface to *John Bull's Other Island* (London: Constable, 1947): "The Anglican Catholics have played and are playing a notable part in the Socialist movement in England in opposition to the individualist Secularists of the urban proletariat" (p. 36). Stewart Headlam's Guild of St. Matthew laid equal stress on socialism and sacramentalism. It was the Anglo-Catholic Headlam who wrote the Fabian tract "Christian Socialism" in 1892. The movement of Anglo-Catholicism away from otherworldiness toward socialism

in the later years of the nineteenth century is illuminatingly traced out by
Lloyd Hubenka in "The Religious Philosophy of Bernard Shaw" (Ph.D.
dissertation, University of Nebraska, 1966). Shaw stated that the clergyman nearest to Morell was Stopford Brooke "with touches of Canon
Shuttleworth and Fleming Williams. I had no models for Candida. When
I began writing the part of the young poet I had in mind De Quincey's
account of his adolescence in his *Confessions*" (*Evening Standard* [London],
November 30, 1944). Shaw was no doubt thinking of De Quincey's youthful shyness, lack of practicality, and effeminacy.

6. Shaw's estimate of Morris is set forth in *Pen Portraits and Reviews*
(London: Constable, 1949) and his 1936 preface to the Oxford edition of
Morris's *Works*. See Yeats on Morris, "The Happiest of the Poets," in
Ideas of Good and Evil. Yeats declared in his *Autobiography* (London:
Macmillan, 1926) that he was "in all things Pre-Raphaelite" (p. 141).
Shaw was still following Pre-Raphaelite principles in *Saint Joan*; see
Chapter Twelve, below. The emphatic rejection of the rhetoric of politics
and social reform on the part of Yeats and other aesthetes in the nineties
is reflected by Shaw in a passage in the British Museum manuscript of
Candida. Burgess conjectures that Eugene is "a swell amusin' hisself by
playin' at Socialism," but Candida sets him straight—"Not a bit in the
world. Poor Eugene hates politics" (50603A, f. 39). Since this chapter was
written, Elsie B. Adams has published an excellent study of the relation of
Candida to English art history: "Bernard Shaw's Pre-Raphaelite Drama,"
PMLA, LXXXI (October 1966), 428–438.

7. In the British Museum version the picture is Raphael's "Sistine
Madonna." Both these paintings, of course, are Pre-Raphaelite by virtue
of their subject matter, not their technique.

8. This was one of the catch phrases of Christian Socialism. See Headlam's tract, *passim*.

9. Shaw wrote to St. John Ervine that Burgess "was born in 1840 in
Oxfordshire, or possibly of Oxonian parents in Hackney; which then had
turnpike gates and pigs running about the road, miles and atmospheres
from the sound of Bowbells. To this day, and certainly to the date of
Candida even Shoreditch is less completely Cockneyfied than Charing X:
cockneyism, being smarty, always went west and not north or east. Burgess, with his emotional rhetorical *h*s, is studied closely from a well known
and long deceased Oxford character. He does not utter a sound of modern
cockney" (*Bernard Shaw: His Life, Work and Friends* [New York:
Morrow, 1956], p. 281].

10. Shaw to Ellen Terry, April 6, 1896, *Bernard Shaw: Collected Letters
1874–1897* (New York: Dodd, Mead, and Co., 1965), p. 623.

11. Walter King's essay, "The Rhetoric of *Candida*" (*Modern Drama*,
II [1959], 71–83), is a perceptive study of the use of oratorical clichés by

Morell. See also Shaw's letter to Charles Charrington, March 16, 1896: "Morell is a very glib, sanguine, cocksure, popular sort of man. His utter want of shyness; his readiness to boss people spiritually; his certainty that his own ideas, being the right ideas, must be good for them; all this belongs to the vulgarity which makes him laugh at Eugene's revelation, and talk of 'calf love.' It is nothing to the point that he is also goodnatured, frank, sympathetic, and capable of admitting Candida's position . . . when it is presented to his *feeling*, in spite of the fact that he would have disputed it hotly had it been presented to him as a purely intellectual position. That rescues him from the odium which would otherwise attach to him as, intellectually and [morally], a clerical bounder . . . . I can see you well enough in the heartstricken passages; but I do not see you facile, cheery, spontaneous, fluent, emphatic, unhesitating and bumptious in the early scenes with Prossy & Burgess & Eugene . . . . I don't hear your boisterous cheery laugh, which should not be refined out of the part merely because I have to refine it out myself in reading the play from sheer incapacity to get quite into that coarse part of his skin. . . . I don't see you as the spoiled child, the superficial optimist, the man who, in spite of his power of carrying everything before him by the mere rush and light & warmth of his good-nature & conviction, is stopped by the least resistance" (*Collected Letters 1874–1897*, p. 611).

12. His emotional attack on what he calls La Rochefoucauld's "cynical" view of marriage suggests that he has not analyzed his "happy marriage" with Candida to the point of understanding it.

13. The epithet "pioneer" (in the sense of pioneer of new moral values) is one Shaw applies to Shelley at the opening of *The Quintessence of Ibsenism*. It does not appear in the revised standard edition of the play (issued in 1931) though it is in earlier ones.

14. At the end of the second act of the British Museum version Shaw has added the note: "Make it perfectly clear that the point left in suspense at the end of 1st Act is whether E M is the man with whom C sympathises & that M's confidence is shattered in himself only & that he has not concluded against his wife but is sensitive to accumulating evidence on that point" (50603B, f. 56).

15. Shaw's unpublished diaries reveal that he lectured to Headlam's Church and Stage Guild on *Parsifal* on October 16, the day after he finished the first act of *Candida*.

16. The reference is to the sword the angel brandishes to keep Adam and Eve out of Eden.

17. Shaw comments on this crisis in his preface to *Getting Married* (London: Constable, 1947): "What an honorable and sensible man does when his household is invaded is what the Reverend James Mavor Morell does in my play. He recognizes that just as there is not room for two

women in that sacredly intimate relation of sentimental domesticity which is what marriage means to him, so there is no room for two men in that relation with his wife; and he accordingly tells her firmly that she must choose which man will occupy the place that is large enough for one only .... In a real marriage of sentiment the wife or husband cannot be supplanted by halves; and such a marriage will break very soon under the strain of polygyny or polyandry. What we want at present is a sufficiently clear teaching of this fact to ensure that prompt and decisive action shall always be taken in such cases without any false shame of seeming conventional . . ." (pp. 230–231).

18. In the British Museum manuscript Candida is described as "A beautiful woman, with the double charm of youth and maternity. A true Virgin Mother" (50603A, f. 3). Later in a cancelled passage Shaw makes Prossy complain of Morell's Candidamania in these terms: "One would think she was the Queen of Heaven herself. He is thinking of her half the time when he imagines that he is meditating on the virtues of Our Blessed Lady." Lexy objects, "Oh Miss Garnett, isn't that a little blasphemous"; and Prossy answers, "Nonsense, facts are facts, whether they are blasphemous or not" (50603A, ff. 15–16). See *Collected Letters 1874–1897*, pp. 623, 632, for further reference to Candida as a "Virgin Mother" play.

19. "The Living Pictures" (April 6, 1895), *Our Theatres in the Nineties* (London: Constable, 1948), I, 82.

20. James Huneker, *Iconoclasts* (New York: Charles Scribner's Sons, 1905), p. 254.

21. *Spectator*, CLXXXV (November 17, 1950), 506.

22. Huneker, *Iconoclasts*, p. 255.

CHAPTER FOUR *The Devil's Disciple*

1. "The Drama Purified" (April 23, 1898), *Our Theatres in the Nineties* (London: Constable, 1948), III, 364–365.

2. For Shaw's attack on jingo nationalism in the theater, see "Mainly about Melodrama" (October 3, 1896), *ibid.*, II, 204–205.

3. "Charles Frohman's Mission" (April 16, 1898), *ibid.*, III, 357–361. In an interview in the *Observer*, August 24, 1930, Shaw explained why the success of the American production of *The Devil's Disciple* was not followed up in London: "George Alexander shrank from a full-dress West-End production because the pre-war playgoing public opinion was not yet educated up to the last act, and I was not prepared to represent the battle of Saratoga as a British victory" (p. 12).

4. "Two Bad Plays" (April 20, 1895), *Our Theatres in the Nineties*, I, 93.

5. "One of the Worst" (December 28, 1895), *ibid.*, I, 287. This review is a criticism of a melodrama based on the Dreyfus case. The last act of *The Devil's Disciple* is a commentary on what Shaw found false in the psychology of this play. Shaw felt that Dreyfus' cry of "Vive la République" (transposed in the English play to "God save the Queen") marked him as guilty and that an English officer, if innocent, might on such an occasion "roundly and heartily damn his country." In the manuscript version of his third act Shaw makes Dudgeon cry out on the gallows "Amen and God damn the king" (50606D, f. 58). This was changed later to "My life for the world's future." Martin Meisel's chapter, "Rebels and Redcoats," in *Shaw and the Nineteenth-Century Theater* (Princeton: Princeton University Press, 1963), gives an interesting discussion of the play in terms of contemporaneous melodramatic formulas.

6. *Major Critical Essays* (London: Constable, 1947), p. 59.

7. The beginning of the British Museum manuscript (Add. MS 50606 A–D) is dated September 10, 1896. The ends of the three acts are dated October 23, November 16, and December 31. A note on 50606D, f. 66, reads "finished the stage business 20/2/97." The play is subtitled "A Drama in 3 Acts."

8. *A Bank Holiday Interlude* (London: Robert Buchanan, 1894), p. 50. The theology of this poem is very close to Shaw's. In it the devil appears in the guise of a clergyman on Hampstead Heath and defends himself as the "foe of all the Churches" and "the friend of man." God is not omnipotent, since that would make him responsible for earthquakes, floods, and shipwrecks. Christ was an outcast, and Buchanan's devil, who identifies himself with Christ, is "the Ishmael of Angels." In a shorthand scenario of the play, dated April 14, 1896, Shaw had originally given Dick the name Ishmael (50606A, f. 1). In the longhand version he is described as "a young man of striking natural grace, with a keen sensitive face, fine eyes, and raven black hair," with a "reckless and sardonic" expression (50606B, f. 38). Shaw wrote Lawrence Langner that "Dick is not a raffish profligate: he is a tragic figure in black, like Hamlet, or Buckingham in Henry VIII" (*G.B.S. and the Lunatic* [New York: Atheneum, 1963], pp. 214–215).

9. *Major Critical Essays*, p. 121.

10. *Three Plays for Puritans* (London: Constable, 1947), p. 15.

11. *The Black Girl in Search of God and Some Lesser Tales* (London: Constable, 1948), pp. 63–64.

12. See his own account of his experience in *A Narrative of Colonel Ethan Allen's Captivity* (1779).

13. "Ibsen Triumphant" (May 22, 1897), *Our Theatres in the Nineties*, III, 143.

14. Shaw wrote to Mrs. Richard Mansfield on December 10, 1897 apropos the American production: "If the end of the second act produces the right

effect, the sympathy goes from the woman for her mistake about Anderson: whenever I read it here the women have always been disgusted at her little faith" (*Bernard Shaw: Collected Letters 1874–1897* [New York: Dodd, Mead, and Co., 1965]), p. 830. The British Museum version contains the following cancelled scene between Judith and Anderson:

> A.—And you let them take the innocent for the guilty?
> J.—Are you guilty?
> A.— I am the man they wanted.
> J.—I tried to speak but my tongue clove to the roof of my mouth. I had to choose between you.
> A.—You should have given me up, ten times over, sooner than let such a wrong be done.
> J.—I tried to. Yes, I tried to. But I could not. Now you know why I want you to say goodbye. It is goodbye. (He looks at her, not very tenderly, and releases her.) Wont you kiss me for the last time?
> A.—Kiss you? What good will kissing do? (50606C, f. 55.)

15. *Major Critical Essays*, p. 102.

16. "Trials of a Military Dramatist," *Review of the Week*, I (November 4, 1899), 8. In this essay Shaw declared: "I had taken some pains to find out what manner of person the real Burgoyne was, and found him a wit, a rhetorician, and a successful dramatic author." Shaw also tells of a British general who confided to him that a firing squad execution was "horrible, sanguinary, and demoralizing even when it was successful (which seldom happened)" and contended that hanging was more humane. Homer Woodbridge charges that Shaw's picture of eighteenth-century New Hampshire is "absurdly and almost unbelievably wrong," and points out that in the first edition Shaw made Burgoyne march south from Boston instead of Quebec and referred to Burgoyne's troops as Continentals (*G. B. Shaw: Creative Artist* [Carbondale: Southern Illinois University Press, 1963], p. 45). Despite these solecisms, Shaw had in fact made a careful study of Edward de Fonblanque's *Political and Military Episodes in the Latter Half of the Eighteenth Century, Derived from the Life and Correspondence of the Right Hon. John Burgoyne, General, Statesman, and Dramatist* (London: Macmillan, 1876) for material on Burgoyne and background for the war.

The University of Texas collection contains a British Museum call slip with detailed notes by Shaw on the article on Burgoyne in the *Dictionary of National Biography*. The jottings dealing with Burgoyne's career in America read as follows: "America/1774 to reinforce Gage (See Fonblanque's Pol. & Military Episodes 120–35 for his private memorandum on his appointment)/ disgusted—nothing to do—returned home Nov. 7 after Bunker's Hill/ 2nd in Com. under Sir Guy Carleton Canada 76/ again disgusted with inaction—returned home/ returned in supreme command of force to make grand march to join Howe in spring 77/ Lieut. Gen.

29/8/77/ Expedition—started spring (May) 77 from Three Rivers 6400 soldiers 649 Indians/ reoccupied Crown Point took Ticonderoga (6 July)/ promoted Lieut. Gen. in August. Failed in attacking Americans at Bennington, crossed Hudson—retreat cut off by Arnold, advance blocked by Schuyler with 16,000 men. Disheartened by hearing that Clinton had not stirred. Advanced, Schuyler retreated & was superseded by Gates, who stood. On 24 Sep. B found American Army, 20,000 strong, entrenched on Behmus' Heights. Attacked it with 5000 men—had to retreat—harassed badly & surrounded at Saratoga—Surrendered to Gates (having no food & no ammunition) 17 Oct. 77 Died 3/6/1792."

General Burgoyne does not appear to have personally occupied any town in New Hampshire. His forces, having taken the water route south from Three Rivers, captured Fort Ticonderoga. Two days later the left flank of his army skirmished with the Americans at Hubbardton, New Hampshire (now Vermont); and on August 16 another party raided Bennington for supplies, but Burgoyne was not himself involved in either of these excursions. The first battle of Bemis' Heights (or Freeman's Farm) took place on September 19 after Burgoyne had crossed to the west bank of the Hudson. A few days before this, Burgoyne discovered that Howe had gone to Pennsylvania instead of marching north to Albany, but he did not learn of the War Office blunder that caused the error until much later. The action of *The Devil's Disciple* takes place in the two days following the demise of Dick's father (who dated his deathbed will September 24). At that time Burgoyne was in fact on the west bank of the Hudson near Still water in New York State. This would place the action of the play after the first and before the second battle of Freeman's Farm (October 7), when Burgoyne, low on provisions, with his retreat cut off, made a gallant last stand and was beaten. He then withdrew to Saratoga, sent an officer to discuss surrender on October 14, and signed terms three days later after the bargaining Shaw describes in his postscript.

17. Shaw to Ellen Terry, March 13, 1897, *Collected Letters 1874–1897*, pp. 734–735.

18. De Fonblanque, *Political and Military Episodes . . . from the Life . . . of John Burgoyne*, p. 492.

19. *Complete Writings of William Blake*, ed. G. Keynes (New York: Random House, 1957), pp. 748, 751–752.

20. Desmond MacCarthy, *Shaw's Plays in Review* (New York: Thames and Hudson, 1951), p. 200.

21. Cf. Ferrovius' speech in *Androcles and the Lion* (London: Constable, 1947): "Today the Christian god forsook me; and Mars overcame me and took back his own. The Christian god is not yet. He will come when Mars and I are dust; but meanwhile I must serve the gods that are, not the God that will be" (p. 144). See also Shaw's postscript to the play: "We were

at peace when I pointed out, by the mouth of Ferrovius, the path of an honest man, who finds out, when the trumpet sounds, that he cannot follow Jesus. Many years earlier, in *The Devil's Disciple*, I touched the same theme even more definitely, and shewed the minister throwing off his black coat for ever when he discovered, amid the thunder of the captains and the shouting, that he was a born fighter." But English clergymen in the Great War did "not take off their black coats and say quite simply, 'I find in the hour of trial that the Sermon on the Mount is tosh, and that I am not a Christian . . . . Have the goodness to give me a revolver and a commission in a regiment which has for its chaplain a priest of Mars: *my* God.' Not a bit of it. They have stuck to their livings and served Mars in the name of Christ, to the scandal of all religious mankind" (pp. 146–147). Raphael's "St. Paul at Athens," a reproduction of which hangs in Anderson's home, shows Paul preaching on the Areopagus and a statue of Mars opposite him.

22. There are also two alternative cancelled endings. The first reads:

> J.—Don't misunderstand me, Dick. You may tell him that I said I loved you if you like. I shall tell him that myself. But don't—*please* don't ever tell him that I lost faith in him.
> R.—I promise.
> J.—Thanks. Now I'll tell you something. I never really loved him before: I only pretended to like most wives. He could never have taught me himself what love is. But you taught me. And now I love *him*. Isn't that funny.
> R.—Quite right. He is a better man than I am.
> J.—But I wish I could have taught you to love too. Is that wicked, do you think?
> R.—If it is, I shall always remain the Devil's Disciple.
> (50606D, ff. 64–65.)

A second alternate ending, also cancelled, reads:

> J.—Promise you will never tell him.
> R.—Don't be afraid.
> J.—I suppose you will marry Essie now.
> R.—(annoyed) Marry Essie! My good madam: the one lesson I have learnt since yesterday is never to marry at all.
> J.—You despise me.
> R.—I *know* you. (She looks at him then covers her face with her hands.) No: thats no use now. Tears have lost their terror for me.
> J.—Since when has that change come in you?
> R.—Since when? (The clock strikes the quarter. He writhes his neck as if to loosen it, pressing his hand around it.) Since exactly [a] quarter of an hour ago. Goodbye. (He leaves her & goes off up the street. She gazes at him. Curtain.)
> (50606D, f. 62.)

CHAPTER FIVE   *Caesar and Cleopatra*

1. See Shaw's statement to Henderson in "George Bernard Shaw Self-Revealed," *Fortnightly Review*, CXXV (April 1926), 438; also his letter to Hesketh Pearson in *G. B. S.: A Full Length Portrait* (New York: Harper & Brothers, 1942), p. 187.

2. "Tappertit on Caesar" (January 29, 1898), *Our Theatres in the Nineties* (London: Constable, 1948), III, 298–299.

3. In "Bernard Shaw's *Caesar and Cleopatra* as History" (Ph.D. dissertation, University of Nebraska, 1968), Gale Larson shows brilliantly how writers under the influence of the Cato-Brutus ideal of aristocratic republicanism and stoic morality condemned Caesar in antiquity. This ideal faded in the Middle Ages, to be revived in the Renaissance under the influence of Plutarch. Shaw's doctrine of self-fulfillment and his utilitarian emphasis on consequences are, of course, the exact opposite of stoicism, with its belief in self-repression, in abstract virtue, and in purity of motive.

4. Theodor Mommsen, *History of Rome*, tr. William Dickson (New York: Charles Scribner's Sons, 1908), V, 324–325. The history was published in Berlin in 1854–1856 and in English translation in 1862–1866. Shaw draws his material from the fifth and last book, *The Establishment of the Millitary Monarchy*. Chapter One, "Marcus Lepidus," gives Mommsen's estimate of Pompey's character; Chapter Four, "Pompeius and the East," sketches the background of Egyptian politics before Caesar's arrival; and Chapter Eight, "The Joint Rule of Pompeius and Caesar," praises Caesar as a social reformer. The most important chapters, however, are Ten ("Brundisium, Ilerda, Pharsalus, and Thapsus"), which covers the Alexandrian War, and Eleven ("The Old Republic and the New Monarchy"), which opens with a ten-page analysis of the character of Caesar as the "sole creative genius produced by Rome." The influence of Mommsen's conception of Caesar's personality on Shaw is traced by Stanley Weintraub in "Shaw's Mommsenite Caesar," in *Anglo-German and American-German Crosscurrents*, ed. P. A. Shelley *et al.* (Chapel Hill: University of North Carolina Press, 1962), II, 257–272. At the University of Texas are several pages of notes by Shaw on Mommsen with the letterhead "Pitfold, Haslemere, Surrey," and dated 1898 in Shaw's hand. These notes read as follows:

Line of Ptolemy Lagides ended on death of Pt. Sotor II
Sulla installed Lathyrus, or Alexander II, killed in his capital in a few days in a tumult.
Alex made a will bequeathing Egypt to Rome.

The Romans grabbed Alex's money in Tyre, but did not take Egypt, allowing Lathyrus's bastards

Auletes (the Flute Blower), the new Dionysos⎱ to take⎰Egypt⎱ 81.
Ptolemy the Cyprian   ⎰   ⎰Cyprus⎰

Explanation—Auletes paid rent for non-disturbance; and the post of governor of Egypt made the holder too powerful.

Yet there was a Roman party in Alex^dria because the royal guard deposed ministers & even kings & besieged the king in his palace when it wanted more pay.

Ptolemy, Cl's uncle, was a miser & would not bribe the Romans. His treasure was 7000 talents (£1,700,000). In 58 Cyprus was annexed by Marcus Cato (armyless) & Pt poisoned himself. Cl was then 6.

Auletes in 59 purchased his recognition as K. of E. by decree of the Roman people for 6000 tal. (£1,460,000). The Egyptians could not stand the consequent taxation & the loss of Cyprus (see above) & chased him out of the country. He appealed to the Romans to be reinstated. They agreed that he had a claim on them, but could not agree who to send, as the job was a desirable one, with lots of pickings.

At last the Triumvirate, at the Conference of Luca, got a promise of an extra 10,000 tal (£2,400,000) from Auletes (total 16,000 tal or £3,860,000) & ordered the governor of Syria, Aulus Gabinius, to go ahead.

Meanwhile the Alexandrians had crowned Archelaus & Berenice. Gabinius got through the desert between Gaza & Pelusium through the cavalry leadership of Mark Antony. The Alexandrians were defeated, Archelaus killed, Auletes restored & Berenice beheaded. It was impossible to extract the ransom from the people; so the Romans left a garrison of Romans & Celtic & German cavalry, who took the place of the old guard & behaved in the same praetorian manner. Later on they intermarry with the Egyptians, & also runaway Italian slaves & criminals & old soldiers of Pompey. This is the stage in which Caesar finds them. Technically, they are the Roman army of occupation.

Caesar comes to Egypt to catch Pompey, but, finding him dead, has nothing to do there & is expected to go on at once to Africa to deal with Juba of Numidia.

Being in want of money, he lands in Alexandria with 2 amalgamated legions (3200 men & 800 Celtic & German cavalry), takes up his quarters in the palace & collects taxes & settles the Egyptian succession. (Pothinus sarcastic.)

Lets Egyptians down easy for 10 million denarii (£400,000).

Invites Cl. & P. D. to submit to arbitration. P. D. already in palace. Cl. comes thither. He makes them marry & gives them Egypt, agreeably to the will of Auletes (their father). He gives Cyprus to Arsinoe & Ptol. junior, cancelling the annexation by Cato in 58.

— Order of Events —

Caesar demands his £400,000, arrears of Auletes's debt.

Pothinus & P. D. send the treasures of the temples & the gold plate of the king to be melted at the mint, so as to make as big a scene as possible. Bare walls & wooden cups.

Pothinus and P. D. plot to attack Caesar with the Roman army of occupation under the command of Achillas. Meanwhile a good deal of sporadic assassination of the Caesarians goes on.

Caesar, detained by the N. W. winds, orders up reinforcements from Asia, & goes in meanwhile for revelry. Suddenly Achillas appears in Alexandria with the army of occupation, and the citizens make common cause with him. Arsinoe and Ganymedes head the insurrection. Caesar siezes the king & Pothinus, fortifies himself in the palace & theatre adjoining, burns his fleet which is in the harbor in front of the theatre & occupies the Pharos (island with lighthouse commanding harbor) with boats. He sends for troop and ships to the Syrians, Nabataeans, Cretans, Rhodians.

Street fighting daily. Caesar is cut off from Marea, the fresh water lake behind the town. He digs wells on the beach & finds drinkable water.

He releases P. D. to propitiate the insurrectionists.

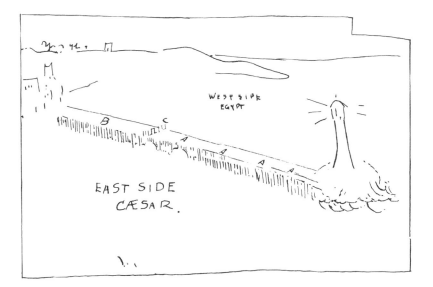

Alexandrians try to introduce fireships into the east harbor & fail.
     ,,   equip a squadron to intercept the towing in by Caesar's ships of a legion from Asia Minor, but are beaten by the Rhodian mariners.

The citizens capture the Pharos & keep continually sea-fighting Caesar in the roadstead. Caesar forced to recover the Pharos at all costs.

He attacks by boats from the harbor & ships from the roadstead. He carries the Pharos & section A of the mole, & builds the wall C. While his troops are crowded near the wall a division of Egyptians rush the part of A nearest the lighthouse, charge the Romans & sailors at the wall C, and drive them into the sea. Some are taken on board by Caesar's ships; but 400 soldiers & more sailors are drowned. Caesar has to swim for it twice—once on jumping off the pier & once when his overcrowded ship founders. The Pharos, and sections of the mole remain in his hands.

The relief by Mithridates followed.

— Relief by Mithridates —

Motley army from Syria—Ityraeans of the prince of the Libanus

Bedouins of Jamblichus, son of Sampsiceramus

Jews under the minister Antipater

contingents from Cilicia & Syria under petty chiefs mostly robbers Mithridates occupies Pelusium on the day of his arrival.

Takes the great road towards Memphis to cross the Nile above the Delta, getting support thereby from the Jewish peasants.

The Egyptians send an army commanded by P. D. to prevent M. from crossing. They meet beyond Memphis at "Jew's Camp" between Onion & Heliopolis. Mithridates outmanoeuvres them & crosses at Memphis.

Caesar, on hearing of the approaching relief, ships part of his troops to the end of Lake Marea (west of Alex^a) & marches round the lake & up the Nile to meet Mit., advancing up the river. Junction affected without molestation.

Battle of the Nile

Caesar marches into the Delta, crosses a deep canal cut by the Egyptians, overthrows their vanguard & storms their camp. Egyptians swept into the Nile by an attack from 3 sides at once. P. D.'s overladen boat sinks; & he is drowned.

Caesar immediately makes straight for the Egypt quarter of Alex at the head of his cavalry. They receive him in mourning, with the images of their gods in their hands. His troops, in the Roman quarter, go wild with enthusiasm.

He lectures them (431 M[ommsen]) grants settled Jews equal rights with Greeks, & replaces army of occupation nominally under king of Egypt by Roman garrison under Rufio, who, as a freedman's son, is not well born enough to make himself formidable.

Cleopatra & Ptol the younger get the throne subject to Rome; Arsinoe is carried off to Italy lest she should become a pretext for dynastic insurrections; and Cyprus is added to Cilicia (a Roman province).

5. "Pompeius . . . for want of faith in himself and his star timidly clung in public life to formal right" (Mommsen, *History of Rome*, IV, 499).

6. Froude's politics in this biography are those of his master, Carlyle. He denounces the patrician party as corrupt and imbecilic and the demo-

cratic one as anarchic, but he leans to the popular side. He is also Carlylean in his anticonstitutionalism, arguing that Republican Rome had become an oligarchy catering to the luxury and ambition of the few.

7. William Warde Fowler, *Julius Caesar and the Foundation of the Roman Imperial System* (London: G. P. Putnam's Sons, 1899), p. 2. Like Mommsen, Warde Fowler takes the view that "Caesar's work marks the consummation of a series of revolutionary tendencies which had been gaining strength for generations" (p. 327).

8. *Major Critical Essays* (London: Constable, 1947), p. 223. "If the next generation of Englishmen consisted wholly of Julius Caesars, all our political, ecclesiastical, and moral institutions would vanish, and the less perishable of their appurtenances be classed with Stonehenge and the cromlechs and round towers as inexplicable relics of a bygone social order" (p. 189).

9. Friedrich Wilhelm Nietzsche, *Complete Works*, ed. Oscar Levy (London: T. N. Foulis, 1910), XV, 367.

10. "*Caesar and Cleopatra*; by the Author of the Play," *New Statesman*, I (May 3, 1913), 112–113. Shaw read a number of classical sources besides Suetonius. In a program note to the copyright performance Shaw stated: "The Play follows history as closely as stage exigencies permit. Critics should consult Manetho and the Egyptian Monuments, Herodotus, Diodorus, Strabo (Book 17), Plutarch, Pomponius Mela, Pliny, Tacitus, Appian of Alexandria, and, perhaps, Ammianus Marcellinus. Ordinary spectators, if unfamiliar with the ancient tongues, may refer to Mommsen, Warde-Fowler, Mr. St. George Stock's Introduction to the 1898 Clarendon Press edition of Caesar's Gallic Wars, and Murray's Handbook for Egypt. Many of these authorities have consulted their imaginations, more or less. The author has done the same" (Archibald Henderson, *Bernard Shaw: Man of the Century* [Appleton-Century-Crofts, 1956], p. 553). It is difficult to tell to what extent Shaw is joking here: obviously he himself did not read Greek or Latin. Of these authorities, only Plutarch, Appian, Mommsen, and Warde Fowler give accounts of the Alexandrian War. The other writers deal with Roman and Egyptian geography and manners. It is surprising that Shaw does not list Dio Cassius' *History*, which provides one of the longest descriptions of Caesar's stay in Egypt, or Caesar's own version of events in his *Civil Wars*, Book III. The play "follows history" only to a degree. The meeting at the sphinx is Shaw's own invention. The treasury scene parallels Plutarch and Mommsen fairly closely. The Pharos episode is roughly historical, except that Caesar did not take his plunge into the harbor from the lighthouse. The carpet trick appears in Plutarch, but in a different context. There is no historical record of Caesar's leave-taking. The most important departure from history, however, occurs in Act Four, where Shaw makes Cleopatra responsible for the death of

Pothinus. Plutarch, Appian, and Caesar himself all state explicitly that Pothinus was killed on Caesar's orders, for various reasons. The relation of Shaw's play to its classical sources is analyzed by Gordon W. Couchman in "Here Was a Caesar: Shaw's Comedy Today," *PMLA*, LXXII (March 1957), 272–285. Couchman also reviews criticism of the play. All modern authorities agree in making Cleopatra twenty-one and not sixteen at the time of Caesar's visit. Froude, however, gives her age as sixteen, and Mommsen mentions this as her age a few pages before his narrative of Caesar's visit in a way which might have misled Shaw. In the Texas notes above, Shaw makes Cleopatra six in 58 B.C., which accords with her age of sixteen in his play.

11. By the term "Nonconformist Conscience," Shaw meant specifically the sexual Puritanism of the English Free Churches as it affected public affairs, particularly in the Dilke and Parnell cases.

12. Letter to *The Times* (London), December 31, 1945, p. 5.

13. "Shakespear in Manchester" (March 20, 1897), *Our Theatres in the Nineties*, III, 78. In this review Shaw chides Janet Achurch for portraying Cleopatra too naturalistically: "One conceives her as a trained professional queen, able to put on at will the deliberate artificial dignity which belongs to the technique of court life." He calls Cleopatra "subhuman" rather than "superhuman" in adversity. She has the "petulant folly of the spoiled beauty who has not imagination enough to know that she will be frightened when the fighting begins," and is full of "weak, treacherous, affected streaks."

14. Shaw to Murray, July 28, 1900, *Drama*, No. 42 (Autumn 1956), p. 24. In this letter Shaw also defends his anachronistic view of Britannus: "In every line that I have come across concerning [the ancient Britons] I see Mr. Podsnap." He contends also that Caesar was an adroit comedian, and that the style of his commentaries on the Gallic Wars does not reflect the man, since Caesar was a literary amateur who was not adept at self-expression.

15. John Pentland Mahaffy, *The Empire of the Ptolemies* (London: Macmillan, 1895), p. 446. "They seem to most readers something new and strange—the pageants and passions of the fratricide Cleopatra as something unparalleled—and yet she was one of a race in which almost every reigning princess for the last 200 years had been swayed by like storms of passion, or had been guilty of like daring violations of common humanity. What Arsinoe, what Cleopatra, from the first to the last, had hesitated to murder a brother or a husband . . . ?" (p. 445).

16. *Three Plays for Puritans* (London: Constable, 1947), pp. 180–181.

17. *New Statesman*, I, 112. MacCarthy's review was published under the title "Bernard Shaw's 'Julius Caesar,'" in the *New Statesman* on April 26, 1913. This critique, and MacCarthy's reply (May 18) to Shaw's rebuttal,

are reprinted in *Shaw's Plays in Review* (New York: Thames and Hudson, 1951).

18. Stark Young sets forth this "biological" view of Caesar admirably in his review of the play, in *Immortal Shadows* (New York: Charles Scribner's Sons, 1948), pp. 57–59.

19. *Man and Superman* (London: Constable, 1947), pp. 129–130.

20. *Ibid.*, p. xxxvii.

CHAPTER SIX   *Man and Superman*

1. Unpublished letter to Siegfried Trebitsch, August 22, 1919, Berg Collection, New York Public Library. In the same letter Shaw refers to these plays as "the big three."

2. James Huneker, *Iconoclasts* (New York: Charles Scribner's Sons, 1905), p. 258.

3. In his letter to Trebitsch cited above in note 1, Shaw compared Tom Broadbent's likable asininity to that of M. Jourdain in *Le Bourgeois gentilhomme*. In both comedies the successful fool's dreams remain unpunctured.

4. "From Phallicism to Purism," *Outspoken Essays on Social Subjects* (London: W. Reeves, 1897), p. 6. Bax, whom Shaw mentions in the preface to *Major Barbara* as one of the overlooked English influences on his thinking, shared with him an interest in Marxist socialism and a Schopenhauerian view of sex. See also "Marriage" in *Outlooks from the New Standpoint* (London: Swan Sonnenschein, 1891). Bax's ideas on marriage had a direct influence on *Getting Married*, especially his essay *The Legal Subjection of Men* (London: New Age Press, 1908). Bax attacks marriage as "trade unionism" and opposes the nonconformist conscience and introspective ascetic sexual morality. According to Bax, sex questions such as birth control, homosexuality, and divorce should be treated, not in terms of traditional taboos or Comtian moral idealism, but simply from the point of view of good social policy.

5. Shaw read Carpenter's *Love's-Coming-of-Age: A Series of Papers on the Relations of the Sexes* (1896) and informed him that he would put his views on sex, marriage, and love—"three entirely different things"—in a play he was engaged on (Stephen Winsten, *Salt and His Circle* [London: Hutchinson, 1951], p. 112). Like Bax, Carpenter is against current legalism in matters of sex and marriage, but his tone is less utilitarian and markedly more transcendental.

Allen's *Falling in Love, with Other Essays on More Exact Branches of Science* (1889) takes the Schopenhauerian view (without acknowledging any debt) that far from being mere foolishness, the tendency to fall in love has fundamental value in the evolution of the race, and finds probable wisdom in men's and women's unconscious choices, holding that in such matters "the sentimentalists are always right, the moralists always wrong." See also *The Woman Who Did* (1895), a controversial novel in which Allen defends the right of unmarried women to bear children.

6. "Mr. Shaw's New Dialogues," *Around Theatres* (London: Rupert Hart-Davis, 1953), p. 270. This review of the published version of the play appeared in the *Saturday Review* on September 12, 1903.

7. Shaw to Iden Payne, February 3, 1911, *University of Buffalo Studies*, XVI (September 1939), 126.

8. Henry Mayers Hyndman, *The Record of an Adventurous Life* (London: Macmillan, 1911), p. 3. Hyndman's *Further Reminiscences* (London: Macmillan, 1912) contains much about Shaw, including a good-natured critique of *Man and Superman*, appreciative of its comedy but critical of the element of "burlesque." In "How Frank Ought to Have Done It," Shaw wrote of *Man and Superman*, "In the final act of that play . . . the scene in which the hero revolts from marriage and struggles against it without any hope of escape, is a poignantly sincere utterance which must have come from personal experience" (*Sixteen Self Sketches* [London: Constable, 1949], p. 129).

9. "William Morris as I Knew Him," in May Morris, *William Morris: Artist, Writer, Socialist* (Oxford: Basil Blackwell, 1936), II, xiii. "Hyndman could talk about anything with a fluency that left Morris nowhere. . . . He was a leading figure in any assembly, and took that view of himself with perfect self-confidence."

10. "The Hyndman-George Debate," *The International Review*, No. 2 (August 1889), p. 54.

11. Arthur Schopenhauer, *The World as Will and Idea*, tr. R. B. Haldane and J. Kemp (London: Trübner, 1886), III, 340.

12. *Iconoclasts*, p. 258.

13. "New Year Dramas" (January 4, 1896), *Our Theatres in the Nineties* (London: Constable, 1948), II, 4–5. The setting of Act Three suggests the opening scene of the epic where Satan rallies his fallen angels. The "mock-parliamentary" debate is also Miltonic. I am indebted to Mr. Brian Sullivan for suggesting these analogies with *Paradise Lost*.

14. The sketch of Louisa was based on Shaw's cook and housekeeper, Mary Farmer (R. F. Rattray, *Bernard Shaw: A Chronicle* (Luton: Leagrave Press, 1951], p. 146).

15. *Selected Essays of Arthur Schopenhauer*, tr. Belfort Bax (London: G. Bell, 1891), pp. 343–344.

16. Shaw to Iden Payne, February 3, 1911 (see n. 7 above).

17. *The World as Will*, III, 366.

18. The list of works inspired by the Don Juan legend in Armand

Edwards Singer's *A Bibliography of the Don Juan Theme: Versions and Criticism* (Morgantown: West Virginia University, 1954) runs to more than eighty pages. Item 3156 lists sixteen reviews of Shaw's Don Juan dialogue, Item 3157, fifty-two reviews of *Man and Superman*. The relation of Shaw's dialogue to other versions of the Don Juan story is traced in Carl Henry Mills's "The Intellectual and Literary Background of *Man and Superman*" (Ph.D. dissertation, University of Nebraska, 1963). For an excellent scholarly interpretation of the connections between the characters and themes of the play and those of the dialogue, see Frederick P. W. McDowell's "Heaven, Hell and Turn-of-the-Century London: Reflections upon Shaw's *Man and Superman*," *Drama Survey*, II (February 1963), 245–268. John Gassner's "Bernard Shaw and the Puritan in Hell," in *The Theatre in Our Times* (New York: Crown, 1954), pp. 156–162, discounts the intellectual side of the Don Juan dialogue but praises its dramatic qualities. Shaw appears to have pronounced "Juan" in the English fashion, as "Jew-un." In "A Glimpse of the Domesticity of Franklyn Barnabas," Shaw makes a character based on G. K. Chesterton pun on the expressions "Don Juan" and "Don Doin'" (*The Black Girl in Search of God and Some Lesser Tales* [London: Constable, 1948], p. 230).

19. John Austen, *The Story of Don Juan: A Study of the Legend and the Hero* (London: Secker, 1939), p. 200; Oscar Mandel, *The Theatre of Don Juan: A Collection of Plays and Views* (*1630–1963*) (Lincoln: University of of Nebraska Press, 1963), p. 550.

20. These plays, stories, and essays were listed by Shaw among books to look up at the British Museum on a page of notes now in the Hanley Collection, University of Texas. The fictional works referred to include Dumas *père, Don Juan de Marana* (1836); Alfred de Musset, *La Confession d'un enfant du siècle* (1836); Prosper Mérimée, *Les Ames du Purgatoire* (1837); and E. T. A. Hoffmann, *Don Juan* (1813). The essays by Pí y Margall, de la Revilla, and Picatoste were translated into French by J. G. Magnabal in *Don Juan et la critique espagnole* (1893). De Latour's essay appears in volume two of his *Etudes sur l'Espagne* (1857), Chasles's in *Voyages d'un critique à travers la vie et les livres: Italie et Espagne* (1865), and Larroumet's in *Nouvelles études d'histoire et de critique dramatiques* (1899). Barrès's essay is called *Du Sang, de la volupté, et de la mort* (1894).

21. Shaw to Jules Magny, December 16, 1890, *Bernard Shaw: Collected Letters 1874–1897* (New York: Dodd, Mead, and Co., 1965), p. 278.

22. *The Black Girl*, p. 176.

23. *Ibid.*, p. 177.

24. *Ibid.*, pp. 186, 187. The description of the heaven-dwellers suggests the Fabian Society.

25. Reprinted in Raymond Mander and Joe Mitchenson, *Theatrical Companion to Shaw* (London: Rockliff, 1954), p. 89.

26. *Three Plays for Puritans* (London: Constable, 1947), p. ix. Since Shaw wrote his prefaces after his plays, the preface to a particular play often reflects closely the ideas which are central to the play germinating in Shaw's mind when he wrote it, that is, the play following it in Shaw's list of works. The opening section of the preface to the *Three Plays for Puritans* is very intimately linked with the Don Juan dialogue. Both show Shaw's revulsion against the theater immediately on leaving his post as critic on the *Saturday Review*.

27. *Pen Portrait and Reviews* (London: Constable, 1949), p. 59.

28. Shaw became interested in the literary traditions of pessimism through his conversations with Thomas Tyler at the British Museum. These are outlined in the preface to *The Dark Lady of the Sonnets*. Shaw repeatedly relates Ecclesiastes, Swift, and Shakespeare to nineteenth-century pessimism; see especially the preface to *Three Plays for Puritans*, pp. xxviii–xxix, and the 1944 postscript to *Back to Methuselah* (London: Constable, 1949), pp. 270–271.

29. Archibald Henderson, *George Bernard Shaw: Man of the Century* (New York: Appleton-Century-Crofts, 1956), p. 262–263.

30. Friedrich Wilhelm Nietzsche, "The Case of Wagner," *Complete Works*, ed. Oscar Levy (London: T. N. Foulis, 1911), VIII, 32. In the eighteenth century in particular, writers often imitated Lucian's *Dialogues of the Dead* when they wished to set forth radical ideas without incurring the wrath of a censor. Traditionally such dialogues have represented famous personages, historical or fictional, from widely divergent eras, arguing controversial philosophical questions. A note in the unpublished diaries records that Shaw read Henry Duff Traill's *The New Lucian, Being a Series of Dialogues of the Dead* (London: Chapman and Hall, 1884). In the fourteenth dialogue Lucretius, Paley, and Darwin discuss evolution. Traill's stilted style contrasts strongly with Shaw's raciness, which is much closer to Lucian's own colloquial verve.

31. Lester Ward, *Pure Sociology: A Treatise on the Origins and Spontaneous Development of Society* (London: Macmillan, 1903), Chap. XIV, "The Phylogenetic Forces."

32. *Ibid.*, p. 324.

33. Havelock Ellis, *Man and Woman* (London: Walter Scott, 1894), p. 397.

34. *Man and Superman* (London: Constable, 1947), p. 214.

35. *Ibid.*, p. 123.

36. Raymond Mander and Joe Mitchenson, *Theatrical Companion to Shaw*, p. 90.

CHAPTER SEVEN   *Major Barbara*

1. See A. B. Walkley, *Drama and Life* (New York: Brentano's, 1907), and Francis Fergusson, *The Idea of a Theater* (Princeton: Princeton University Press, 1949).

2. See Charles Frankel, "Efficient Power and Inefficient Virtue," in *Great Moral Dilemmas in Literature*, ed. R. M. MacIver (New York: Harper, 1956).

3. R. F. Rattray, *Bernard Shaw: A Chronicle* (Luton: Leagrave Press, 1951), p. 161.

4. *Gilbert Murray: An Unfinished Autobiography* (New York: Oxford, 1960), pp. 87, 99.

5. Dorothy Henley, *Rosalind Howard: Countess of Carlisle* (London: Hogarth Press, 1959), p. 146.

6. Murray wrote to Dorothy Henley: "Your Mother was not only a remarkable character in herself, but she was a representative of a social type which has probably quite disappeared from the modern world never to emerge again: the Whig aristocrat in an extreme form, with all the authoritarianism and fearlessness of the aristocrat and the rebellious idealism of the radical. One might add, the puritanism of English nineteenth-century Liberalism" (*Ibid.*, p. 147).

7. Shaw to Gilbert Murray, October 7, 1905, *An Unfinished Autobiography*, p. 156. Shaw apparently chose the name Adolphus Cusins both for its feminine-sounding diminutive and as a reference to the Swedish king, Gustavus Adolphus, who began life as a brilliantly precocious linguist, and then mastered the art of war.

8. Of his life as a professor in Glasgow in the nineties, Murray wrote, "I believe I struck people at the time as being over-serious and over-enthusiastic. I combined—or tried to combine—an enthusiasm for poetry and Greek scholarship with an almost equal enthusiasm for radical politics and social reform" (*Unfinished Autobiography*, p. 97).

9. Gilbert Murray, *A History of Ancient Greek Literature* (New York: Appleton, 1897), p. 250. See also Murray's *Euripides and His Age* (New York: Henry Holt, 1913).

10. Murray wrote to Russell: "I preferred you to other philosophers because, while they mostly tried to prove some horrible conclusion—like Hobbes, Hegel, Marx &c, you were, I believed, content if you could really prove that $2 + 2 = 4$, and that conclusion, though sad, was at least bearable" (*Unfinished Autobiography*, p. 210).

11. Murray called *The Trojan Women* a play of pity: "Pity is a rebel passion. Its hand is against the strong, against the organized force of

society, against conventional sanctions and accepted Gods. It is the Kingdom of Heaven within us fighting against the brute powers of the world" (*The Trojan Women*, tr. Gilbert Murray [London: George Allen & Sons 1908], p. 7).

12. Murray wrote of Dionysos in *Euripides and His Age*: "This spirit that I call Dionysus, this magic of inspiration and joy, is it not . . . the great wrecker of men's lives?" (p. 187). Murray was himself largely responsible for the revival of interest in Greek religion at the turn of the century. His *Four Stages of Greek Religion* first appeared in 1912 and was reissued as *Five Stages of Greek Religion* in 1925. The latter title is the title of a lecture Cusins is shown delivering at the beginning of the Penguin screen version of Shaw's play. Murray accepted Shaw's portrait good-naturedly, though he thought the particularity of the identification of Cusins with an Australian professor of Greek was an artistic error. Murray advised Shaw on his revisions of Act Three and even wrote some dialogue Shaw incorporated into the play. See Murray's letters of October 2 and 7, 1905, in the Hanley Collection, University of Texas.

13. The lines are quoted from page 126 of Murray's *The Bacchae of Euripides* (London: George Allen and Unwin, 1904).

14. *Time*, LXVIII (November 12, 1956), 72; Fergusson, *The Idea of a Theater*, p. 183.

15. Rattray, *Bernard Shaw: A Chronicle*, p. 161.

16. British Museum Add. MS 50616B, f. 53.

17. The epithet "Undershaft" was applied to the church because of the custom of setting up a maypole outside its doors.

18. *John Bull's Other Island, How He Lied to Her Husband and Major Barbara* (London: Constable, 1947), p. 279.

19. Add. MS 50616E, ff. 35–36. The end of Act One in this manuscript is dated April 4, 1905; the end of Act Two, July 23. Shaw wrote the first version of Act Three in Derry, Ireland. The beginning and end of Scene One are dated July 24 and August 3, of Scene Two, August 4 and September 8. Shaw wrote to Murray of this "Irish" version of Act Three, Scene Two: "I am writing the whole scene over again. The moisture which serves for air in Ireland spoiled it hopelessly" (*Unfinished Autobiography*, p. 156). The revision was begun on October 4 and finished on October 15.

20. Cf. Frankel's comment that the play "invokes the audience's own deepest convictions, and employs them to upset what the audience thinks it believes or would like to believe. The political thinking in *Major Barbara* is in the tradition of Machiavelli and Hobbes, Nietzsche and Marx. These were not when Shaw wrote, and they are not now, pleasant names to conjure with. They are all 'materialists,' antimoralists, the great doctrinaires of Power. But *Major Barbara* makes us see that they are speaking for us, and that we dislike them only because they are telling everybody's

secret. And it makes us see that there is no choice between Power and Virtue. There is only an undiscriminating and a discriminating use of power, an unimaginative and an imaginative use, a use for ends that are imposed on us and a use for ends we choose for ourselves freely and responsibly" ("Efficient Power and Inefficient Virtue," p. 17).

21. Add. MS 50616E, f. 18.

22. Add. MS 50661, ff. 81–82.

23. Though the analogies with Dante are occasionally strained, Joseph Frank's "*Major Barbara*—Shaw's Divine Comedy" (*PMLA*, LXXI [March 1956], 61–74) is an excellent essay on the religious side of the play.

24. The man was H. N. Brailsford; see *An Unfinished Autobiography*, p. 97.

25. *Ibid.*, pp. 156–157.

CHAPTER EIGHT   *The Doctor's Dilemma*

1. Following the great comedies, these three domestic dramas make up the fifth cycle of Shaw's plays. *The Shewing-Up of Blanco Posnet*, the first play of the sixth cycle (a series of religious parables which includes also *Fanny's First Play* and *Androcles and the Lion*), was written before *Misalliance*. The beginning of *The Doctor's Dilemma* (Add. MS 50619A–D is dated August 11, 1906. Shaw finished the five acts on August 21 and 28 and September 3, 10, and 12, respectively, and the revisions of the last four acts on October 3, 8, 9, and 11.

2. Leonard Colebrook, *Almroth Wright: Provocative Doctor and Thinker* (London: William Heinemann, 1954), p. 154.

3. William James, *The Will to Believe and Other Essays* (New York: Longmans, Green, and Co., 1897), p. 4.

4. "DISCARDS from the Fabian lectures on IBSEN & DARWIN when publishing them as the Quintessence of Ibsenism & the Methuselah Preface," British Museum Add. MS 50661, ff. 56–57.

5. The British Museum version makes it clear that Schutzmacher is visiting Ridgeon for purely sentimental reasons. J. Percy Smith calls Schutzmacher a man "who has made a fortune by conscious and deliberate fraud" and describes Sir Ralph and Walpole as "more comical figures—though no more scrupulous" ("A Shavian Tragedy: *The Doctor's Dilemma*," *The Image of the Work* [University of California Publications, English Studies 11, 1955], p. 197). But in *Doctors' Delusions* (London: Constable, 1950), Shaw contends that "the general education of our citizens (the patients) leaves them so credulous and gullible, that the doctor, to whom they attribute magical powers over life and death, is forced to treat them according to their folly lest he starve" (p. xi).

6. It has been pointed out, quite justly, that, far from being a slashing attack on medical ethics, Shaw's play represents all its medical men as models of professional integrity, even to the point of overidealization. In the British Museum version Shaw had at first included a conversation about an unethical surgeon. It is significant that the following passage was later cancelled before the play was published:

W[alpole]—Paddy doesnt appreciate the fine arts.
Sir P[atrick]—Mr. Walpole: do you appreciate Paul Flasher's surgery?
W.—What has Flasher got to do with it?
Sir P.—Never mind. Is he a good surgeon or is he not?
W.—He's a better surgeon than I am in his special cases.
Sir P.—Then why did you pretty nearly cut him?
W.—Well, I draw a certain professional line; and he overstepped it. You know Flasher's specialty: trephanning.
Sir P.—Trepanning. Talk English.
W.—Trepanning then. Well, Flasher wanted ready money to furnish a house he had just built in Surrey. He didnt want to sell out anything; and he didnt want to borrow when he could earn just as easily. Some anti-vivisectionist rotter wrote to the Times just then to say that vivisection had never led to anything—you know: the usual cackle. Flasher wrote and said that Ferrier's experiments on monkeys had shewn how to cure epilepsy by trepanning, and as good as said he could do the trick: at all events there was his home and address at the end of the letter. Of course his waiting room and doorstep were crowded for the next fortnight with epileptics and the fathers and mothers husbands wives of epileptics. Well, he couldnt cure them—probably most of the cases were really only blood poisoning—but he got his fee all the same for telling them so, and furnished his house all right.
Ridgeon—That was a cruel sell.
W.—Sell! It was *worse*. I dont know what you call it, Sir Paddy; but I call it simple, flat, barefaced advertising. And I draw the line at advertising.
Sir P.—Flasher was a very agreeable man, wasnt he?
W.—Personally, very. I admit it.
Sir P.—And a clever surgeon.
W.—Wonderful. I am not disputing it for a moment.
Sir P.—Well, this young Dubedat is a very agreeable young fellow, and a wonderful sketcher. What does that prove about him? He may be as big as rascal as Flasher, who'd do anything for money.
B.B.—But my dear Sir Patrick, you can *see* that this is a very different case. Young Dubedat is not a bit like Flasher. Not the least in the world. Besides, after all, what could be wrong with him? *Look* at him. What *could* be wrong with him? [Add. MS 50619B, ff. 39–42.]

7. Readers often tend to discount Shaw as a medical critic on account of his stand against vaccination. The case of the anti-vaccinationists rested

on the fact that though the United Kingdom made vaccination compulsory in 1853, the smallpox epidemic of 1871 killed eight thousand people in London, twice as many as the worst eighteenth-century outbreak. Shaw, who had been vaccinated, caught smallpox in another epidemic a decade later. Anti-vaccinationsists argued that the waning of the disease simply paralleled the decrease in diseases like cholera, bubonic plague, and typhus, for which no serums were given. In the last two decades of the nineteenth century, the Register General listed about fifty deaths a year as due to "effects of vaccination." In 1898 the protests of parents whose children had died from it forced the government to drop compulsory vaccination. *Time* magazine reports (May 20, 1966) that there has not been a death from smallpox in the United States since 1949. On the other hand, more than two hundred people in that period have been reported as dying as a result of vaccination. *Time* estimates that probably another four hundred have been infected, since the death rate runs at about thirty percent (pp. 50–51).

8. British Museum Add. MS 50661, f. 19.

9. "The Independent Theatre" (January 26, 1895), *Our Theatres in the Nineties* (London: Constable, 1948), I, 23.

10. Lillah McCarthy, *Myself and My Friends* (London: Thornton Butterworth, 1933), p. 78.

11. *Ibid.*, pp. 5–6.

12. H. M. Hyndman, *Further Reminiscences* (London: Macmillan, 1912), pp. 138–148.

13. Archibald Henderson, *George Bernard Shaw: Man of the Century* (New York: Appleton-Century-Crofts, 1956), p. 607.

14. *Misalliance* (London: Constable, 1949), p. 99.

15. *Major Critical Essays* (London: Constable, 1947), p. 288.

16. British Museum Add. MS 50619B, f. 14.

17. In the British Museum draft of the play Jennifer's name appears several times as "Andromeda." Shaw was satirizing Ridgeon's quixotic desire to save her from Louis as Perseus saves Andromeda from the sea monster in the Greek myth.

18. "Ibsen," *Clarion* (London), June 1, 1906, p. 5.

19. *Tribune* (London), July 14, 1906, p. 2.

20. Henderson, *Man of the Century*, pp. 606–607.

21. Hesketh Pearson, *G.B.S.: A Full Length Portrait* (New York: Harper & Brothers, 1942), p. 103.

22. Arthur Nethercot, *First Five Lives of Annie Besant* (London: Rupert Hart-Davis, 1961), p. 206.

23. Shaw to Granville Barker, August 21, 1906, *Bernard Shaw's Letters to Granville Barker*, ed. C. B. Purdom (New York: Theatre Arts Book, 1957), p. 69. Redford was the British censor. The "blasphemy" was the

parody of the creed in Louis's speech on art. The motion picture version of the play deleted the words "I believe," making the speech unintelligible.

24. Richard Wagner, *Prose Works*, tr. W. Ashton Ellis (London: Kegan Paul, Trench, Trübner, 1898), VII, 66–67.

25. Shaw to Siegfried Trebitsch, May 5, 1910, Berg Collection, New York Public Library.

26. Critics have generally missed the irony of Jennifer's role in the death scene. J. Percy Smith (see note 5, above) remarks, "She, who up to this point is one of the least satisfactory figures in the play, lacking both firmness and clarity, here takes on a strength and dignity that are the most moving things in the scene" (p. 200).

27. A. B. Walkley, *Drama and Life* (New York: Brentano's, 1907), p. 244. Shaw did, however, revise Act Five considerably in manuscript. The cancelled first draft in the British Museum version reads as follows:

Supposing herself, after a look round, to be alone [Jennifer] seats herself at the secretary's table, and begins to admire her memoir. Ridgeon reappears, face to the wall, scrutinizing the drawings. He makes a noise. She hastily closes the book, pushes it aside, looks round, but does not recognize Ridgeon's back.

Mrs. Dubedat—I am so sorry the catalogues have not come.

(He turns with a violent start; and she is almost equally taken aback.)

Ridgeon—I thought I was alone. Where did you come from?

Mrs. D.—I thought *I* was alone. (She looks at her watch.)

R.—I am before my time.

Mrs. D.—Yes.

R.—Shall I go?

Mrs. D.—Not at all. The secretary will be back presently. I need not disturb you. I have a little private room here.

R.—In justice to myself I must explain that I came before my time expressly that I might see the pictures and get away before you came, to spare you the sight of me. I know you bear malice against me for not saving his life.

Mrs. D.—What right have you to say that?

R.—I stay away from BB's dinners by arrangement when you are at them. When you spend week-ends with the Walpoles, I dont. You have adopted Sir Paddy as your grandfather. Theyve given up talking to me about you now, the subject is such a sore one. I'm on the black list. You have really had me almost boycotted.

Mrs. D.—Please do not blame me for that. I have made a particular point of never mentioning your name.

R.—Yes: I guessed you had done something of that kind. However, you are entitled to drop me when I can no longer be of any service to you.

Mrs. D.—Oh!

R.—Forgive me for intruding. Good morning.

Mrs. D.—You are accusing me of ingratitude.

R.—I am not accusing you of anything.

Mrs. D.—You are making me out to be ungrateful and disloyal. That is not fair. Have I ever said one word of reproach to you since—since—

R.—Have you ever said one word to me of any sort to me since—since—? What have you to reproach me with?

Mrs. D.—Oh, you have no conscience. Surely you must know—you must have acknowledged to yourself at least that you made a dreadful mistake about Louis. . . . Can you deny that except on that one night at Richmond, when you were under the first spell of Louis's wonderful conversation, and when you had perhaps taken a little more wine than usual (Ridgeon starts) you hated him.

R.—You really have taken my breath away this time. Was I drunk at Richmond?

Mrs. D.—I did not say so. Your manner was sentimental: that was all. When you were quite yourself again you gave him up, with undisguised callousness. And you are talking about him now with just the same callousness. When he was dying there were tears in Sir Ralph's eyes; and I shall never forget how gentle Sir Patrick's gruffness became. But you were so hard that when you spoke Louis said your voice was devilish. And you lied to me.

R.—Lied! Oh!

Mrs. D.—Yes: you lied. You saw that you could not save Louis and that you could save Dr. Blenkinsop. So you threw the case which would have discredited you on Sir Ralph, and kept for yourself the case that would prove the value of your discovery. That was bad enough; but to excuse yourself to me you pledged your word that Sir Ralph would cure Louis. And in my joy & gratitude & belief in you I—poor fool!—I—I kissed your hand. Oh, I could cut my lips off.

R.—Oh, the female mind! the female mind! It is ingenious. No: I never promised you that BB would cure him.

Mrs. D.—(with cold disgust) Oh, if you deny it, I think we had better say no more. (She turns her back on him.) I shall not contradict you.

R.—You are wrong. You forget the pledge, and you mistake the motive. His case was not hopeless. But for me, he would have been alive today.

Mrs. D.—Of course, he died because he was another doctor's patient; and Dr. Blenkinsop lived because he was yours. How can you be so mean —so envious of Sir Ralph!

R.—Yes: I suppose it looks like that.

Mrs. D.—What else is it?

R.—I am astonished at the lengths you drive me to. The professional instinct is so strong in me—so much part of my personal honor—that I have let people die sooner than meddle with another doctor's case or give him away. And yet here I am, without thinking twice about it, giving away BB. However, there's nobody listening; so here goes. That night at Richmond, your husband was not as far gone as Blenkinsop. Well, have you seen Blenkinsop lately?

Mrs. D.—I met him at dinner at Sir Ralph's.

R.—Have you ever seen a man so wonderfully changed for the better?
Come! confess. He looks twenty years younger. [50619D, ff. 47–49,
54–60.]

28. This is not to say that Shaw is not concerned with the concept of
honor in *The Doctor's Dilemma*. "Honorable" and "honest" are un-
questionably the key words of the play and the preface. All the doctors, are
as we have seen, honorable men, and Shaw regards the medical profession
as generally dishonorable on only one score—its countenancing of vivisection. On the other hand, Louis is radically lacking in a sense of honor,
and so is the farcically egregious newspaperman.

29. Almroth Wright, "On Feminine Psychology," *Alethetropic Logic*
(London: William Heinemann, 1953), p. 217.

30. Almroth Wright, *The Unexpurgated Case Against Woman Suffrage*
(London: Constable, 1913), p. 45. "Woman's mind . . . is over-influenced
by individual instances; arrives at conclusions on incomplete evidence;
has a very imperfect sense of proportion; accepts the congenial as true,
and rejects the uncongenial as false; takes the imaginary which is desired
for reality, and treats the undesired reality which is out of sight as non-
existent—building up for itself in this way, when biased by predilections
and aversions a very unreal picture of the external world" (pp. 35–36).
Shaw would have accepted this as an accurate description of human
psychology, female or male.

CHAPTER NINE *Pygmalion*

1. *My Fair Lady: A Musical Play based on "Pygmalion" by Bernard
Shaw*, adaptation and lyrics by Alan Jay Lerner (New York: New American Library), 1964, [p. i].

2. Milton Crane, "*Pygmalion*: Bernard Shaw's Dramatic Theory and
Practice," *PMLA*, LXVI (December 1951), 879–885. Crane rejects the
epilogue as "something less than serious" and argues that Shaw condoned
"the tenderly romantic conclusion" of the film. In the original stage
version Shaw perversely "turned on his unsuspecting audience and denounced it for expecting the normal conclusion of a comic romance."
Crane further contends that if the audience "had believed Liza's statement
in Act V that she was going to marry Freddy, Shaw doubtless had another
Epilogue already in type to prove that Liza was in fact going to marry
Higgins." As Crane sees it, at the end of the play, Higgins' "confusion is
complete. Galatea has subdued Pygmalion; the comedy is ended."

3. Shaw based Higgins largely on Henry Sweet (1845–1912), the Anglo-
Saxon scholar and phonetics specialist. See Bertrand Wainger, "Henry
Sweet—Shaw's Pygmalion," *Studies in Philology*, XXVII (July 1930),

558–572. Shaw himself described Sweet in a letter to Florence Farr (June 30, 1904) as "having a genius for making everything impossible both for himself and everybody else. He is the most savagely Oxonian and donnish animal that ever devoted his life to abusing all the other dons" (*Florence Farr, Bernard Shaw, W. B. Yeats: Letters*, ed. C. Bax [New York: Dodd, Mead, and Co., 1942], p. 26).

4. "G.B.S., Eliza, and the Critics," *Daily News and Leader* (London), April 17, 1914, p. 1. Shaw contended also that "the flower girl's conversation is much more picturesque, much better rhetoric, much more conscise, interesting, and arresting than the conversation of the drawing-room, and that the moments she begins to speak beautifully she gains an advantage by the intensity of her experience and the strength of her feeling about it."

5. *Androcles and the Lion, Overruled, Pygmalion* (London: Constable, 1949), p. 209.

6. "The nearest approach to *Tendenz* in the play is Alfred Doolittle. . . . His felicity depends on the studied neglect of organized charity. But the long and brainless arm of American philanthropic wealth reaches out and plunges him into a lifelong hell of respectability by endowing him as lecturer on ethics to the world-wide Wannafeller Societies" (William Irvine, *The Universe of G.B.S.* [New York: Whittlesey House, 1949], p. 289).

7. In an unpublished letter to Siegfried Trebitsch, dated May 8, 1914, in the Berg Collection, New York Public Library, Shaw admits that Doolittle in the play analyzes his character with an articulateness more typical of Balzac than of a workingman.

8. It is worth noting that when Shaw subtitled his play "A Romance in Five Acts," he was using the word to refer to the transformation of Eliza into a lady, not in the sentimental-erotic sense. Compare his ironic use of the term "tragedy" in connection with *The Doctor's Dilemma*.

9. Page 82 of the typescript in the Hanley Collection, University of Texas, has the following cancelled speech by Mrs. Higgins: "I have tried to make Eliza understand that this kind of stupidity is part of what people call manliness. I did my best to persuade her at the same time, that you, Henry, are not quite incapable of feeling; but I dont think I should have convinced her if you hadnt fortunately parted from her with some words which betrayed some sort of sensibility on your part."

10. In another cancelled passage, on page 72 of the Hanley Collection typescript, Mrs. Higgins calls Henry selfish, to which he retorts, "O very well, very well, very well. Have it your own way. I have devoted my life to the regeneration of the human race through the most difficult science in the world; and then I am told I am selfish. Go on. Go on."

11. Shaw to Mrs. Shaw, April 12, 1914; quoted by Meisel, *Shaw and the Nineteenth-Century Theater* (Princeton: Princeton University Press, 1963), p. 177 n.

12. Shaw to Gabriel Pascal, April 16, 1938, "Letters and Telegrams to Grabriel Pascal About the Motion Picture *Pygmalion,* London 1937–1938," photostatic copies in the library of the University of California at Berkeley.

13. Shaw to Pascal, February 24, 1938: "I have given my mind to the Pygmalion film seriously, and have no doubt at all as to how to handle the end of it. . . . I am sorry I have had to stick in the flower shop; but it need not cost more than it is worth and you will save by getting rid of the wedding rubbish. It is not a Bond Street shop but a South Kensington one: half florist's, half greengrocer's and fruiterer's with a fine bunch of property grapes for Freddy to weigh for a lady customer" (*ibid.*).

14. Valerie Delacorte, "GBS in Filmland," *Esquire,* LXII (December 1964), 288.

15. *Androcles and the Lion, Overruled, Pygmalion,* pp. 289–290.

16. In the 1914 version, Higgins gives Eliza orders for various household items. She then rebels and the play ends as follows:

LIZA [*disdainfully*] Buy them yourself. [*She sweeps out*]
MRS. HIGGINS. I'm afraid youve spoiled that girl, Henry. But never mind dear: I'll buy you the tie and gloves.
HIGGINS [*sunnily*] Oh, dont bother. She'll buy em all right enough. Good-bye.
   They kiss. Mrs. Higgins runs out. Higgins, left alone, rattles his cash in his pocket; chuckles; and disports himself in a highly self-satisfied manner.

In the 1941 screen version, Liza replies to Higgins's request that she buy a ham, a Stilton cheese, number eight gloves, and a new tie in this way:

LIZA [*disdainfully*] Number eights are too small for you if you want them lined with lamb's wool. You have three new ties that you have forgotten in the drawer of your washstand. Colonel Pickering prefers double Gloucester to Stilton: and you dont notice the difference. I telephoned Mrs Pearce this morning not to forget the ham. What you are to do without me I cannot imagine. [*She sweeps out.*]
MRS. HIGGINS. I'm afraid youve spoilt that girl, Henry. I should be uneasy about you and her if she were less fond of Colonel Pickering.
HIGGINS. Pickering! Nonsense: she's going to marry Freddy. Ha ha! Freddy! Freddy!! Ha ha ha ha ha!!!! [*He roars with laughter as the play ends.*]

Shaw reprinted the screen version in the Constable standard edition of his works, where it superseded the earlier stage play. The screen version, however, differs at many points from the actual filmed scenario. See Donald P. Costello, *The Serpent's Eye: Shaw and the Cinema* (Notre Dame: University of Notre Dame Press, 1965), Appendix C, where Mr. Costello reprints the play, the published screen version, and the actual sound track of Act Five for comparison. Folio 11, British Museum Add. MS 50628,

"Pygmalion: a Scenario by Bernard Shaw," contains the following very explicit instructions to the movie producer:

> *Higgins is not youthful. He is a mature, well built, impressive, authoritative man of 40 or thereabouts, with a frock coat, a broadbrimmed hat, and an Inverness cape.*
>
> *It is important that in age and everything else he should be in strong contrast to Freddy, who is 20, slim, goodlooking, and very youthful.*

(The producer should bear in mind from the beginning that it is Freddy who captivates and finally carries off Eliza, and that all suggestion of a love interest between Eliza and Higgins should be most carefully avoided.)

17. *My Fair Lady*, p. 128.

CHAPTER TEN   *Heartbreak House*

1. Cf. Stark Young, *Immortal Shadows*, pp. 207–209. F. P. W. McDowell reviews criticism of the play and also discusses its Chekhovism in "Technique, Symbol, and Theme in *Heartbreak House*," *PMLA*, LXVIII (June 1953), 335–356.

2. "Bernard Shaw on 'Heartbreak House,'" *Illustrated Sunday Herald*, October 23, 1921, p. 5.

3. Chekhov to Alexei Suvorin, November 25, 1892, *The Portable Chekhov*, ed. A. Yarmolinsky (New York: Viking, 1947), pp. 624–625.

4. Shaw remarked to Paul Green, of Heartbreak House, that "it is a sort of national fable or a fable of nationalism" (*Dramatic Heritage* [New York: Samuel French, 1953], p. 127).

5. The epithet "black" presumably does not mean Negro here. The reference is more likely to the baleful black magic the tropical beauty exercised.

6. On July 28, 1929, Shaw wrote to Mrs. Campbell: "Of course we are a pair of mountebanks; but why, oh why do you get nothing out of me, though I got everything out of you? Mrs. Hesione Hushabye in *Heartbreak House*, the Serpent in *Methuselah*, whom I always hear speaking with your voice, and Orinthia [in *The Apple Cart*]: all you, to say nothing of Eliza, who was only a joke. You are the Vamp and I the victim; yet it is I who suck your blood and fatten on it whilst you lose everything! It is ridiculous!" (*Bernard Shaw and Mrs. Patrick Campbell: Their Correspondence*, ed. Alan Dent [New York: Alfred A. Knopf, 1952], p. 334).

7. "Bernard Shaw on 'Heartbreak House,'" *Illustrated Sunday Herald*, October 23, 1921, p. 5.

8. Desmond MacCarthy, *Shaw's Plays in Review* (New York: Thames and Hudson, 1951), p. 151.

9. F. J. Osborn, preface to Ebenezer Howard, *Garden Cities of To-morrow* (London: Faber and Faber, 1946), pp. 22–23.

10. When St. John Ervine objected that Ellie seemed out of place in the play, Shaw replied that he had intended to give such an impression and had emphasized the effect by choosing the Irish actress Ellen O'Malley for the part because he thought she was a strong "Lady Macbeth" type, and not an ingenue or a "sweet little sexual attraction" (unpublished letter, October 28, 1921, Hanely Collection, University of Texas).

11. *Dramatic Heritage*, p. 127.

12. Shaw to St. John Ervine, October 28, 1921, Hanley Collection.

13. Later, during the war, Beatrice Webb complained that Lloyd George had handed over each ministry to a special interest: "the Food Controller is a wholesale Grocer"—"the egregious Devonport" (February 22, 1917, *Beatrice Webb's Diaries 1912–1924*, ed. Margaret Cole [London: Longmans, Green and Co., 1952], p. 83).

14. Preface to Sidney and Beatrice Webb, *English Prisons Under Local Government* (London: Longmans, Green and Co., 1922), p. xxi.

15. Manuscript note in typescript of French translation, p. 86, Hanley Collection.

16. *Dramatic Heritage*, pp. 125–126.

17. Stark Young at first agreed with Edmund Wilson that *Heartbreak House* was "probably the best of the Shaw plays." Reviewing a performance in 1938, however, he attacked it as "garrulous, unfelt, and tiresome" (*Immortal Shadows*, pp. 206–207).

CHAPTER ELEVEN   *Back to Methuselah*

1. Edmund Wilson, "Bernard Shaw at Eighty," *The Triple Thinkers* (London: John Lehmann, 1952), p. 188.

2. Shaw began his writing of the cycle with Part II, continued with Part III, then interrupted Part IV to write Part I, and finally extended the tetralogy to a pentateuch by adding Part V. In British Museum Additional MS 50531, Part II is dated March 19, 1918, to April 9, 1918; Part III was finished on May 16 and Part IV begun on May 21, 1918. The fragment published with Shaw's prose stories under the title "A Glimpse of the Domesticity of Franklyn Barnabas," which was originally to have formed Act Two of Part II is dated November 12, 1918. Part I was finished February 14, 1919, and Part IV taken up again and completed on March 15, 1920. Part V was begun March 16, 1920, and completed on May 27 of the same year.

The most extensive scholarly treatment of *Back to Methuselah* is H. M. Geduld's six-volume variorum edition of the play submitted as a doctoral thesis at Birkbeck College, University of London (1961). This thesis, which runs to fourteen hundred pages, includes a discussion of the intellectual and literary background, a collation of some forty editions of the text, annotations to the five parts, preface, and postscript, and an account of the theatrical history of the play. I am particularly indebted to the notes. Mr. Geduld's bibliographical findings have been published as "The Textual Problem in Shaw," *Shaw Review*, V (May 1962), 54–60. The relation of Shaw's cycle to the Utopias of Plato, More, Swift, and Bulwer-Lytton has been analyzed in detail by Bill Knepper in "*Back to Methuselah* and the Utopian Tradition" (Ph.D. dissertation, University of Nebraska, 1967).

3. *Back to Methuselah* (London: Constable, 1949), p. 270.

4. Shaw to Siegfried Trebitsch, July 20, 1919, unpublished letter in the Berg Collection, New York Public Library. Since Shaw indicated when he wrote this letter that he was already at work on Part IV, Part V seems to have been conceived only at a very late stage in the process of writing the cycle.

5. August Weismann, *Essays upon Heredity*, 2nd ed. (Oxford: Clarendon Press, 1891). Shaw, in his preface, draws heavily on the historical side of Weismann's *The Evolutionary Theory*, tr. J. A. Thomson (London: E. Arnold, 1904).

6. Preface to *Misalliance* (London: Constable, 1949), p. 3.

7. *Bernard Shaw: His Life, Work and Friends* (London, New York: Morrow, 1956), p. 383.

8. Quoted by Geduld (see note 2, above), Vol. II, Appendix K, p. 87. The actor who played Cain was Scott Sunderland.

9. Bernard Shaw, *What I Really Wrote About the War* (London: Constable, 1932), pp. 347–348.

10. For Shaw's estimate of Asquith, see *ibid.*, p. 300, and *Pen Portraits and Reviews* (London: Constable, 1949), pp. 149–150.

11. March 1 and December 12, 1918, *Beatrice Webb's Diaries 1912–1924*, ed. Margaret Cole (London: Longmans, Green, 1952), pp. 111, 139.

12. "Personalities and Politics: Mr. Shaw to His Critics," *The Times*, February 25, 1924, p. 13.

13. *Back to Methuselah*, p. 68.

14. Julian Huxley, *Evolution: The Modern Synthesis* (London: George Allen and Unwin, 1942), p. 458.

15. Hugo de Vries, *The Mutation Theory: Experiments and Observations on the Origin of Species in the Vegetable Kingdom*, tr. J. B. Farmer and A. D. Darbishire, 2 vols. (Chicago: Open Court, 1909–1910).

16. Book VIII, *Dialogues of Plato*, tr. B. Jowett, 3rd ed. (London: Oxford University Press, 1892), III, 269.

17. *Back to Methuselah*, p. 159.

18. Untitled lecture, dated April, 1887, British Museum Add. MS. 50702, ff. 238–239.

19. "Population decays under conditions that cannot be charged to the presence or absence of misery, in the common sense of the word. These exist when native races disappear before the presence of the incoming white man. . . . It is certainly not wholly due to misery, but rather to listlessness, due to *discouragement* [italics added]" (Francis Galton, *Inquiries into Human Faculty* [London: Macmillan, 1883], p. 319).

20. In drawing the personal characteristics of the Elderly Gentleman, however, Shaw seems to have had in mind one of the most "discouraged" of contemporary theologians and social critics—his good friend William Ralph Inge, the so-called Gloomy Dean of St. Paul's. Critics, always keen to catch him in a despairing mood, have from time to time identified Shaw himself with the Elderly Gentleman. But the latter's ruling passion is reverence for the past, a very un-Shavian trait. By contrast, Inge, though Shaw admired him greatly as a liberal theologian strongly opposed to bigotry, and as a Platonic philosopher who bore the "undying fire," was a social conservative with a strong class feeling, who found himself markedly out of sympathy with the "young Bolsheviks" of the postwar period, and with twentieth-century literature, which he compared unfavorably to Tennyson's *Idylls*. In *Truth and Falsehood in Religion* (1906), Inge takes Dürer's "Melencolia" as the leading symbol of modern civilization, laments the passing of the old order, and quotes Austin Dobson—"But O Unmerciful, O Pitiless!/ Leave us not thus with sick men's hearts to bleed." Shaw even includes an arcane reference to Inge's controversial opinions on polar exploration.

21. Chapter XXXII, "Coercions and Sanctions," *Everybody's Political What's What?* (London: Constable, 1945), p. 287. Shaw compares this power of "Awe" with Prospero's power over Caliban and a headmaster's power over a mob of riotous schoolboys. The entire chapter cited here is a philosophical discussion of the problem of social power which Shaw is concerned with in *Back to Methuselah*.

22. Henri Bergson, *Creative Evolution*, tr. Arthur Mitchell (New York: Henry Holt, 1911), p. 264.

23. H. D. Rankin (see note 24, below). The pseudo-Greek setting for the children's play seems to owe something to the "Festival of Pan" in Keats's *Endymion*. In an essay written for the Keats centennial in 1921, Shaw attacked Keats's "two idle epics" as "voluptuously literary" (*Pen Portraits*, p. 184).

24. C. E. M. Joad points out similarities to Plato in his *Shaw* (London: Victor Gollancz, 1949), pp. 149–152, 191–193. H. D. Rankin's "Plato and Bernard Shaw: Their Ideal Communities," *Hermathena*, XCIII (May 1959), 71–77, touches on parallels between the two men's views of art and morals, but not on politics. Other analogies are drawn by Margery M. Morgan in "*Back to Methuselah*: The Poet and the City," in *G. B. Shaw:*

A Collection of Critical Essays, ed. R. J. Kaufmann (Englewood Cliffs, N.J.: Prentice Hall, 1965), pp. 130–142. For a fuller treatment of the relation of the *Republic* to Shaw's play, see Knepper, "*Back to Methuselah* and the Utopian Tradition."

25. *Back to Methuselah*, pp. 218–219.

26. Shaw develops this distinction in the section of his preface subtitled "The Homeopathic Reaction against Darwinism." There he tells us that "the New Vitalist only half extricated from the Old Mechanist" objected "to be called either." He is presumably referring to Scott Haldane's demurrers in his *Mechanism, Life, and Personality* (London: John Murray, 1913); see Shaw's "Foundation Oration" of 1920 in *Platform and Pulpit*, ed. Dan H. Laurence (New York: Hill and Wang, 1961), p. 153. In the 1947 edition of the preface Shaw added some explanatory sentences to clarify the point: "The Old Vitalists, in postulating a Vital Force, were setting up a comparatively mechanical conception as against the divine idea of the life breathed into the clay nostrils of Adam, whereby he became a living soul. The New Vitalists, filled by their laboratory researches with a sense of the miraculousness of life that went far beyond the comparatively uninformed imaginations of the authors of the Book of Genesis, regarded the Old Vitalists as Mechanists who had tried to fill up the gulf between life and death with an empty phrase denoting an imaginary physical force" (*Back to Methuselah*, p. lxix). Another Neo-Vitalist work sympathetic to Shaw's point of view is Hans Driesch's *The History and Theory of Vitalism*, tr. C. K. Ogden (London: Macmillan, 1914). For a good statement of the antivitalist position, see Sir Peter Chalmers Mitchell's *Materialism and Vitalism in Biology* (Oxford: Clarendon Press, 1930).

27. *Shaw on Vivisection*, ed. Russell F. Knutson (Chicago: Alethea, 1950), p. 10.

28. Shaw to St. John Ervine, September 21, 1921, *Bernard Shaw*, p. 490.

29. In Talmudic lore, Lilith was Adam's first wife. She appears as such in poems by Rossetti and Browning, and in the Walpurgis Night scene of Goethe's *Faust*, where she is represented as a kind of vampire.

30. *The Religious Speeches of Bernard Shaw*, ed. Warren S. Smith (University Park: Pennsylvania State University Press, 1963), p. 49.

31. Shaw wrote to Granville Barker (December 18, 1918) apropos of the first draft of Part II: "The idea is not to get comic relief (they are not really comic, if you come to that); but to exhibit the Church, marriage, the family, and parliament under [shortlived] conditions before reproducing them under longlived conditions. The stuttering rector develops into an immortal archbishop and the housemaid into a Minister of Public Something or other.... [The characters seem] dull and in fact are dull and irritating, just as in real life. [In] the end I may have to disregard the boredom of the spectator who has not mastered all the motifs, as Wagner had

to do; but I daresay I shall manage to make the people more amusing, some of them more poetic, and all of them more intelligible than they are now in this first draft. . . . You see, if I make them all satisfactory, the reason for making them live 300 years vanishes. What I have to do is not to make them satisfactory but to find an artistic treatment of their unsatisfactoriness, which will prevent its being as disagreeable to the audience as the real thing" (*Bernard Shaw's Letters to Granville Barker*, ed. C. B. Purdom [New York: Theatre Arts Book, 1957], pp. 198–199). Shaw was obviously aware of the difficulty Part II posed, but he does not seem to me to have overcome it.

CHAPTER TWELVE *Saint Joan*

1. Shaw mentioned these sources in an interview with Archibald Henderson, "Bernard Shaw Talks of His *Saint Joan*," *Literary Digest International Book Review*, II (March 1924), 286–289. Shaw singles out Marcel Poullin's "La Libératrice d'Orléans" as showing "the greatest insight," but I have been unable to locate any book or essay with this title. Poullin's *Jeanne d'Arc* (1887) appears to be merely a run-of-the-mill study.

2. Michelet's essay on Joan, a minor French classic, first appeared in Volume V of his *Histoire de France* in 1841. It is Shavian in the emphasis it places on Joan's common sense, robustness, political practicality, bravery, and national feeling, un-Shavian in its emphasis on her beauty and purity.

3. Archibald Henderson, *Table-Talk of G.B.S.* (London: Chapman and Hall, 1925), pp. 40–41.

4. Hans Stoppel's "Shaw and Sainthood," *English Studies*, XXXVI (April 1955), 49–63, is a penetrating analysis of its subject to which I am much indebted.

5. The text of this broadcast was published in *The Listener*, V (June 3, 1931), 921–922, 947; it has been reprinted in *Platform and Pulpit*, ed. Dan Laurence (New York: Hill and Wang, 1961).

6. T. S. Eliot, "*Mr. Shaw and 'The Maid*,'" *Criterion*, IV (April 1926), 389–390. Eliot calls Shaw's play "one of the most superstitious of the effigies which have been erected to that remarkable woman."

7. *Mr. Shaw and "The Maid"* (London: Richard Cobden-Sanderson, 1925), p. 40. This book-length attack on the historicity of *Saint Joan* ends with the prophecy that "it may plausibly be doubted whether posterity three hundred—or thirty—years hence will be discussing *Saint Joan*. The didactic aim, in art, is notoriously susceptible of self-frustration" (p. 98).

8. T. Douglas Murray, *Jeanne d'Arc, Maid of Orleans, Deliverer of France* (London: William Heinemann, 1902), pp. 281, 239–240.

9. In his BBC broadcast Shaw compared Joan to Sylvia Pankhurst.

10. Andrew Lang published his *The Maid of France* (London: Longmans, Green, and Co.) in 1908 as a counterblast to France's skepticism. The book is close to Shaw in many respects, especially in the parallels it draws between Joan's military genius and Napoleon's and between her visionary tendencies and those of Socrates, Mahomet, Luther, and Shelley. However, Lang makes Joan "the flower of chivalry" and "the most perfect daughter of her church " (p. 1).

11. "A Crib for Home Rulers" (1888); reprinted in *The Matter with Ireland*, ed. Dan H. Laurence and David H. Greene (New York: Hill and Wang, 1962), p. 23.

12. Lawrence Langner, *G. B. S. and the Lunatic* (New York: Atheneum, 1963), pp. 70–71.

13. Karl Hase, *Neue Propheten: drei historisch-politische Kirchenbilder* (1851). See Charles Lightbody, *The Judgments of Joan* (Cambridge: Harvard University Press, 1961), p. 156.

14. Among modern historians who have written on the play, J. Van Kan, in "Bernard Shaw's *Saint Joan*: An Historical Point of View," *Fortnightly Review*, CXXIV (July 1, 1925), 36–46, refuses to see Joan as a proto-Protestant. Charles Sarolea calls the play a triumph from the theatrical point of view, but unhistorical. He accuses Shaw of making a heretic out of a pious mystic, misunderstanding the Middle Ages (which he claims were nationalistic all the way through), and thinks the judges believed in the justice of their cause, but saw the issues as ultimately political ("Has Mr. Shaw Understood Joan of Arc?" *English Review*, XLIII [August 1926], 175–182). Lightbody, however, adopts Shaw's evaluation of Cauchon in *The Judgments of Joan*.

15. "*Saint Joan* Banned: Film Censorship in the United States," *London Mercury*, XXXIV (October 1936), 494.

16. Many readers assume that this is a piece of frivolous stage supernaturalism added by Shaw for dramatic effect. In fact, he is satirizing popular religious psychology. After men are convinced that a particular person is a saint, "miracles" are inevitably discovered as proofs of his sainthood. We may compare modern canonization procedure, where dangerously ill patients are always discovered to have recovered "miraculously" after prayers to the candidate for sainthood.

17. Walter Tittle, "Mr. Shaw Talks about St. Joan," *The Outlook*, CXXXVII (June 25, 1924), 313.

18. Edmund Wilson, "Bernard Shaw Since the War," *New Republic*, XL (August 27, 1924), 381.

19. There is a good discussion of this point in Sylvan Barnet, "Bernard Shaw on Tragedy," *PMLA*, LXXI (December 1956), 888–899.

20. Arthur Schopenhauer, *The World as Will*, tr. R. B. Haldane and

J. Kemp (London: Trübner, 1883), p. 27. Many of Schopenhauer's comments on tragedy at the conclusion of Book III are of interest in relation to Shaw. Like Shaw and Hegel, he rules out the accidental in tragedy and favors the dramatization of "inevitable" conflicts. On the other hand, Schopenhauer regards the Maid of Orleans, like Hamlet and Gretchen, as dying "purified by suffering," i.e., as having abrogated the will to live. Shaw would have attacked the pessimism implicit in such a view.

21. Louis Martz, in "The Saint as Tragic Hero: *Saint Joan* and *Murder in the Cathedral*," quotes Butcher's interpretation of Aristotle: "Impersonal ardour in the cause of right [does not have] the same dramatic fascination as the spectacle of human weakness or passion doing battle with the fate it has brought upon itself." Martz notes Joan's superficial resemblance to the Aristotelian hero, but goes on: "Her extreme self-confidence, her brashness, her appearance of rash impetuosity—all this becomes in the end a piece of Shavian irony, for her only real error in the play is the one point where her superb self-confidence breaks down in the panic of recantation" (*G. B. Shaw: A Collection of Critical Essays*, ed. R. J. Kaufmann [Englewood Cliffs, N.J.: Prentice-Hall, 1965], pp. 143, 149–150). In the main, this is right; but for a different view of Joan's recantation, see below.

22. John Fielden, in "Shaw's *Saint Joan* as Tragedy," *Twentieth Century Literature*, III (July 1957), 59–67, argues for reading the play as classical tragedy. Of the Archbishop's mention of *hubris*, he says, "How a playwright could make this reference to classical tragedy and not mean to communicate anything to his audience is difficult to imagine. And when a speech such as this fits in perfectly with other indications in the play and in the preface that Shaw was at least considering his play from the standpoint of classical tragedy, it is of a significance difficult to cast aside" (p. 65). Fielden suggests Joan's *hubris* is her superiority to the godlike forces of evolution. This is ingenious but, to me, not convincing.

23. Cf. Shaw's criticism of a production of Ibsen's *John Gabriel Borkman*: "John Gabriel Borkman is no doubt technically a tragedy because it ends with the death of the leading personage in it. But to stage-manage or act it rhetorically as such is like drawing a Dance of Death in the style of Caracci or Giulio Romano. Clearly the required style is the homely-imaginative, the realistic-fateful—in a word, the Gothic. I am aware that to demand Gothic art from stage managers dominated by the notion that their business is to adapt the exigencies of stage etiquette to the tragic and comic categories of our pseudo-classical dramatic tradition is to give them an order which they can but dimly understand" ("*John Gabriel Borkman*," [May 8, 1897], *Our Theatres in the Nineties* [London: Constable, 1948], III, 124).

24. Georg Wilhelm Friedrich Hegel, *The Philosophy of Fine Art*, tr.

F. P. B. Osmaston (London: G. Bell and Sons, 1920), IV, 317. Nearly everything Hegel has to say about tragedy, and about drama in general, closely parallels Shaw, since Hegel sees drama as essentially a conflict between "old and new gods."

25. Quoted in Walter Pater, *Plato and Platonism* (London: Macmillan and Co., 1910), pp. 91–92, from Hegel's *Lectures on the History of Philosophy*, Part I, Section I, Chap. Two, B, § 3.

26. *Bernard Shaw 1856–1950* (Norfolk, Conn.: New Directions, 1957), p. 169. Mr. Bentley's treatment of *Saint Joan* in his chapter, "Bernard Shaw, Caesar, and Stalin," in *A Century of Hero-Worship* (New York: J. B. Lippincott, 1944) is hostile. He thinks that the play is morally ambiguous because "the religious tone of such speeches as Joan's last is not suited to the theory expounded in the preface and in earlier scenes," that "the sublime parts are bad in themselves," and that Shaw wrote with the purpose of edifying headmasters and clergymen (pp. 191–192). This chapter was omitted from later editions as a result of a change in Mr. Bentley's views on Stalin. The remarks on *Saint Joan* in *Bernard Shaw* (pp. 168–172) are much more sympathetic.

27. *Major Critical Essays* (London: Constable, 1947), p. 75.

28. Shaw's apparently paradoxical judgment of the Inquisitor has been, in fact, the traditional view of sophisticated free thought as opposed to vulgar anti-Catholicism. Gibbon, after relating the sensational crimes of John XII, remarks, "Protestants have dwelt with malicious pleasure on these characters of Antichrist; but to a philosophic eye the vices of the clergy are far less dangerous than their virtues" (*The History of the Decline and Fall of the Roman Empire*, Chap. Forty-nine; *Works*, VIII, ed. J. B. Bury [New York: Fred de Fau, 1907], 379). Cf. also John Stuart Mill's comments on his father, James Mill: "He blamed as severely what he thought a bad action, when the motive was a feeling of duty, as if the agents had been consciously evil doers. He would not have accepted as a plea in mitigation for inquisitors, that they sincerely believed burning heretics to be an obligation of conscience" (*Autobiography* [New York: Columbia University Press, 1924], p. 35).

29. *Saint Joan* and *The Apple Cart* (London: Constable, 1949), pp. 127–128.

30. Archibald Henderson, *George Bernard Shaw: Man of the Century* (New York: Appleton-Century-Crofts, 1956), p. 741.

31. "Inquisition," *Catholic Encyclopedia* (1910), VIII, 31.

32. H. C. Lea, *A History of the Inquisition of the Middle Ages*, I (New York: Harper and Brothers, 1900), 106.

33. Preface to Sidney and Beatrice Webb, *English Prisons Under Local Government* (London: Longmans, Green and Co., 1922), p. xxiv.

34. *Saint Joan*, pp. 142–143.

35. Presumably Shaw drew his conception of De Stogumber from the testimony at Joan's rehabilitation: "A certain Englishman, a soldier, who hated her greatly, had sworn to bring a faggot for the stake. When he did so, and heard Jeanne calling on the name of Jesus in her last moments, he was stupified, and as it were, in an ecstasy at the spectacle: his companions took him and led him away to a neighboring tavern. After refreshment, he revived. In the afternoon the same Englishman confessed in my presence, to a Brother of the Order of Saint Dominic, that he had gravely erred and that he repented of what he had done against Jeanne" (Murray, *Jeanne d'Arc*, p. 191). The executioners and others are represented as going through similar crises.

36. "Satan Saved at Last" (June 16, 1897), *Our Theatres in the Nineties*, III, 18.

37. Henderson, *Table-Talk of G. B. S.*, p. 42.

Acknowledgments

I am grateful to Dan H. Laurence for the unstinting fashion in which he has let me draw on his great wealth of bibliographical information about Shaw. I am also appreciative of the courtesy of the staff of the manuscript department of the British Museum, who responded cheerfully to what might have seemed like inordinate demands on their time and energy. The students of my seminars in Shaw at the University of Nebraska have been a constant source of intellectual stimulus. I am particularly indebted to Gordon Bergquist, Barbara Brooks, Sherrill Daniels, Kathleen Dillon, Terry Ford, Garitt Griebel, Robert Griffin, Lowell Lamberton, Robert Samuelson, Donald Savera, and Sister Thérèse Ann Wass, who gave me valuable editorial assistance with the next-to-final version of the text, to Lloyd Hubenka and Gale Larson, who read parts of the manuscript, and to Mrs. Hilayne Cavanaugh, who has helped in the proofreading.

Permission has been granted by the Public Trustee and the Society of Authors to quote from Shaw's published works and from unpublished writings in the British Museum and elsewhere. I am also obliged to the Lenox and Tilden Foundations for permission to quote from manuscripts in the Henry W. and Albert A. Berg Collection of the New York Public Library, and to the University of Texas to quote from manuscripts in the Academic Center Library and the Hanley Collection. In quoting from both published and unpublished material an attempt has been made to follow Shaw's unorthodox and often irregular usage, including his verbal contractions. The references to manuscript numbers in the British Museum collection are those of August, 1968, but readers should note that they are liable to subsequent revision.

I am also indebted to Miss Bernice Slote for kind permission to reprint material that originally appeared in slightly altered form in the *Prairie Schooner*.

The Research Council of the Graduate Council has made work on this book possible through leaves and through grants for travel and microfilms.